Corporate Environmental Responsibility and Pollution Control Laws

This book critically examines the corporate environmental responsibility of major oil companies operating in Nigeria's Niger Delta, focusing on oil spills and comparing regulatory frameworks in Nigeria, the US, the UK, and the EU. It provides a theoretical foundation for holding these companies to the same environmental standards in Nigeria as they adhere to in more advanced jurisdictions.

Analysing Shell's oil spill environmental performance data, the book assesses how its operations in Nigeria compare with global performance figures. Additionally, it evaluates Nigerian environmental laws, highlighting deficiencies that may contribute to persistent oil pollution. Furthermore, it explores issues of regulatory capture, corporate environmental crime, and the transnational litigation of Nigerian oil spill cases in the US, the UK, and the EU. The Petroleum Industry Act (PIA) 2021 is comprehensively assessed in the context of corporate environmental governance and oil pollution control.

To propose solutions, the book examines legal frameworks for strengthening corporate due diligence and accountability. It advocates for a robust legal regime to address the clean-up liability of pre-existing (stale) oil spills in the Niger Delta, drawing insights from the UK/EU laws on contaminated land, the US Comprehensive Environmental Response, Compensation, and Liability Act (CERCLA or the Superfund), and the UK laws on oil infrastructure decommissioning. Additionally, the book introduces a novel *failure to prevent* oil spill offence in Nigeria, an omission-based liability inspired by the UK Bribery Act 2010 and the UK Criminal Finances Act 2017.

This book will be of interest to researchers and practitioners in the field of environmental law, pollution, and land law.

Millicent Nwabu Ele is a UK-based law lecturer and academic researcher focusing on corporate environmental responsibility, clean energy, and pollution control laws. She has a PhD in environmental and energy law from University of Aberdeen, Scotland, UK, and an LL.M from Columbia University School of Law, New York, USA. Before her law degree at University of Nigeria, Nsukka, she read Zoology/Botany/Education at University of Ibadan, Nigeria and taught biology and human physiology for many years. Millicent is well-published in law and has broad legal experience. She has been admitted to practice law in Nigeria and the State of New York, USA.

Routledge Research in International Environmental Law

Environmental Liability and the Interplay between EU Law and International Law
Dr Emanuela Orlando

Implementing International Environmental Law and Policy
An Interactive Approach to Environmental Regulation
Joanna Miller Smallwood

Environmental Law and Governance in India
Sairam Bhat and Centre for Environmental Law, Education, Research, and Advocacy (CEERA)

Environmental Law and Policy in India
Sairam Bhat and Centre for Environmental Law, Education, Research, and Advocacy (CEERA)

Protection of the Environment under International Law during Occupation
International Humanitarian, Human Rights and Environmental Law
Waad Abualrob

State Accountability for Environmental Damage in International Armed Conflict
Aïda Tamer Chammas

Corporate Environmental Responsibility and Pollution Control Laws
The Case of Oil Spills in the Niger Delta
Millicent Ele

https://www.routledge.com/Routledge-Research-in-International-Environmental-Law/book-series/INTENVLAW

Corporate Environmental Responsibility and Pollution Control Laws

The Case of Oil Spills in the Niger Delta

Millicent Ele

Routledge
Taylor & Francis Group
LONDON AND NEW YORK

First published 2026
by Routledge
4 Park Square, Milton Park, Abingdon, Oxon OX14 4RN

and by Routledge
605 Third Avenue, New York, NY 10158

Routledge is an imprint of the Taylor & Francis Group, an informa business

British Library Cataloguing-in-Publication Data
A catalogue record for this book is available from the British Library

ISBN: 978-1-032-56363-3 (hbk)
ISBN: 978-1-032-56797-6 (pbk)
ISBN: 978-1-003-43515-0 (ebk)

DOI: 10.4324/9781003435150

Typeset in Times New Roman
by Apex CoVantage, LLC

To ongoing and sustained commitment to learning and scholarship and to all determined to provide impactful education and research to solve problems both local and global.

Contents

Preface

This book examines the case of oil spills in Nigeria and selected advanced jurisdictions – the US, the UK, and the EU. It analyses the conduct of major oil companies operating in the Niger Delta – specifically the Royal Dutch Shell (RDS) and its Nigerian Subsidiary the Shell Petroleum Development Company (Nig.) Ltd (SPDC) for onshore operations with occasional reference to the Shell Nigeria Exploration & Production Company (SNEPCo) for offshore operations; the US ExxonMobil Corporation and its Nigerian subsidiaries Mobil Producing Nigeria, Unlimited (MPN), and ESSO; the Italian Eni and its subsidiary, the Nigerian AGIP Oil Company (NAOC); etc. The work, however, also draws examples from BP Plc although BP ceased to have a Nigerian subsidiary since 1979.

Focus is placed mainly on Shell because it is the biggest, oldest, and the most dominant player in Nigeria's oil industry. It also has one of the worst records on oil spills in the Niger Delta. The Nigerian oil spill data analysed in this book are limited mainly to figures from 2010 to 2021. Particular attention is placed on operational spills rather than spills from oil pipeline vandalism because the former is under the direct control of the operator. The work did not cover the spill activities of the indigenous oil companies. Occasional reference is made, where relevant, to RDS's Annual Reports, and BP's Statistical Review of World Energy.

The hypothesis that oil spills in the Niger Delta appear not to be cleaned up in the same way as in the advanced jurisdictions was validated in this work by producing factual evidence of differential behaviour of the MNOCs to oil spill response and clean-up in the Niger Delta and the selected advanced jurisdictions.

This book also offers an analysis of Shell's oil spill environmental performance data as presented in the RDS's Annual Sustainability Reports from 2010 to 2021 and discovered that Shell's operational spills in Nigeria were disproportionately high, accounting for at least 30 percent of the global volume and 12 percent of the global number. This is very significant considering that Shell operates in more than 70 countries globally and that the operational spills are completely within the control of the operator.

The problem of oil spills in the Niger Delta have so far defied solution and therefore, there is a clear and present need to find an answer to it. This book proposed the enactment of a new *failure to prevent* oil spills offence in Nigeria with extraterritorial application modelled on the UK Bribery Act, 2010 and its progeny the UK

Criminal Finances Act, 2017. This is a fresh idea shown to be very comprehensive and far reaching both in its scope of operations and available sanctions. If adopted in Nigeria, the new law will apply extraterritorially in oil spill matters to any oil company that has a link with Nigeria, the same way the UK Bribery Act applies extraterritorially to any company with links to the UK.

The Niger delta is replete with pre-existing (stale) oil spills, which has no direct equivalence in the advanced jurisdictions. Current legal scholarship has not developed an effective way of managing and remediating the environment polluted by these spills. It is difficult to apportion clean-up liabilities to operators involved especially because some of the spills are from multiple sources and have existed for decades and without reliable spill records that will enable a definitive isolation of responsible parties for purposes of liability. In this book, a legal framework for solving this problem was developed with insights from the UK/EU regimes on contaminated land, the US CERCLA (the Superfund), and the UK laws on oil infrastructure decommissioning.

The book critically analysed the provisions of the Petroleum Industry Act (PIA) 2021. In line with the focus of this work, this analysis was limited to the sections that relate to environmental protection and pollution control in the upstream petroleum sector of the Nigerian oil and gas industry. Other ancillary issues such as regulatory capture and corporate environmental crime were also discussed making this book a compendium of detailed information on oil spill laws and corporate environmental responsibility.

The book would be of interest to academics, postgraduate researchers, and professionals in environmental management and policy, environmental law, energy resource management, and environmental justice. Additionally, it will be a valuable source of reference for environmental policy makers, regulators, government officials responsible for policy design and implementation, and environmental NGOs. It will also be of interest to those in the oil industry such as environmental managers and strategists and oil and gas legal practitioners both for the purposes of litigation and consultancy work on oil spill control and clean-up. It can also be recommended for teaching modules in environmental and energy law in universities.

Acknowledgments

It has been a journey filled with ebbs and flows, but I thank God for enabling me to get to the finish line. Thanks are also due to Professor John Paterson and Professor Tina Soliman Hunter for their guidance and encouragement. There are others too numerous to mention, my family and friends, and the entire editorial team at Routledge. I thank you all most sincerely.

Acronyms

ABNJ	Areas Beyond National Jurisdiction
ACP	Area Contingency Plan (USA)
AJA	Administration of Justice Act 1920 (UK)
API	American Petroleum Institute
ASME	The American Society of Mechanical Engineers
ATS	(United States) Alien Tort Statute
AU	The African Union
BA	(UK) Bribery Act
BAAC	Bonn Agreement Appearance Code
BAOAC	Bonn Agreement Oil Appearance Code
BAT	Best Available Technology
BEIS	(UK Department of) Business Energy and Industrial Strategy
EIICL	British Institute of International and Comparative Law
CAC	Corporate Affairs Commission (Nigeria)
CAMA	Company and Allied Matters Act (Nigeria)
CCPCJ	(UN) Commission on Crime Prevention and Criminal Justice
CCPCJ	UN Congress on Crime Prevention and Criminal Justice
CDDCA	Corporate Due Diligence and Corporate Accountability (EU)
CDP	The Carbon Disclosure Project
CEHRD	The Centre for Environment, and Human Rights Development
CERCLA	Comprehensive Environmental Response, Compensation and Liability Act
CFA	Conditional Fee Arrangement
CFCs	Chlorofluorocarbons
CITES	The Convention on International Trade in Endangered Species of Wild Fauna and Flora
CNA	The Clean Nigeria Associate
CoRA	Chain of Responsibility Act (Australia)
CSDDD	The Corporate Sustainability Due Diligence Directive (EU)
CSR	Corporate Social Responsibility
CWA	Clean Water Act (USA)

DCCP	Dutch Code of Civil Practice
DECC	Department of Energy and Climate Change (UK)
DES	Department of Environment and Science (Australia)
DoJ	(US) Department of Justice
DPR	Department of Petroleum Resources (Nigeria)
DRD	Decommissioning Relief Deed (UK)
DSA	Decommissioning Security Agreement
ECCJ	European Coalition for Corporate Justice
ECD	Environmental Crime Directive (EU)
ECOSOC	UN Economic and Social Council
ECOWAS	Economic Community of West African States
ECT	Environmental Courts and Tribunals
EFFACE	The European Union Action to Fight Environmental Crime
EGASPIN	Environmental Guidelines and Standards for the Petroleum Industry in Nigeria
EI	Energy Institute (London)
EIA	Environmental Investigation Agency
ELD	Environmental Liability Directive (EU)
EMAS	Eco-Management and Audit Scheme
ENRD	Environmental and National Resources Division
EPA	Environmental Protection Act
EPA	Environmental Protection Agency
EPO	Environmental Protection Order
ESG	Environmental, Social and Governance
ESO	Environmental service order (Australia)
EU	European Union
EWCA	England and Wales Court of Appeal
FCPA	(US) Foreign Corrupt Practices Act
FHC	Federal High Court (Nigeria)
FIRS	Federal Inland Revenue Services
FOEI	Friends of the Earth International
FPP	Forest Peoples Programme
FRN	Federal Republic of Nigeria
FSA	The Financial Service Authority
GHGs	Green House Gases
HCD Trust	Host Community Development Trust
HCFCs	Hydrochlorofluorocarbons
HSE	Health, Safety & Environment
HYPREP	The Hydrocarbon Pollution Remediation Project
ICC	International Chamber of Commerce
ICCWC	International Consortium on Combating Wildlife Crime
INTERPOL	The International Criminal Police Organisation
MEAs	Multilateral Environmental Conventions and Agreements
IJVC	Incorporated Joint Venture Company
ISO	International Standards Organization

IUCN	International Union for Conservation of Nature
JIV	Joint Investigation Visit
JOA	Joint Operating Agreement
JSI	Joint Spill Investigation
JV	Joint Venture
KCM	Konkola Copper Mines plc
LDS	Leak Detection System
LFN	Laws of the Federation of Nigeria
MMS	The Mineral Management Service (USA)
MNC	Multinational Company
MNOC	Multinational Oil Company
MPN	Mobil Producing Nigeria Unlimited
NACGOND	The National Coalition on Gas Flaring and Oil Spills in the Niger Delta
NAOC	Nigeria AGIP Oil Company
NCP	National Contingency Plan
NCS	Norwegian Continental Shelf
NDP	Niger Delta Development Programme
NESREA	National Environmental Standards and Regulations Enforcement Agency
NGO	Non-Governmental Organisation
NNPC	Nigerian National Petroleum Corporation
NNPC Ltd	Nigerian National Petroleum Company Limited
NOGP	National Oil and Gas Policy
NOSCP	National Oil Spill Contingency Plan
NOSDRA	National Oil Spill Detection and Response Agency
NPRC	Nigeria Petroleum Regulatory Commission
NSW	New South Wales, Australia
NSW LEC	New South Wales Land and Environment Court (Australia)
ODS	Ozone Depleting Substances
OECD	Organisation for Economic Co-operation and Development
OGA	Oil and Gas Authority (UK)
OGIC	Oil and Gas Sector Reform Implementation Committee
OHCHR	UN Office of the High Commissioner for Human Rights
OPA	Oil Pollution Act 1990 (USA)
OPEP	Oil Pollution Emergency Plans
OPRC	(International Convention on) Oil Pollution Preparedness and Response Cooperation
OPRED	Offshore Petroleum Regulator for Environment and Decommissioning
OSDAR	Oil Spill Damage Assessment Regulations
PEOA	Protection of the Environment Operations Act (NSW, Australia)
PES	Personnel Executive Secretary
PHCB	Petroleum Host Community Bill
PIA	Petroleum Industry Act

PIAB	Petroleum Industry Administration Bill
PIB	The Petroleum Industry Bill
PIFB	Petroleum Industry Fiscal Bill
PIGB	The Petroleum Industry Governance Bill
PON	Petroleum Operations Notice
PPPRA	Petroleum Products Pricing Regulatory Agency
PSC	Production Sharing Contracts
RCP	Regional Contingency Plan (Alaska)
RDS	Royal Dutch Shell
RILO AP	Regional Intelligence Liaison Office for Asia and the Pacific
SDGs	Sustainable Development Goals
SLCS	South Luangwa Conservation Society (Zambia)
SNEPCo	Shell Nigeria Exploration and Production Company
SPDC	Shell Petroleum Development Corporation
SPV	Special Purpose Vehicles
TCC	Technology and Construction Court (UK)
TFEU	Treaty on the Functioning of the European Union
TPH	Total Petroleum Hydrocarbon
UK	United Kingdom
UKCS	UK Continental Shelf
UKSC	UK Supreme Court
UNEP	United Nations Environment Programme
UNICRI	UN Interregional Crime and Justice Research Institute
UNDP	United Nations Development Programme
UNCAC	United Nations Convention against Corruption.
UNFCCC	UN Framework Convention on Climate Change
UNGC	UN Global Compact
UNGPs	UN Guiding Principles on Business and Human Rights
UNODC	UN Office of Drugs and Crime
WCO	World Customs Organisation
WHO	World Health Organization

1 Introduction

1. Introduction and Background

Nigeria is blessed with huge deposit of crude oil and natural gas, particularly in the rich wetlands of the Niger Delta. The Niger Delta located in the southernmost part of Nigeria covers a total land mass of about 70,000 km^2 with a population of about 30 million people.[1] It is the largest Delta in Africa and the third largest in the world.[2]

In the pre-oil and gas era, this region was characterised by lush brackish swamp and rain forest vegetation, expansive mangrove forest with a wide variety of flora and fauna.[3] The land was fertile for agriculture and the crisscrossing creeks housing many varieties of freshwater fishes – and other aquatic resources – were excellent for fishing by the local inhabitants.[4] However, oil exploration and production in the region has resulted in massive oil spills polluting the land and negatively impacting soil fertility.[5] The oil pollution penetrated far deeper underground than expected,[6] contaminating drinking and domestic water supplies.[7] Both the recurring spills and the ones accumulated over the years have thus resulted in lasting damage to the environment of this previously pristine and productive region.[8]

1 United Nations Environment Programme (UNEP), 'Environmental Assessment of Ogoniland' (2011) 20 <https://postconflict.unep.ch/publications/OEA/UNEP_OEA.pdf> accessed 04 September 2024.
2 UNEP (n 1).
3 O Adekola and G Mitchell, 'The Niger Delta Wetlands: Threats to Ecosystem Services, their Importance to Dependent Communities and Possible Management Measures' (2011) 7 Int J Bio-resour Stress Manage 50, 51–52.
4 MAO Aluko, 'Sustainable Development, Environmental Degradation and the Entrenchment of Poverty in the Niger Delta of Nigeria' (2004) 15(1) J Hum Ecol 63, 63–65; JC Ebegbulem, D Ekpe and T O Adejumo, 'Oil Exploration and Poverty in the Niger Delta Region of Nigeria: A Critical Analysis' (2013) 4(3) Int J Business Soc Sci 279, 280.
5 S Pegg and N Zabbey, 'Oil and Water: The Bodo Spills and the Destruction of Traditional Livelihood Structures in the Niger Delta' (2013) 48(3) OUP Commun Dev J 391; TA Abii and PC Nwosu, 'The Effect of Oil-Spillage on the Soil of Eleme in Rivers State of the Niger Delta Area of Nigeria' (2009) 3(3) Roman J Engl Stud 316.
6 UNEP (n 1) 20.
7 IL Worika, U Etemire and PS Tamuno, 'Oil Politics and the Application of Environmental Laws to the Pollution of the Niger Delta: Current Challenges and Prospects' (2019) 17(1) Oil Gas Energy Law 1, 3.
8 Damilola S Olawuyi, *The Principles of Nigerian Environmental Law* (Rev edn, Afe Babalola University Press 2015) 172.

DOI: 10.4324/9781003435150-1

Records indicate that oil spills occur frequently in the Niger Delta.[9] In 2021 alone, there were 409 publicly available oil spill records[10] and between 2010 and 2021 there was a yearly average of 893 oil spills in the Niger Delta.[11] Although figures vary markedly,[12] it is an undeniable fact that an unacceptable number and volume of oil spills have occurred and are still occurring in the Niger Delta today.[13] What is also true is that the bulk of the spilt oil has not been cleaned up[14] and has, thus, accumulated over the years in most parts of the Niger Delta. Most of these were onshore oil spills usually caused by aging pipelines, poor oil infrastructure maintenance, equipment failure, operational error, well blowout, accidents, corrosion, oil theft and bunkering, as well as acts of vandalism and sabotage.[15]

Table 1.1 Summary of Oil Spill Data in the Niger Delta 2010–21[16]

s/n	*Year*	*Total No. of Spills*	*Major**	*Med**	*Minor**	*Under 10 Barrels*	*No Category**	*Total Volume in Barrels*	*No JIV*	*Spills with No Vol.*
1	2021	409	2	6	257	186	139	23,489.38	32	133
2	2020	433	0	23	301	205	105	21,328.54	35	90
3	2019	709	5	28	452	310	209	38,446.21	70	193
4	2018	696	0	27	480	376	188	25,485.85	104	154
5	2017	595	4	15	380	304	195	32,181.15	73	178
6	2016	684	5	19	447	355	211	42,734.53	129	173
7	2015	920	4	27	582	459	304	47,701.63	158	268
8	2014	1521	8	30	903	713	580	78,890.46	284	540
9	2013	1666	1	29	823	625	813	32,292.16	450	762
10	2012	1135	4	34	698	505	399	41,802.00	179	391
11	2011	1058	2	23	663	455	370	73,131.01	218	359
12	2010	889	3	37	575	399	274	47,261.02	262	261
2010–21		10715	38	298	6561	4892	3787	504,743.94	1994	3502

* The minor spills include spills under ten barrels. Therefore, the total number of spills is made up of the major, medium, and minor spills and spills not categorised.

9 NOSDRA Oil Spill Monitor <https://nosdra.oilspillmonitor.ng/> accessed 04 September 2024. Nigerian Oil Spill Monitor <https://oilspillmonitor.ng/> accessed 04 September 2024.
10 NOSDRA and Nigerian Oil Spill Monitor (n 9) TABLE 1.
11 TABLE 1 (NOSDRA and Nigerian Oil Spill Monitor (n 9) TABLE 1).
12 For instance, the oil spill data summary from the NOSDRA Oil Spill Monitor for 12 years covering 2010–2021 gives the total volume of oil spilled during this period as 504,744 barrels (Table 1). But records on file at the Department of Petroleum Resources (DPR), Lagos, Nigeria in February 2016, indicated that a total of 773,727 barrels of oil were spilt in Nigeria in the 15 years between 1999 and 2014 – Dickson E Omukoro, 'Environmental Regulations in Nigeria and Liability for Oil-Pollution Damage: Musings from Norway and the US (Alaska)' (2017) 8 Interact Entertain Law Rev 324–30, 324.
13 NOSDRA and Nigerian Oil Spill Monitor (n 9).
14 Niger Delta Human Development Report (UNDP 2011) 87.
15 K Sam, F Coulon and G Prpich, 'Management of Petroleum Hydrocarbon Contamination Sites in Nigeria: Current Challenges and Future Direction' (2017) 64 Land Use Policy 133–34; D Olawuyi, 'Legal and Sustainable Development Impacts of Major Oil Spills' (2012) 9(1) J Sustain Dev 1–15; Nigerian Oil Spill Monitor (n 9).
16 NOSDRA and Nigerian Oil Spill Monitor (n 9).

Although oil was first discovered in Nigeria by Shell D'Arcy[17] in 1956 at Oloibiri in the present-day Bayelsa State, and a year later in Ogoniland, the latter soon became the focal point of oil exploration and production in the Niger Delta. Ogoniland covers about 1,000 km^2 in the south-eastern part of the Niger Delta with a population close to 832,000 consisting mainly of Ogoni people.[18] It has been the site of oil exploration and production mainly by Shell since the late 1950s with numerous oil spills.[19] However, Shell stopped drilling oil in this region in early 1990s (about 30 years ago) following continuous conflicts with the local community.

The UN Environment Programme (UNEP) on the invitation of the Nigerian government conducted a thorough environmental assessment of Ogoniland in 2011.[20] This remains, to date, the most comprehensive independent assessment of the environmental and public health impacts of oil contamination of any part of the Niger Delta. For about a year, the UNEP team worked with the agreement and support of the Ogoni communities, the Rivers State Government and other partners, gathering information from regulators, the Shell Petroleum Development Company (SPDC),[21] and community members within and around Ogoniland. They inspected hundreds of locations and more than a hundred kilometres of oil pipelines. They visited oil wells, spill sites, and oil-related facilities in Ogoniland.[22] They also reviewed Shell's oil spill response, clean-up, and remediation manual;[23] conducted water tests at various locations; and analysed the air in and around Ogoniland, the creeks including fishes and other aquatic resources, as well as sediments from the creeks.[24] This environmental assessment highlighted the enormous environmental damage done by oil spills in Ogoniland and, by extension, the Niger Delta.

The ongoing oil spills in the Niger Delta and the fact that these spills appear not to be cleaned up in the same way as in advanced jurisdictions[25] could indicate that Shell and the other multinational oil companies (MNOCs) operating in the region apply different standards in different places with respect to oil spills. This hypothesis was confirmed in 2010 when Richard Steiner on behalf of Friends of the Earth (*Milieudefensie*) published a report revealing the double standard that Shell practices in Nigeria compared to international standards for oil spill prevention and

17 A company formed by the Royal Dutch/Shell Group in 1936. It later entered a joint venture relationship with the British Petroleum to form Shell-BP in 1956 <https://www.shell.com.ng/about-us/shell-nigeria-history.html> accessed 2 September 2024.

18 The 2006 Nigerian National Census; UNEP (n 1) 22.

19 UNEP (n 1) 8, 24.

20 UNEP (n 1) 20.

21 The Nigerian subsidiary of the Royal Dutch Shell (RDS).

22 UNEP (n 1) 6–9.

23 UNEP (n 1) 85.

24 UNEP (n 1) 6–9.

25 'Advanced Jurisdictions' in this book refers to economically developed and industrialised countries with advanced technological infrastructure e.g., the US, the UK, and most countries of the EU. Lynge Nielsen, 'Classifications of Countries Based on Their Level of Development: How it is Done and How it Could be Done' (IMF Working Paper, WP/11/31, February 2011).

control.[26] Evidence indicates that Shell and the other MNOCs conduct petroleum operations in Nigeria far below commonly accepted international standards used in the advanced jurisdictions to prevent and control oil spills.[27] This is in violation of their corporate social responsibility (CSR),[28] international guidelines, and standards. This book, in part, investigates this differential corporate behaviour focusing on corporate environmental responsibility.

It is regrettable that there is marked absence of international legal obligations directly *binding* on multinational corporations and the domestic laws are generally too weak to effectively hold them accountable for their actions. So, though their activities cause severe negative impact on human health and the environment, there is much reliance on self-regulatory tools and voluntary initiatives, guidelines, and codes of conduct for regulating corporate behaviour. Soft law instruments are developed as a reference guide and standard for measuring corporate responsibility and good corporate behaviour.[29] Although these are not binding on the multinational corporations, they nevertheless provide uniform parameter for measuring corporate obligations generally and provide global standards for corporate environmental responsibility expected of businesses irrespective of the jurisdiction in which they operate. Thus, they provide the basis for holding the MNOCs operating in the Niger Delta to the same standard for oil spill control and clean-up applied in advanced jurisdictions. They are discussed in the following section.

2. Self-regulatory Tools and Voluntary Initiatives, Guidelines, and Codes of Conduct (Soft Law Instruments) for Regulating Corporate Behaviour

- The Rio Declaration on Environment and Development (in Agenda 21), 1992
- The International Standards Organisation (ISO) 14001 and related standards on Environmental Management Systems, 1996; as well as ISO 26000 (2010), which provides guidance on social responsibility (including standards on environmental sustainability)
- The UN Global Compact (UNGC) (Particularly Principles 7–9) (2000)

26 Richard Steiner, 'Double Standard: Shell Practices in Nigeria Compared with International Standards to Prevent and Control Pipeline Oil Spills and the Deepwater Horizon Oil Spill' *Milieudefensie*(November2010)4,6.<https://www.foei.org/wp-content/uploads/2014/01/20101109-rapport-Double-Standard.pdf> accessed 04 December 2022.

27 Numerous oil spill records in the Nigerian Oil Spill Monitor (n 9).

28 CSR has been defined as 'the responsibility of enterprises for their impacts on society.' See European Commission, Memo/11/730, Brussels, 25 October 2011 – the European Commission's new strategy on corporate social responsibility (CSR). <https://ec.europa.eu/commission/presscorner/detail/en/MEMO_11_730> accessed 22 August 2023.

29 A comprehensive list categorised by sector could be found in Deborah Leipziger, *The Corporate Responsibility Code Book* (3rd edn, Routledge 2017).

- The Organisation for Economic Co-operation and Development's (OECD) Guidelines for Multinational Enterprise (Part VI on Environment) (2011) and the 2023 Update
- The UN 17 Sustainable Development Goals (2015)
- Company Codes of Conduct

Companies are expected to adopt and comply with these instruments in support of their policy and practice as evidence of corporate responsibility, both for their parent and subsidiaries abroad. Despite being mostly self-regulatory in nature, they all help to strengthen corporate environmental responsibility and sustainable development. When they are publicly adopted by an enterprise, they form the basis for activists and non-governmental organisations (NGOs) to hold them accountable to the adopted standards and values, and this ultimately improve compliance. Although it is not quite certain how much they have helped to improve the environmental performance of oil companies or to prevent oil spills,[30] companies and businesses know that adherence to them reduces business risk and improves public image, consumer loyalty, reputation, and goodwill. Also, with the increase in environmental consciousness in recent decades,[31] potential investors, procurement agents, and customers are likely to reject goods and services that do not meet adequate environmental standards. As a result, enterprises tend to integrate social and environmental concerns into their business strategies. Unfortunately, this may also lead to box-ticking and phoney compliance in which a company may have excellent codes and at the same time very dishonest business practices. For instance, companies like Enron, WorldCom, Parmalat, etc. involved in monumental corporate scandals were known to have good declarations on codes of corporate responsibility.[32] So, genuine and accurate voluntary reporting and transparency remains very important. Next is a discussion of the listed soft law instruments.

2.1. The 1992 Rio Declaration on Environment and Development

The 1992 Rio Declaration on Environment and Development is a performance-oriented treaty that reaffirms and builds on the 1972 Stockholm Declaration.[33] It recognises that long term economic progress is only assured if it is linked with the protection of the environment. It encourages the establishment of

30 JG Frynas, 'Corporate Social Responsibility or Government Regulation? Evidence on Oil Spill Prevention' (2012) 17(4) Ecol Soc 4.

31 Caroline Flammer, 'Corporate Social Responsibility and Shareholder Reaction: The Environmental Awareness of Investors' (2012) 56(3) Acad Manage J 1 <https://doi.org/10.5465/amj.2011.0744>.

32 Bahram Soltani, 'The Anatomy of Corporate Fraud: A Comparative Analysis of High Profile American and European Corporate Scandals' (2014) 120(2) J Business Ethics 251–74; See generally: Paul H Dembinski and others (eds), *Enron and World Finance: A Case Study in Ethics* (Palgrave Macmillan 2005).

33 Declaration of the United Nations Conference on the Human Environment, Stockholm, Sweden, 5–16 June 1972, UN Doc. A/CONF.48/14/Rev (16 June 1972).

global partnerships among States, key sectors of the society, and people. It provides them with the inspiration to work towards international agreements that respect the interests of all and protect the integrity of the global environmental and developmental system. It has 27 principles[34] among which are Principle 4, which provides for sustainable development through environmental protection, and Principle 6, which prioritises the needs of developing countries and those most environmentally vulnerable in international actions on the environment and development even as the interests and needs of all countries are considered. Although many States have signed the 1992 Rio Declaration on Environment and Development,[35] it is neither binding on States nor directly on non-state actors like the multinational corporations, which are the usual culprits in environmental damage in transnational business.[36]

2.2. ISO 14001 and Related Standards

ISO 14001 and related standards are international voluntary environmental certifications used to track corporate environmental compliance. They set out the criteria for environmental management systems and provide practical tools for companies or organisations to follow in managing their environmental responsibilities.

Historically, BS 7750[37] is a forerunner to ISO 14001 first published in 1996 setting some minimum requirements for environmental management that an organisation needed to define. The ISO 14001, 2015 revision ushered in a harmonised approach with other ISO management systems ultimately aimed at positive environmental outcomes.[38] This is, so far, the world's most recognised standard for the assessment of an organisation's environmental management system against defined requirements.

34 The Rio Declaration on Environment and Development adopted by the UN Conference on Environment and Development 'Earth Summit' in Rio de Janeiro, Brazil, 3–14 June 1992, U.N. Doc. A/CONF.151/26 (Vol I).

35 Rio Declaration (n 34) which embodies such instruments as the precautionary approach.

36 Commentary on the environment provided under Chapter VI of the OECD Guidelines 2011 which states that 'None of these instruments is explicitly addressed to enterprises, although enterprise contributions are implicit in all of them.' – para 68 of the Commentary on the Environment chapter (VI) of the OECD Guidelines for Multinational Enterprises (2011) <http://mneguidelines.oecd.org/2011Environment.pdf> accessed 04 December 2024.

37 British Standards (BS) are the standards produced by the British Standards Institution (BSI) Group, which eventually became the national standards body (NSB) for the UK. In 1992 the BSI established BS 7750 as a standard for environmental control in the manufacturing and services sector. BS 7750 introduced an international standard that *contains a specification for an environmental management system that* enables organisations to develop publicly available environmental policies and objectives, targets, programmes and appropriate work instructions, which are then verified.

38 Adam Faiers, 'A Brief History of ISO 14001 Environmental Management' (*Spedan Blog*, 6 August 2018) <https://spedan.co.uk/blog/iso-14001-environment/a-brief-history-of-iso-14001-environmental-management#:~:text=BS%207750%20laid%20the%20foundation,the%20organisation%20needed%20to%20define> accessed 16 December 2023.

ISO 14001 can be certified to—and it provides assurances to—all stakeholders (internal and external) that environmental impact is being assessed and improved. It is a good business strategy and a show of corporate environmental responsibility to make obtaining international environmental certification a corporate obligation and a condition for all tender participants especially in sectors that are highly impactful on the environment e.g., Oil & Gas, Mining, and Power Generating Sectors etc.

ISO 26000 – Launched in 2010, provides guidance on social responsibility for businesses and organisations who recognise that respect for society and the environment is not only necessary for success but also the right thing to do. It was an expanded version of 14001 standards for companies and organisations of all kinds looking to manage their environmental responsibilities.[39] It is a comprehensive guideline on process and performance relating to governance, the environment, human rights, labour practices, etc.[40] It applies globally to all organisations and is linked to the UNGC, the OECD Guidelines for Multinational Enterprises, and the 2030 UN Agenda for Sustainable Development.[41]

Other environmental management standards include the Eco-Management and Audit Scheme (EMAS) – a voluntary environmental management instrument launched by the European Commission (EC) in 1993[42] to help companies and businesses to evaluate, report, and improve their environmental performance.[43] Then there is the Business Charter for Sustainable Development, which complements environmental management systems and provides a practical framework for companies and businesses to use in shaping their sustainability strategy. In line with this goal, the United Nations Environment Programme (UNEP) and the International Chamber of Commerce (ICC) among others have developed kits to assist companies and businesses integrate environmental management systems in their daily management practices.[44]

2.3. The UN Global Compact

The UNGC[45] is a non-binding UN initiative intended to get businesses all over the world to adopt and implement sustainable and socially responsible policies. It covers human rights, the environment, labour, anti-corruption, etc., and applicable

39 Hans van Loon, 'Principles and Building Blocks for a Global Legal Framework for Transnational Civil Litigation in Environmental Matters' (2018) 23 Unif Law Rev 298, 303.

40 Leipziger (n 29) 69–77.

41 Leipziger (n 29) 69; ISO 26000 – Social Responsibility <https://www.iso.org/iso-26000-social-responsibility.html> accessed 01 December 2023.

42 Regulation 1993/1836 – European Council Regulation (EEC) No: 1836/93, 29 June 1993.

43 Leipziger (n 29) 263–98; The European Commission Green Business <https://green-business.ec.europa.eu/eco-management-and-audit-scheme-emas_en> accessed 20 April 2023.

44 Leipziger (n 29) 258–62; ICC Business Charter for Sustainable Development, Document No 213/18–12 ABH – November 2014.

45 UN Global Compact (2000) <https://unglobalcompact.org/what-is-gc/mission/principles> accessed 04 December 2024; Leipziger (n 29) 56–66.

to all jurisdictions in which a company practices and throughout its value chain. The Compact has 10 Principles, and Principles 7–9 derived from the Rio Declaration and the Environment relate to the environment. They cover a precautionary approach to dealing with environmental challenges, the adoption of initiatives that promote greater environmental responsibility, and encourage the development and diffusion of environmentally friendly technologies. As of December 2023, almost 44 thousand participants, 167 countries, and 69 local networks had subscribed to it.[46]

2.4. The OECD Guidelines for Multinational Enterprise (Part VI on Environment)

The OECD Guidelines for Multinational Enterprise (Part VI on Environment) (2011) and the 2023 Update: The 2011 Guidelines requires multinational corporations to respect the wider goal of sustainable development. It also requires them to assess, and address in decision-making, the foreseeable environmental, health, and safety-related impacts associated with the processes, goods, and services of the enterprise over their full life cycle.[47] The OECD Guidelines on Responsible Business Conduct (2023)[48] that replaced the 2011 edition encourage positive contributions that enterprises can make to economic, environmental, and social progress, by minimising the adverse impacts caused through their operations, products, and services. If their operations result in severe negative impact on the environment or public health, the corporations/enterprise could be sued for damages and be held accountable.

The Guidelines cover all areas of responsible business conduct including human rights, labour rights, technology, the environment, health and safety, etc.[49] It encourages enterprises to work to raise the level of environmental performance in all jurisdictions in which they operate, even where this may not be formally required by existing practice in those jurisdictions. This would be especially relevant to business operations in developing countries.[50]

The guidelines also enjoin enterprises to operate within the framework of laws, regulations, and administrative practices and in consideration of relevant international agreements, principles, objectives, and standards.[51] In essence, they should conduct their business in a manner protective of the environment and contributing more broadly to sustainable development. They are, therefore, to avoid and address

46 The UNGC <https://www.unglobalcompact.org/> accessed 04 December 2024.

47 The OECD Guidelines for Multinational Enterprises (n 36) 42–43.

48 OECD, 'The OECD Guidelines for Multinational Enterprises on Responsible Business Conduct' (2023), Pt VI, with relevant commentaries on the environment, 33–38 <https://www.oecd.org/en/publications/oecd-guidelines-for-multinational-enterprises-on-responsible-business-conduct_81f92357-en.html> accessed 05 September 2024.

49 OECD (n 48) 33, introductory paragraph.

50 OECD (n 48) 37, para 82.

51 OECD (n 48) 33, introductory paragraph.

adverse environmental impacts relating to climate change, biodiversity loss, degradation of land, marine and freshwater ecosystems, deforestation, air, water and soil pollution, as well as proper waste management.[52] Although the Guidelines are non-binding, they require adhering countries to set up updated implementation procedures for the National Contact Points for Responsible Business Conduct.[53] This and the recommendations for enterprises to align with internationally agreed goals on climate change, biodiversity, business integrity, supply chain due diligence, and the use of technology are the key updates to the OECD guidelines in 2023.[54]

2.5. The UN Sustainable Development Goals (SDGs)

The 2030 United Nations Agenda for Sustainable Development, *Transforming Our World,*[55] adopted by all the UN Member States in 2015, has 17 Sustainable Development Goals. The aim is to bring together governments, the private sector, and civil society to work together to end poverty, improve health and education, reduce inequality, and spur economic growth while at the same time preserving the environment and tackling the challenges posed by climate change. In other words, sustainable development has three pillars – economic, social, and environmental, and it involves the interdependent protection of human rights and the environment[56] while stimulating economic growth. The Ruggie Principles on Business and Human Rights[57] and the SDGs fully support corporate responsibility for sustainable development. Also, John Knox in his report on human rights obligations relating to the environment concluded that human rights law includes obligations to the environment.[58] This shows a clear connection between human rights obligations of the States and corporations as outlined in the UNGPs by John Ruggie and their obligations to the environment as outlined in the Knox reports.[59] Therefore, corporate environmental responsibility should be measured against the fulfilment of

52 OECD (n 48) 33.
53 OECD (n 48) 77.
54 OECD (n 48).
55 The UN Agenda for Sustainable Development adopted by the UNGA on 25 September 2015, 'Effective 1 January 2016' (A/RES/70/1) UN SDGs <https://sdgs.un.org/goals> accessed 30 November 2023.
56 van Loon (n 39) 302.
57 Report developed by John Ruggie, the Special Representative of the Secretary-General on the Issue of Human Rights and Transnational Corporations and Other Business Enterprises (2008) UN Doc. A/HRC/8/35, paras 25 and 58. The Special Representative annexed the Guiding Principles to his final report to the Human Rights Council (A/HRC/17/31). The Human Rights Council endorsed the Guiding Principles in its resolution 17/4 (A.HRC.RES.17.4) of 16 June 2011. This Framework outlined the states' obligations to protect human rights and fundamental freedoms, corporate responsibility to respect human rights in business operations, and need for transnational corporations and other businesses to provide appropriate and effective remedies when these rights are breached.
58 John H Knox, 'Report of the Independent Expert on the Issue of Human Rights Obligations Relating to the Enjoyment of a Safe, Clean, Healthy and Sustainable Environment' John H Knox Mapping Report, UNHRCGAOR, 25th Sess (2013) A/HRC/25/53 1, para 79 <https://www.ohchr.org/en/special-procedures/sr-environment/mapping-report> accessed 15 April 2023.
59 Knox (n 58) paras 79–83 (Obligations relating to non-State actors).

environmental obligations both in terms of environmental sustainability and remedies for environmental harm (including harm caused by private actors/corporations).[60] It should be noted that the UN General Assembly (UNGA) endorsed access to a safe, clean, healthy, and sustainable environment as a universal human right in July 2022.[61]

2.6. Company Codes of Conduct

These are codes of conducts declared by individual companies. They vary in scope and content from company to company and from sector to sector. While service and manufacturing industries may focus on their responsibilities to customers, oil companies may focus on codes that address environmental sustainability. But in general, these codes provide valuable guide for companies and help to raise awareness about corporate responsibility among employees, develop corporate identity, and enhance stakeholder trust and value.[62]

3. Core Principles, Values, and Rights Underpinning Environmental Law

Apart from the codes and standards, there are core principles, values, and rights that underpin environmental law and are relevant to pollution prevention and control. These include:

- The Polluter-pays Principle
- The Precautionary Principle
- The principle of preventive action, and the principle that environmental damage should be rectified at source
- The principle of sustainable development
- Civil Actions in Tort

3.1. The Polluter-pays Principle

The polluter-pays principle provides that those who are responsible for pollution must pay for its clean-up and restoration of the polluted environment as well as compensation to the victims of such pollution. Proper implementation of this principle is hoped to incentivise the polluter (corporation or business) to adopt pollution-prevention or pollution-reduction methods of production and services to avoid liabilities. However, this principle does not necessarily provide guidance on the precise way financial liability for environmental damage may be imposed and the extent of that liability. For instance, it is difficult to correctly

60 Knox Mapping Report (n 58) (summary).
61 UNGA Resolution A/76/L.75 and A/76/L.75/Add1 (28 July 2022).
62 Leipzige (n 29) 27–28.

quantify environmental damages for the purposes of full remediation and payment of compensation when damages to natural resources are involved as these could be underestimated. Also, there are variations in standards in different jurisdictions regarding what polluters pay for damages resulting from the pollution. In Europe, the possibility of not fully paying for the costs of pollution or evading liability for full payment of pollution damage was part of the reasons for the enactment of the Environmental Liability Directive (ELD).[63]

The polluter-pays principle is rooted on the environmental principles set out in Article 191 (2) of the Treaty on the Functioning of the European Union (TFEU).[64] The polluter-pays principle was also preserved in the 1972 Stockholm Declaration, principle 21, and the 1992 Rio Declaration, principles 2 and 6.[65] In Nigeria, this principle is not explicitly provided for, in any legislation. Although the Nigerian courts generally hold polluters liable for their action under the torts of negligence,[66] nuisance, and the strict liability rule in *Ryland v Fletcher*,[67] they do not necessarily do this as environmental matters involving the polluter-pays principle.

3.2. The Precautionary Principle

The precautionary principle arises in situations when policy makers must make decisions about environmental regulation of an activity, product, or process in the face of uncertainties about potential risk of harm to the public or the environment resulting from the outcome of such decision. This is either because the activity, product, or process is novel or because the functioning of the environment regarding that activity, product, or process is not understood. In such instances, the precautionary principle dictates that protective action should be taken before there is complete scientific proof of environmental harm or human health hazard. This principle, therefore, gives regulators the authority to take action to prevent possible but unproven harm. It emphasises caution and review before embarking on new productions and developments that may be harmful. For example: Article 3 of the United Nations Framework Convention on Climate Change (UNFCCC) establishes that 'parties should take precautionary measures to anticipate, prevent, or minimize the causes of climate change and mitigate its adverse effects.' As a result, the precautionary principle has been invoked to justify a policy of aggressive

63 Directive 2004/35/CE on environmental liability regarding the prevention and remedying of environmental damage [2004] OJ L143/56, art 14(1). See also ELD, arts 2(16) and 8(1).

64 These principles are the precautionary principle, the principle of preventive action, the principle that environmental damage should be rectified at source as well as the 'polluter-pays' Principle.

65 The Stockholm Declaration (n 33); The Rio Declaration (n 34).

66 *SPDC (Nig) Ltd v Tiegbo VII* (2005) 9 NWLR (Pt 931) 439 (2005) 3–4 S.C 137; *Chief Pere Ajuwa & Others v Shell Petroleum Development Company Nig Ltd* (2011) 18 NWLR (Pt 1279); *Shell Petroleum Development Company Limited* vs *Abel Isaiah and others* (2001) 11 NWLR (Pt 723) 168.

67 *Ryland v Fletcher* (1866) L.R.1 Ex 265; (1868) L. R. 1 H. L. 330. The Nigerian courts have reaffirmed that the strict liability rule established in this case is applicable to the petroleum industry because the use of land for petroleum operation is a non-natural use – *Umudje v Shell Petroleum Development Co. of Nigeria Ltd* (1975) 11 SC 155.

greenhouse gas (GHG) emission controls to reduce global warming, even before complete proof of the harmful effect of GHG to the global temperature.

3.3. The Principle of Preventive Action and the Principle that Environmental Damage Should be Remedied at Source

The principle of preventive action requires that proactive and preventive measures be taken to avoid environmental damage before it happens. It allows action to be taken to protect the environment at an early stage and to prevent damages occurring in the first place. However, where environmental damage has occurred, it must be remedied at source. This makes sense, but the principle remains vague in terms of the exact actions required of States to prevent environmental harm.

3.4. The Principle of Sustainable Development

The concept of sustainable development was described in the 1987 Brundtland Commission Report as 'development that meets the needs of the present without compromising the ability of future generations to meet their own needs.'[68] For example, the unrestrained exploitation of natural resources generates waste and pollution that damages the environment and are thus detrimental to the interest of the future generation.

The concept of sustainable development is extremely significant on policy and law for environmental protection. The first international attempt to introduce sustainable development was in the 1992 UN conference on Environment and Development in Rio.[69] It recognised the fact that environmental protection is imperative if sustainable development is to be achieved.[70] However, both the Rio Declaration and the OECD Guidelines on Multinational Enterprises, which requires multinational corporations *to respect* the wider goal of sustainable development,[71] are not binding on non-state actors like transnational businesses and corporations. Yet, these are the usual culprits of environmental damage. So, the voluntary nature of this guideline arguably weakens its impact on corporate environmental responsibility and accountability.

3.5. Civil Actions in Tort

Environmental pollution control and prevention could also be through enforcement of environmental laws, liability for environmental damage, and remedies for environmental harm. These are accomplished through civil actions in torts of negligence, trespass, nuisance, and strict liability. In fact, most transnational private

68 World Commission on Environment and Development, *Our Common Future*, The Brundtland Report (OUP 1987).

69 The Rio Declaration (n 34).

70 The Rio Declaration (n 34) Principles 4 and 8.

71 The OECD Guidelines for Multinational Enterprises (n 36) 42–43.

litigations on environmental matters are based on human rights and civil liability (tort) law and these could involve extraterritorial application of domestic tort law to damages caused by transnational companies abroad. This is a common way of enforcing transnational corporate responsibility[72] and seeking redress for environmental harm committed by a company.

Recent decisions in the United Kingdom (UK) and the Netherlands indicate that a parent company domiciled in the UK and the EU may be sued as an anchor defendant for an environmental damage cause by its subsidiary abroad.[73] Although opportunities to litigate Nigerian oil spill cases against MNOCs remain open in the USA under the Alien Tort Statute, albeit small, following the US Supreme Court decision in the Kiobel case,[74] the opening for bringing such a suit is greater in Europe based on jurisdiction granted under the Recast Brussels Regulation.[75] *Forum non conveniens* may be an issue under the US Alien Tort Statute but it does not arise under the Brussels Regulation.[76]

4. Conclusion

In conclusion, the soft law instruments and core environmental principles and values, as well as civil actions in tort law, have great significance in environmental law and policy and underpin corporate environmental accountability and responsibility. The totality of all of them informs the impetus for the expectation that transnational corporations should maintain the same standard of environmental practice in all jurisdictions in which they operate.

As already stated, apart from being the oldest and most dominant player in the oil and gas industry in Nigeria, Shell also has one of the worst records in oil spills in the Niger Delta as seen from the oil spill summary (in number and volumes) of the subsidiaries of major oil companies in the Niger Delta, from 2010–21.[77]

72 van Loon (n 39) 298.

73 *Okpabi and Others v RDS plc and SPDC (Nig) Ltd* [2021] UKSC 3; *Oguru, Efanga and Milieudefensie v RDS and SPDC*, ECLI:NL:GHDHA:2021:132; *Dooh and Milieudefensie v RDS and SPDC*, ECLI:NL:GHDHA:2021:133; *Akpan and Milieudefensie v RDS and SPDC*, ECLI: NL: GHDHA: 2021: 134.

74 *Kiobel v Royal Dutch Petroleum Co* 569 US 108 (2013) 5.

75 Regulation (Eu) No 1215/2012 of the European Parliament and of the Council on jurisdiction and the recognition and enforcement of judgments in civil and commercial matters (recast) (Recast Brussels Regulation) art 63(1) read together with art 4(1).

76 *Andrew Owusu v N. B. Jackson* CJEU (1 March 2005) C-281/02.

77 NOSDRA and Nigerian Oil Spill Monitor (n 9) updated 11 July 2023. See the pie charts showing number and volume of spills. Volume is measured in barrels (bbls). [SPDC 2618=164147bbls; NAOC 4985=101373bbls; Chevron 462=3963bbls; Total 124=4724bbls; MPN 695=44118bbls; ESSO 22=99bbls; Addax 44=2212bbls; SNEPCo 7=40563bbls.]

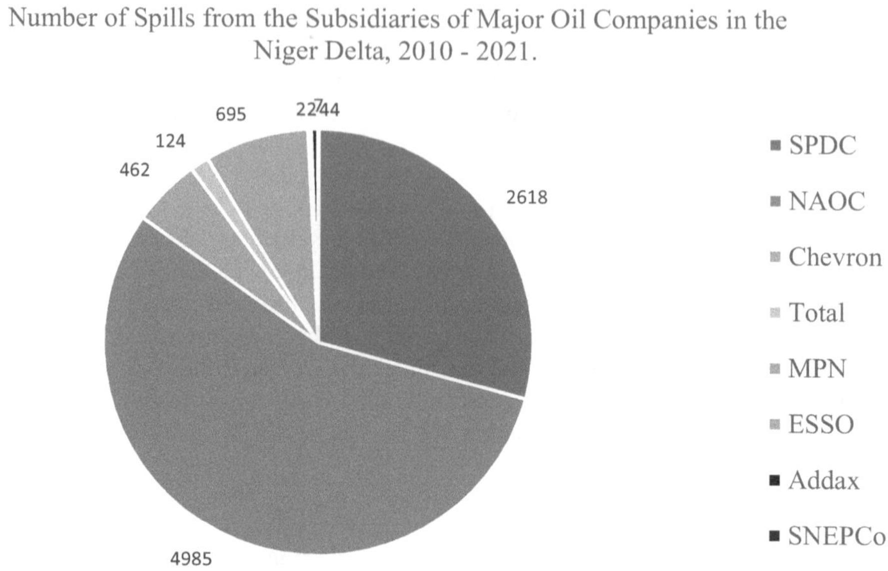

Figure 1.1 Number of Spills from the Subsidiaries of Major Oil Companies in the Niger Delta, 2010–21.

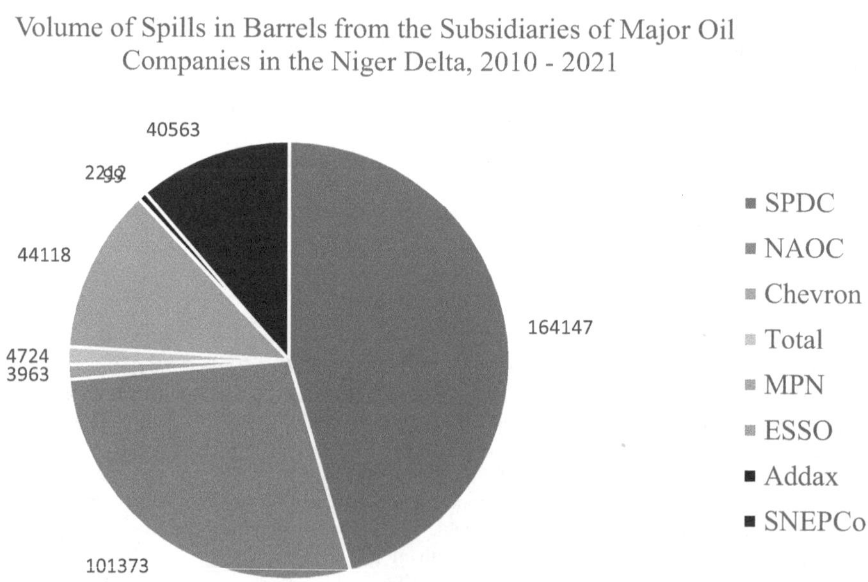

Figure 1.2 Volume of Spills in Barrels from the Subsidiaries of Major Oil Companies in the Niger Delta, 2010–21.

Sources: Volume of spills, measured in barrels (Bbls) and 1 bbl = 42 US gallons.

- The Shell Petroleum Development Company (SPDC) and the Shell Nigeria E&P Company (SNEPCo) are the Nigerian subsidiaries of Royal Dutch Shell (RDS)
- Nigerian AGIP Oil Company (NAOC) is the Nigerian subsidiary of the Italian Eni
- Chevron Nigeria Ltd is the Nigerian subsidiary of the US Chevron
- Total E&P Nigeria Ltd is the Nigerian subsidiary of the French Total
- Mobil Producing Nigeria Unlimited (MPN) and ESSO E&P Nigeria Ltd are the Nigerian subsidiaries of the US ExxonMobil
- Addax Petroleum Nigeria Ltd is the Nigerian subsidiary of Chinese Sinopec Group

Note: This work did not cover indigenous oil companies although at the time of this writing, there are 38 of them recorded by NOSDRA in the NOSDRA Oil Spill Monitor, some with significant spills.[78] However, this number may be below the actual operative indigenous oil companies in the Niger Delta because NOSDRA acknowledged that some companies may have no spill data available.

Although NAOC, on the average, have a greater number of spills in the twelve-year study period (4,985) than SPDC (2,618), SPDC has a larger volume of spills (164,147 bbls) than NAOC (101,373 bbls). The two companies are, by far, the heaviest spillers in the Niger Delta, and when the SPDC figures are added to the SNEPCo figures (seven spills totalling 40,563 bbls), then one can rightly say that Shell is the worst oil spiller in the Niger Delta. Thus, it merits special attention.

78 NOSDRA and Nigerian Oil Spill Monitor (n 9).

2 Oil Spill Prevention, Sanctions, and Payment of Compensations

1. Introduction

Chapter one of this book highlighted commonly accepted international standards for pollution control, offering a theoretical basis for expecting the same standard of behaviour from the MNOCs operating in Nigeria as is expected when they operate in the selected advanced jurisdictions. However, it appears as if they behave differently in different jurisdictions and this chapter will attempt to show factual evidence of differential corporate behaviour of the MNOCs in relation to oil spills in Nigeria and the selected advanced jurisdictions. This will be presented under five sub-headings as follows:

1. Compliance with petroleum laws and regulations.
2. Determination of cause and volume of spills.
3. Oil spill response and clean-up.
4. Contingency Plan for Oil Spill Response and Clean-up.
5. Oil Spill Sanctions and Payment of Compensations.

2. Compliance with Petroleum Laws and Regulations

Nigerian law provides that oil spill incidents should be reported to the National Oil Spill Detection and Response Agency (NOSDRA) in writing, by fax, or by electronic mail by the oil company/spiller within 24 hours of the onset of the spill.[1]

The Nigerian Oil Spill Monitor is replete with evidence of non-compliance to this requirement by the MNOCs as shown through the Joint Investigation Visit (JIV) forms and reports posted in the site.[2] Both the oil spill incident forms filled

1 The National Oil Spill Detection and Response Agency (NOSDRA) (Establishment) Act 2006 s 6(2). Hereinafter, NOSDRA (Est) Act 2006; Environmental Guidelines and Standards for Petroleum Industries in Nigeria (EGASPIN) 2018, Part VIII, s 6(1)(i).

2 Nigerian Oil Spill Monitor <https://oilspillmonitor.ng/> accessed 07 September 2024; The NOSDRA Oil Spill Monitor <https://nosdra.oilspillmonitor.ng/> accessed 07 September 2024.

DOI: 10.4324/9781003435150-2

by the NOSDRA and the ones completed by the oil companies show widespread non-compliance with this requirement.[3]

In the US, the Environmental Protection Agency (EPA) requires that the operator *reports immediately* any oil spill incident.[4] In the UK, telephone notifications of onset of spills (offshore) must also be made *immediately* within one hour while the electronic Petroleum Operations Notice (PON) submissions must be made within six hours in accordance with the BEIS PON1 Guidance.[5] Evidence indicates that the MNOCs comply with these provisions. For example, when a Shell pipeline ruptured in May 2016 near Tracy California, the company immediately shut down the pipeline and reported the spill with the Governor's Office of Emergency Services as the law requires.[6] Also, when an Exxon-operated pipeline ruptured near Torbert in Louisiana, USA in April 2012, Exxon shut down the pipeline the same day and immediately reported the leak to the appropriate authority as the law required.[7]

In the UK, the oil companies are known to report spills and deal with it promptly even when the spill is below the threshold level for reporting. For instance, in December 2017 when a threat of oil spill incident involving a mere *hairline crack* in the onshore portion of the BP Forties crude oil pipelines occurred in the North Sea, INEOS, the new owners, shut down the pipelines and reported the incident.[8]

> The Nigerian Law provides that response to and clean-up of oil spills is to commence within 24 hours of the onset of the spill.[9]

Evidence of non-compliance with this law by the MNOCs abound in the Nigerian Oil Spill Monitor as shown through the JIV forms and reports posted on the site.

3 Nigerian Oil Spill Monitor and NOSDRA (n 2).

4 The US Clean Water Act as amended by the Oil Pollution Act of 1990, s 311(j)(1)(C); 40 CFR s 110(1) – (3); For Alaska: Alaska Regional Contingency Plan, Version 1, Final, August 2018, 17, 36, 68 <https://dec.alaska.gov/spar/ppr/contingency-plans/response-plans/regional-contingency-plan/> accessed 07 September 2024.

5 BEIS Department, 'Guidance Notes for Preparing Oil Pollution Emergency Plans (OPEPs) for Offshore Oil and Gas Installations and Relevant Oil Handling Facilities' (2022) <https://assets.publishing.service.gov.uk/media/62a9992ad3bf7f036cb7a22e/OPEP_Guidance_-_Rev_7_-_June_2022.pdf> accessed 07 December 2024.

6 Ted Goldberg, 'Pipeline at Centre of Altamont Pass Oil Spill Also Ruptured Last September' *KQED News* (24 May 2016) <https://www.kqed.org/news/10966238/pipeline-at-center-of-altamont-pass-oil-spill-alsoruptured-last-september> accessed 07 September 2024.

7 State of Louisiana, Department of Environmental Quality, 'In the Matter of: ExxonMobil Pipeline Company – Settlement Tracking No: SA-WE-15–0077' (4 March 2016) <http://deq.louisiana.gov/assets/docs/General/Settlement_Agreements/2016/Exxon0077_Final.pdf> accessed 07 September 2024; Janet McGurty and Matt Daily, 'Exxon Mobil Shuts Louisiana Oil Pipeline after Leak' *Reuters Business New* (30April2012)<https://www.reuters.com/article/us-exxon-spill/exxon-mobil-shuts-louisiana-oil-pipeline-afterleak-idusbre83t0k120120430> accessed 07 September 2024.

8 Christopher E Smith, 'Ineos Shuts Forties Crude Oil Pipeline Following Leak' (2017) Oesophago-Gastric Junct (12 December 2017) <https://www.ogj.com/articles/2017/12/ineos-shuts-forties-crude-oil-pipeline-following-leak.html accessed 07 September 2024.

9 EGASPIN (n 1) Part VIII B 2.6.3.

Clean-up of oil spills in the Niger Delta is often slow and below international best practices[10] where it is done at all.[11] For instance, the 2008 Bodo oil spill caused by operational error was not contained by Shell for weeks[12] and clean-up was very slow and arguably still not completed at the time of this writing. The contrary seems to be the case when oil spills occur in the advanced countries. For instance, in 2011 when oil leaked from Shell's Gannet Alpha platform in the UK North Sea, Shell quickly stopped the leak and cleaned up the spill.[13] In July 2011 when an Exxon-operated crude oil pipeline ruptured and spilled oil into the Yellowstone River and floodplains of Montana, USA, the company quickly stopped the spill and immediately started an extensive clean-up.[14] It is on record that the clean-up of the Gulf after the 2010 oil spill was started immediately by the Bp plc and was so thoroughly done within four months that President Barack Obama was able to have a demonstration swim in the beach waters after the clean-up just to show the waters were safe.[15] This cannot be said of oil polluted land and creeks in the Niger Delta where most of them remain unsuitable for agriculture and fishing even after clean-up.

> The Nigerian law provides that a joint investigation visit should be carried out within 24 hours of spill notification to investigate the spillage and determine the cause and the impact.[16]

The Environmental Guidelines and Standards for the Petroleum Industry in Nigeria (EGASPIN) requires that a Joint Spill Investigation (JSI) team be activated by the Operator of the affected facility within 24 hours of spill notification to conduct a Joint Investigation Visit (JIV).[17] However, reports indicate that it takes Shell an

10 United Nations Environment Programme (UNEP), 'Environmental Assessment of Ogoniland' (2011) 146–47, 175 – SPDC's clean-up value was set at 5,000 mg/kg Total Petroleum Hydrocarbon (TPH) corresponding to the risk threshold of 1/10,000. But WHO's guidelines are based on clean-up standard of 500 mg/kg TPH, corresponding to a risk threshold of 1/100,000.

11 Nigerian Oil Spill Monitor (n 2); Amnesty International, 'Shell in Nigeria Briefing: Shell – Own UP, Pay Up and Clean Up' *Amnesty International* (2012) <http://www.amnesty.org.uk/sites/default/files/shell_briefing_2012_lores_0.pdf> accessed 07 September 2024.

12 Nigerian Oil Spill Monitor (n 2).

13 Fiona Harvey, 'Oil Spill Investigation begins as Shell Plugs North Sea leak' *The Guardian* (22 August 2011) <https://www.theguardian.com/environment/2011/aug/22/shell-north-sea-oil-leak> accessed 07 September 2024.

14 McGurty and Daily (n 7).

15 Suzanne Goldenberg, 'BP Oil Spill: Barack Obama Dives into Safety Debate with Gulf of Mexico Swim' (15 August 2010) <https://www.theguardian.com/environment/2010/aug/15/barack-obama-swim-gulf-florida> accessed 07 September 2024.

16 EGASPIN (n 1) Pt II, para 5.6.3.

17 EGASPIN (n 1). The JSI team usually comprise of the Licencee/Operator/Spiller/oil company, representative of the Community, any third party responsible for the spill (where known), the appropriate government agency – mainly the Department of Petroleum Resources (DPR, now the Nigerian Upstream Regulatory Commission or the Commission) pre-2006 or the NOSDRA from 2006, the Ministry of Environment, and the Local Government Council. Representatives of a coalition of major NGOs in the Niger Delta – The National Coalition on Gas Flaring and Oil Spills in the Niger

average of 5.35 days to conduct JIV on land and 9.68 days to conduct it for spills on water.[18] This evidence of non-compliance with the Guideline is corroborated by Shell's report in 2019 stating that JIVs now commence within three days compared to six days in 2016.[19]

JIVs are not conducted in the USA. Rather, the EPA requires that the operator/ the person in charge of the facility (or vessel) *reports immediately* any oil spill and supplies the cause of the spill.[20] JIVs are also not conducted in the UK, but the operator is expected to furnish the regulators with the cause of spill and the circumstances surrounding it which the latter will then investigate in line with the enforcement policy.[21] Nothing suggests that Shell and the other MNOCs do not comply with these requirements as opposed to their conduct in the Niger Delta.

3. Determination of Cause and Volume of Spill

> The Nigerian law also requires that the cause and volume of spill as well as the degree or level of impact be determined during the JIV by the JSI team within 24 hours of spill notification.[22]

Although oil pipeline sabotage/vandalism is rampant in the Niger Delta, the method of establishing cause of spill in the region may be biased in favour of that conclusion. In the Niger Delta cause of spill could be determined by the visual observation of the position of the spill hole on the oil pipeline – the o'clock rule or cross-sectional method.[23] By this method, if the spill hole is at or above the three and nine 9 o'clock mark on a cross section of the oil pipeline, the spill is ruled to be caused by sabotage (third party interference), but if the hole is at the six o'clock mark on the cross section of the pipeline, then it is ruled most likely to be due to corrosion.[24] There is no clear provision on who has the final authority to decide the cause of spill if there is a disagreement among the members of the JIV team. These

---

Delta (NACGOND) are now allowed as part of the JIV with observer status and the right to publish their observation independently – Shell Sustainability Report, 2014, 37.

18 Amnesty International, 'Negligence in the Niger Delta: Decoding Shell and Eni's Poor Records on Oil Spills' *Amnesty International* (16 March 2018) 7<https://www.amnesty.org/en/documents/afr44/7970/2018/en/> accessed 07 September 2024.

19 RDS Sustainability Report, 2019, 75.

20 The US Clean Water Act (n 4) s 311(j)(1)(C).

21 Mick Creary, Offshore Environmental Inspector, UK Department of Business, Energy and Industrial Strategy (BEIS), Aberdeen, Scotland. The BEIS and Offshore Petroleum Regulator for Environment and Decommissioning (OPRED) Enforcement Policy <https://www.gov.uk/guidance/oil-and-gas-decc-publicregisters-of-enforcement-activity#enforcement-policy accessed 5 April 2020. (BEIS was replaced in February 2023 by Department for Business and Trade (DBT), the Department for Energy Security and Net Zero (DESNZ) and the Department for Science, Innovation and Technology (DSIT)).

22 EGASPIN (n 1) Pt II, para 5.6.3; Appendix VIII-B5 (JIV Form).

23 Amnesty International and the Centre for Environment, Human Rights Development (CEHRD), 'Bad Information: Oil Spill Investigations in the Niger Delta' *Amnesty International* (7 November 2013) 21 <www.amnesty.org/en/documents/AFR44/028/2013/en/> accessed 07 September 2024.

24 Amnesty International and CEHRD (n 23).

observations are recorded accordingly on the NOSDRA JIV Form.[25] This method has been criticised as inaccurate and unscientific.[26]

Not making use of a more objective method of determining the cause of spill in the Niger Delta makes the outcome questionable. Additionally, this induces oil companies to claim that oil pipeline sabotage is the cause of most spills in the Niger Delta. In March 2018, Amnesty International published the result of crowdsourcing research by thousands of Amnesty International supporters and activists which delved into the operational practices of the oil industry in the Niger Delta.[27] The research analysed thousands of documents and photographs relating to oil spills that have been made public by the Royal Dutch Shell and the Italian Eni. The findings from this research exposed the systemic flaws in the JIV process and noted that at least 89 spills may have been wrongly attributed to sabotage or theft by Shell and Eni.[28]

There is no information on the frequency of pipeline rupture at specific points on the cross section of oil pipeline in the UK or the USA, to enable a comparison. There is also no indication that the o'clock method is used by Shell or any other MNOC in the advanced jurisdictions. Rather, in the US, the EPA requires that the operator immediately reports any oil spill into navigable waters or adjoining shorelines and also supplies the cause of the spill.[29] Similarly, in the UK, the operator is expected to furnish the regulators with the cause of spill, which the latter will then investigate in line with the enforcement policy.[30] The UK does not have anything similar to the JIV but the regulators have the powers to visit the installations involved in the oil spills (the *locus in quo*) and to investigate and take statements.[31] The difference in the methods of determining cause of spill in Nigeria and the advanced jurisdiction increases the probability of differential behaviours of the MNOCs between the two jurisdictions.

Volume of spill in the Niger Delta is visually estimated.[32] This is unreliable and could lead to underestimation.[33] The usual delay between the onset of the spill and JIV[34] could affect the determination of volume of the spill because some of the oil

25 NOSDRA JIV Form para 5(i) covers visual observation of hole position and para 5(iv) covers cause of spill which could be corrosion, equipment failure, third-party interference, accident, operational error, and others.

26 Michael Watts and Anna Zalik, 'Consistently Unreliable Oil Spill Data and Transparency Discourse' (2020) 7(3) Extr Ind Soc 790, 793.

27 Amnesty International, 'Negligence in the Niger Delta' (n 18).

28 Amnesty International, 'Negligence in the Niger Delta' (n 18) 7. In that research, Shell and Eni's poor record on oil spills in the Niger Delta was made plain by analysing thousands of oil spill documents and photographs made public by the two companies.

29 The US Clean Water Act (n 4) s 311(j)(1)(C).

30 Creary, Offshore Environmental Inspector, BEIS (n 21).

31 The Offshore Petroleum Activities (Oil Pollution Prevention and Control (OPPC Regulations 2005), s 12(1)–(3), s 12(3).

32 Amnesty International and CEHRD (n 23) 28–29.

33 Amnesty International and CEHRD (n 23).

34 JIVs don't usually occur within 24 hours of the onset of spill as the law requires.

would have been absorbed by the soil if on land[35] or carried away by water if the spill was in the creeks. This further supports the argument that the credibility and legitimacy of the JIV reports for volume of spill in the Niger Delta are doubtful.[36] Yet, this affects the determination of cause and volume of spills and the quantum of compensation payable in the Niger Delta. Despite the JIV, however, the volume of spill is generally supplied by the oil industry from whose facility the spill issues.[37] This does not necessarily make it more reliable without scientific means of calculating or estimating the volume.

In the UK, the operator must ensure that the amount of oil released to sea (offshore) is quantified as accurately as possible[38] by any of the following means:

1. Based on level indication, tank drop, tank volume, metering etc.[39]
2. Based upon a known flow rate (size of the leak point and oil flow per unit of time)[40] or more accurately through *Mass Balance* calculation[41] – calculated from known quantities and known concentrations.
3. By using the *Bonn Agreement Oil Appearance Code* (BAOAC).[42] Although this is also a visual estimate of the volume of spill on Sea surface, it presents a more objective estimate because of the colour code and the even and visible nature of the sea surface as opposed to the swamps and creeks of the Niger Delta.

Each of these methods ensures a more objective estimation of the volume of spill than the visual method often employed in the Niger Delta.

4. Oil Spill Response and Clean-up

> The Nigerian Law provides that oil spill response and clean-up should commence within 24 hours of the onset of the spill.[43]

Evidence of non-compliance with this provision by the oil companies in the Niger Delta abound from the records in the Nigerian Oil Spill monitor. Records indicate

35 Although the rate will depend on the absorption and adsorption co-efficient of the soil, impacted by soil type, porosity, permeability, and previous rainfall.

36 Amnesty International and CEHRD (n 23) 7.

37 Watts and Zalik (26).

38 BEIS (n 5) Appendix A5 (Guidance on Requirements for Consolidated OPEPs) 28.

39 BEIS (n 5) 35.

40 BEIS (n 5).

41 Mark Reed and others, 'Numerical Model for Estimation of Pipeline Oil Spill Volumes' (2006) 21(2) Environ Model Softw 178 <https://www.sciencedirect.com/science/article/pii/S1364815204002506> accessed 30 April 2023.

42 BAOAC is derived from the Bonn Agreement Appearance Code (BAAC), first developed in 1993 and used to estimate the volume of oil on the sea surface. The BAAC had a seven-colour code that used visual inspection to estimate the amount of oil spilled on the sea surface – each colour representing different thickness of spilled oil. In 2004, the BAAC was renamed the Bonn Agreement Oil Appearance Code (BAOAC) when the colours were reduced from seven to five to make it easier to use.

43 EGASPIN (n 1) Part VIII B 2.6.3.

that similar oil companies operating in the advanced countries act speedily in response to oil spills. For instance, in 2011 when a subsea pipeline started leaking oil from Shell's Gannet Alpha platform in the UK North Sea, Shell quickly stopped it and cleaned up the leak.[44] In March 2006 when a BP-operated pipeline started spilling oil into the Prudhoe Bay in Alaska, USA, BP quickly stopped the spill and cleaned it up.[45] Exxon did the same in July 2011 when its crude oil pipeline ruptured and spilled oil into the Yellowstone River and the floodplains in Montana, USA,[46] The same quick response was repeated in March 2013, when an Exxon-operated oil pipeline ruptured and spilled bitumen near Mayflower, Arkansas.[47]

The preceding examples show the same MNOCs operating in Nigeria and the advanced jurisdictions (the UK and the USA) with totally dissimilar response to oil spills. However, in Nigeria, occasional denial of access to the oil spill site by the local communities and militant groups as well as general security problems could present challenges that may delay the onset of clean-up activities.

> The Nigerian law also requires the licensee/lessee or the operator to adopt all possible precautions and take all practicable steps to prevent oil spill[48] and when it occurs to take immediate action to control or end it and to clean it up.[49]

The oil pipeline license holder is required *to institute mechanisms for prevention of* oil spill and for the remediation of the polluted environment following a spill.[50] This would involve proper and timely maintenance and integrity checks of oil pipelines, flowlines, and equipment. This does not always happen in the Niger Delta. For instance, untimely maintenance was recorded as the cause of the oil spill incident number 2017–1826306 involving the Shell Oil and Gas Bonny Storage Tank 9 in 2017. Records indicate that proper appraisal, maintenance, and timely replacement of worn-out pipelines and flowlines reduces the number of operational spills.[51]

44 Harvey (n 13).

45 Graeme Wearden, 'BP Shuts Alaska Pipeline after Leak' *The Guardian* (10 January 2011) <https://cpb-us-e1.wpmucdn.com/share.nanjing-school.com/dist/1/43/files/2013/01/BP-shuts-Alaska-pipeline-after-leak-Business-theguardian.com-1zcdy2f.pdf> accessed 07 September 2024.

46 USA Department of Justice, Office of Public Affairs, 'Public and Environment to Benefit from Proposed $12 Million Settlement with ExxonMobil for Natural Resource Damages from 2011 Yellowstone River Oil Spill' *Justice News* (21 September 2016) <https://www.justice.gov/opa/pr/public-and-environment-benefit-proposed-12-million-settlement-exxonmobil-natural-resource> accessed 07 September 2024.

47 Steven Mufson, 'Exxon Mobil Pipeline Leaks 'A Few Thousand' Barrels of Crude Oil in Arkansas' *Washington Post* (31 March 2013) <https://www.washingtonpost.com/business/economy/exxon-mobil-pipeline-leaks-a-few-thousand-barrels-of-crude-oil-in-arkansas/2013/03/31/6868d6f6–9a2e-11e2-a941-a19bce7af755_story.html?noredirect=on&utm_term=.d48476ada2c8> accessed 07 September 2024.

48 Petroleum (Drilling and Production) Regulations (1969), s 37 (d)(e).

49 Petroleum (Drilling and Production) Regulations (n 48) ss 25 and 36; EGASPIN (n 1) Part VIII B 1.4.2.

50 *Centre for Oil Spill Watch v NNPC* [2019] 5 NWLR (Pt 1666) 518.

51 Shell Sustainability Report, 2018, 41.

Modern technology has made it possible to detect oil spills much faster by a reduction in pipeline pressure signalling oil leakage. Also, with advanced technology, it is now possible to know the exact point in the pipeline system where the spill is occurring, to immediately alert the operator to leak incidents,[52] and/or to automatically and remotely shut down the flow with an inbuilt mechanism. It is now also possible to install a system that provides valuable information about *leak* size, location, and amount of product lost when a *leak* occurs and to ensure reliable pipeline integrity and pipeline leak detection generally by remote technology.[53] Installation of state-of-the-art leak detection systems in all pipelines and improved protection of pipelines and facilities from vandalism will reduce, prevent, or control oil spills in the Niger Delta.

When oil spill occurs from a pipeline or facility owned or controlled by an operator, that operator is required to take immediate action to control or end the spill and clean it up. This clean-up obligation is irrespective of the cause – whether it is from operational error or third-party interference (sabotage/vandalism) Also, where the spilt oil is discovered within the operational area of an oil company, that operator is obligated to clean it up irrespective of source.[54] However, an operator is entitled to reimbursement of all expenses incurred in such clean-up, through funds established by the government *or* the oil industry for that purpose.[55]

In cleaning up the spill, the operator is required to adopt *good international petroleum industry practices.*[56] This means that the clean-up must be in line with practices generally accepted in the international petroleum industry as 'good, safe, economical, environmentally sound, and efficient.'[57] Also, the operator must use state-of-the-art or otherwise appropriate technology and apply standards 'no less rigorous than those in use by petroleum companies in global operations.'[58] This means that all MNOCs operating in Nigeria must apply the same standard to oil spill response and clean up in Nigeria as they do in the US, the UK, and the Netherlands/

52 Arafat Aloqaily, 'Cross-Country Pipeline Risk Assessments and Mitigation Strategies' (2018) <https://www.sciencedirect.com/book/9780128160077/cross-country-pipeline-risk-assessments-and-mitigation-strategies> accessed 04 December 2022.

53 Some of the pipeline leak detection brands available in the market today include: PSI software used to monitor gas grids and oil pipelines <https://www.psigasandpipelines.com/en/home/>; The TTK oil/hydrocarbon leak detection system <https://www.ttkuk.com/oil-leak-detection/applications/pipelines/>; Sensornet Leak Detection System for Oil and Gas Pipelines <https://www.sensornet.co.uk/oil-and-gas-pipelines/>; OptaSense pipeline leak detection system <https://www.optasense.com/pipeline-monitoring/leak-detection/>; Atmos International leak detection system <https://www.atmosi.com/en/solutions/leak-detection/>; Emerson pipeline integrity and leak detection <https://www.emerson.com/en-gb/industries/automation/oil-gas/pipeline-integrity-leak-detection>; PipePatrol Leak Detection with patented Leak Pattern Recognition module <https://pipeline-management.com/leak-detection/> all accessed 19 November 2022.

54 EGASPIN (n 1) Part VIII B 2.4; Part VIII B 2.11. Petroleum (Drilling and Production) Regulations (n 48) s 25.

55 EGASPIN (n 1) Part VIIIB 4.1; UNEP (n 10) 15.

56 Petroleum Industry Act (PIA) 2021, s 318. This is equivalent to the old requirement of 'good oil field practice' in Petroleum Act 1969 s 8(1)(g) and s 25(1)(a)(iii).

57 PIA (n 56).

58 PIA (n 56).

EU, otherwise, the Minister of Petroleum resources would revoke the petroleum prospecting or petroleum mining licence.[59] Despite this requirement, clean-up efforts are often slow and below international best practices in the Niger Delta.[60]

5. Contingency Plan for Oil Spill Response and Clean-up

> The Nigerian law require all operators in the Nigerian petroleum industry to have an oil spill contingency plan approved by the Director of Petroleum Resources and to activate the same within 24 hours of the onset of the spill.[61]

An Oil Spill Contingency Plan is an organised and predetermined course of actions (usually contained in a document), to be pursued in the event of a spill/leakage of oil, to contain and control the incident.[62] This is to ensure environmental protection and that manpower, equipment, and funds are available to effectively control and clean up the spills when they occur.[63] Additionally, a contingency plan would provide for proper recordkeeping of spill incidents and the dissemination of the same to the public and the government.[64] The law requires each operator to identify beforehand all sensitive areas that should be protected in the event of a spill[65] and locate all potential sources of spills.[66] Niger Delta being a 'high consequence area'[67] merits protection in every area.

Further requirements for oil spill contingency plan in Nigeria include the need to have appropriate plan containment equipment or the capability to mobilise them; proper containment and clean-up procedures; a contemporary communication network system; a disposal plan for the spilt oil and debris; procedure for press release of information; accurate record of spill history and cost of clean-up; as well as a plan for remediation/rehabilitation of the affected area.[68] The purpose of all these is to mitigate the impact of oil spills on the environment. The achievement of this purpose in the Niger Delta is questionable in view of the extent of oil pollution in that region.

59 PIA (n 56) s 96(1)(a).

60 Nigerian Oil Spill Monitor (n 2); UNEP (n 10) 146–47, 175. For detailed comparison of the responses to spills in the Niger Delta and the Deepwater Horizon disaster – Richard Steiner, 'Double Standard: Shell Practices in Nigeria Compared with International Standards to Prevent and Control Pipeline Oil Spills and the Deepwater Horizon Oil Spill' *Milieudefensie* (November 2010) 4, 6 <https://www.foei.org/wp-content/uploads/2014/01/20101109-rapport-Double-Standard.pdf> accessed 07 December 2024.

61 EGASPIN (n 1) Part VIII B, ss 1–2, 6.3.

62 EGASPIN (n 1) Part VIII B s 1.

63 EGASPIN (n 1) Part VIII B, s 2.2.

64 EGASPIN (n 1).

65 EGASPIN (n 1) s 2.3.1.

66 EGASPIN (n 1) s 2.3.1.1.

67 Since *High Consequence Area* has been defined to include a highly populated urban area and/or very sensitive area with very dynamic ecosystem, it means that most parts of the Niger Delta qualify as a *High Consequence Area* – 49 CFR s 195.450 <https://www.law.cornell.edu/cfr/text/49/195.450> accessed 23 September 2024.

68 EGASPIN (n 1) s 2(4)–2(11).

The National Oil Spill Detection and Response Agency (NOSDRA) co-ordinates and implements the National Oil Spill Contingency Plan (NOSCP) for Nigeria.[69] The NOSCP 2010[70] was modelled after the International *Convention* on Oil Pollution Preparedness, Response and Co-operation (*OPRC Convention*) 1990, which has been ratified by Nigeria.[71] Under the NOSCP small spills between 0–25 barrels in inland waters/onshore or 0–250 barrels offshore are designated Tier 1 spills (the Company plan). Individual companies are required to have a contingency plan to respond to and clean-up spills within the Tier 1 size.[72] The medium sized spills between 25–250 barrels in inland waters/onshore or 250–2,500 barrels offshore are designated Tier 2 spills (the Cooperative plan).[73] This category of spills require a collaborative response approach in which a company confronted with it seeks assistance from other oil companies, government agencies, and local cooperatives such as the Clean Nigeria Associate (CNA) set up by the oil industry operators in Nigeria.[74] Major spills greater than 250 barrels in inland waters/onshore or above 2,500 barrels offshore are designated Tier 3 spills (the National or Government plan).[75] This requires substantial assistance, support, and resources from national or international co-operatives. The government is required to provide the necessary command and control, organisational structure, communication network, etc., to ensure proper spill response. Therefore, the government agency, NOSDRA, is responsible not only to activate the response but for a safe, timely, effective, and appropriate response to major oil spills in Nigeria.[76] However, logistic challenges and funding issues often limit the agency's effectiveness in discharging this responsibility.

In the UK, all UK continental shelf (UKCS) pipelines with the potential for an oil pollution incident must have an approved oil pollution emergency plan (OPEP)[77] in compliance with the *OPRC*. The responsibility for OPEP submission for onshore spills rests with the operator.[78] This must include such details as all relevant oil pollution response training; details of the arrangements with any specialist oil spill response contractor and its response capabilities etc.; response strategies to facilitate a prompt and effective response to a pollution event; and the positions of the person authorised to initiate emergency response procedures as well as the position of the person responsible for directing the internal emergency response.[79]

69 OPRC(1990,art3)<https://treaties.un.org/doc/Publication/UNTS/Volume%201891/volume-1891-I-32194-English.pdf> accessed 09 September 2024; Eghosa Osa Ekhator, 'Environmental Protection in the Oil and Gas Industry in Nigeria: The Roles of Governmental Agencies' [2013] Int Energy Law Rev 196, 198.

70 Relating to marine oil pollution incidents in Nigerian waters (both inland/onshore and offshore).

71 OPRC (n 69).

72 National Oil Spill Contingency Plan (NOSCP) para 9.2.

73 NOSCP (n 72) para 9.3.

74 Second Schedule to the NOSDRA Act for an outline of the responsibilities of the various agencies that are co-opted by NOSDRA in the event of such spills.

75 NOSCP (n 72) para 9.4.

76 NOSCP (n 72) paras 6 & 10.2.

77 BEIS (n 5).

78 BEIS (n 5).

79 BEIS (n 5) Appendix A1–A3 for the content requirements of an onshore OPEP and Appendix A5 for the detailed guidance, 18–39.

In the US, oil spill contingency planning is in layers from national to regional and area contingency plans, down to each facility's (or vessel's) response plans.[80] The National Contingency Plan (NCP), is the federal government's blueprint for responding to both oil spills and hazardous substance releases[81] while the Regional Contingency Plan (RCP) serves as guidance to planners preparing for a coordinated federal, state, and local response to an oil spill or substantial threat of it.[82] The RCP in conjunction with the NCP is used to guide and support the Area Committee[83] within each planning area in building their respective Area Contingency Plan (ACP).

There is no indication that oil companies do not comply with oil spill contingency requirements in the UK and the USA. In fact, according to Ann Pickard, Shell's Executive Vice President for the Arctic and Alaska:

> [i]n Alaska we have the capability to mount an effective oil spill response within 60 minutes, 24 hours a day, with a dedicated on-site fleet, near-shore barges and onshore response teams. We regularly test our plans and take part in large-scale joint exercises with other industry partners, government agencies, scientists and oil spill experts.[84]

This is indicative of an ever-ready oil spill response team and a contingency plan by Shell, which could be activated in a moment's notice.

In the UK North Sea, after the Shell Gannet Alpha spill (about 200 tonnes) in 2011, the company, in addition to the swift response and clean-up, went beyond the requirement of the law and conducted a comprehensive review of their North Sea pipeline system[85] and reportedly applied the result across their UK upstream operations.[86] Also in 2011, a major spill occurred at Bonga field in Nigeria[87] when Shell was making a routine transfer of crude oil from a floating platform to an oil tanker. Although Shell reported that action was swiftly taken by the Shell Nigeria Exploration and Production Company (SNEPCo)[88] staff working with international oil spill

80 Alaska Regional Contingency Plan (n 4) 7.

81 EPA, 'National Oil and Hazardous Substances Pollution Contingency Plan (NCP) Overview' <https://www.epa.gov/emergency-response/national-oil-and-hazardous-substances-pollution-contingency-plan-ncp-overview> accessed 07 December 7, 24.

82 For instance, Alaska Regional Contingency Plan following section 300.210 of the National Contingency Plan and Alaska Statute 46.04.200; Alaska Regional Contingency Plan (n 4) 1.

83 Area Committees are spill preparedness and planning bodies made of federal, state, and local agency representatives, tribal representatives as well as owner/operator and stakeholders – 40 CFR 300.210.

84 Shell Sustainability Report, 2014, 32.

85 Adam Barnett, 'Shell's £22,500 Fine for North Sea Oil Spill Slammed as 'Paltry' by Campaigners' *Independent News* (24 November 2015) <https://www.independent.co.uk/climate-change/news/shell-s-ps22–500-fine-for-north-sea-oil-spill-slammed-as-paltry-by-campaigners-a6747536.html> accessed 7 December 2024.

86 Barnett (n 85).

87 Shell Sustainability Report, 2011, 30.

88 SNEPCo is wholly owned by the RDS, see RDS Sustainability Report (n 19) 2013, 23. And SNEPCo pioneered Nigeria's deep-water oil and gas production at the Bonga field.

experts and the Nigerian government to stop the leak,[89] 4.8 thousand tonnes of oil, as admitted by Shell,[90] was spilt before containment. This was, in every account, a much larger spill than the Gannet Alpha spill, yet Shell has not been seen to do more that the law requires of them. Shell may appear unwilling to do this because it does not make business sense to spend a lot of money in Nigeria as in the North Sea when the enforcement machine in Nigeria is not as tough as in the UK. Based on a simple cost-benefit analysis and the lessons from the Ford-Pinto case,[91] the cost of compliance with the Nigerian oil spill laws far outweighs the risk or the cost of non-compliance for the MNOCs. Sanctions for non-compliance are inadequate[92] and there is little risk of revocation of licence or injunction from continuous production of petroleum because oil is the mainstay of the Nigerian economy. Therefore, there is no real incentive to spend a lot of money on comprehensive review and improvement of the oil pipeline system in the Niger Delta especially when the regulators are not necessarily breathing down their neck. For the same reason, it is also unlikely that Shell would attempt to replicate the principle behind the Alaska model in Nigeria. Because Shell's oil operation in Nigeria is now mostly offshore,[93] without replicating the principle behind the oil spill contingency plan in Alaska for SNEPCo and other offshore operations in Nigeria, it is reasonable to predict that another spill in the category of the 2011 Bonga field spill is a disaster waiting to happen in Nigeria and there is little to show that the government and oil companies are better prepared for it.

6. Oil Spill Sanctions and Payment of Compensation

6.1. Sanctions

The Nigerian Law provides that any operator guilty of avoidable oil spill shall pay a fine not less than N500,000 (£1055) 'to be deducted at source'[94] and an additional fine of N100,000 (£211) for every day the offence subsists[95]

Additionally, the operator should report an oil spill to NOSDRA within 24 hours of the onset of the spill or pay a fine of N500,000 for every day it fails to make that report to the agency.[96] A fine of N1,000,000 is also imposed on the operator under the Nigerian law for failure to clean-up the spill to all practical extent.[97]

89 RDS Sustainability Report (n 19) 2011, 4, 18, 20.

90 RDS Sustainability Report (n 19) 20, 30.

91 *Grimshaw v Ford Motors Company* 119 Cal. App.3d 757 (1981) 174 Cal. Rptr. 348, 1981. This case epitomises risk allocation and economic efficiency in decision making. Companies generally chose the least costly option if they can get away with it.

92 EGASPIN (n 1) Part IX 4.6.2 (a); IL Worika, U Etemire and PS Tamuno, 'Oil Politics and the Application of Environmental Laws to the Pollution of the Niger Delta: Current Challenges and Prospects' (2019) 17(1) Oil Gas Energy Law 1, 5–6.

93 Shell Sustainability Report, 2013, 22.

94 Deduction of the fine at source implies taking it from the operator's profit share before it gets its share of profit.

95 EGASPIN (n 1) Part IX 4.6.2 (a).

96 NOSDRA (Est) Act (n 1) s 6(2).

97 NOSDRA (Est) Act (n 1) s 6(3).

A fine of N500,000 or N1,000,000 may appear significant, but at the present currency exchange rate they are equivalent to £232 ($304) or £465 ($608).[98] Therefore, in relative terms, the fine is a pittance for a MNOC to pay, and it impedes the full application of the polluter-pays principle. In the UK, the English Court of Appeal suggested in *R v Thames Water Utilities Ltd*[99] that fines in millions of pounds could be imposed for serious environmental offences.[100] In the US, the fine for failing to notify the appropriate Federal agency of a discharge is a maximum of $250,000 for an individual or $500,000 for an organisation or a maximum of five years' imprisonment.[101] And civil penalties for each day of violation are $25,000 or $1,000 per barrel of oil discharged.[102] In view of this, it is recommended that the fines in Nigeria be significantly increased if they are expected to have a deterrent effect on the oil companies. But levying fines and compensations, no matter how high, may never have enough deterrent effect on rich companies as such costs will generally be passed on to the consumers or be written off in some other way. More effective deterrence is likely to be achieved by holding corporate executives (officers and directors) personally liable for the company's civil or criminal offences especially if they made or influenced the corporate decisions on the illegal act.[103] Queensland, Australia, has the *Chain of Responsibility* legislation, which could make individuals and entities with *'relevant connection'* to a company liable in certain circumstances for breach of corporate environmental obligations.[104] The New South Wales (NSW), Australia's *'special executive liability,'*[105] could be relied on, subject to certain exceptions, to prosecute directors and management personnel for corporate offences even if the company has not been prosecuted or convicted.[106] Holding officers and directors of a company personally liable for corporate offence is a rapidly growing area of company law[107] and Nigeria should consider adopting

98 Currency Converter online <http://www.convertmymoney.com/> accessed 10 September 2024.

99 *R v Thames Water Utilities Ltd* [2015] EWCA Crim 960.

100 UK Oil and Gas Authority's Financial Penalty Guidance, 2017, s 14< 9.

101 Oil Pollution Act 1990 (as amended in 2000), s 4301 (a)(c). Oil Pollution Act Review <https://archive.epa.gov/emergencies/content/lawsregs/web/html/opaover.html> accessed 10 September 2024.

102 Oil Pollution Act (n 101), s 4301(b).

103 Michael Nietsch, 'Corporate Illegal Conduct and Directors' Liability: An Approach to Personal Accountability for Violations of Corporate Legal Compliance' (2018) 18(1) J Corporate Law Stud 151–84; Kara D Schwee, 'Red Sky at Morning: A Look at Responsible Corporate Officer Liability for Cyber Breaches' (2020) 45(3) J Corporat Law 787–813; Queensland *Environmental Protection Act 1994* (Qld) Australia, s 493; Amy J Sepinwall, 'Denying Corporate Rights and Punishing Corporate Wrongs' (2015) 25(4) Business Ethics Q 517–34.

104 The Queensland Environmental Protection (Chain of Responsibility) Amendment Act 2016 (CoRA) (under chapter 7, part 5, division 2 of the EPA, 1994).

105 Protection of the Environment Operations Act (PEOA) 1998 (NSW) s 169.

106 Protection of the Environment Operations Act (n 105), ss 143(1) and 144(1); *EPA v Foxman Environmental Development Services*; *EPA v Botany Building Recyclers Pty Ltd; EPA v Foxman* (No 2), [2016] NSWLEC 120.

107 Nietsch (n 103). Here, the patterns and standards of executive liability for corporate non-compliance under common law and civil law were examined drawing examples from various jurisdictions including the USA, the UK, Australia and Germany; Kara D. Schwee (n 103); Relevant case laws include: *Westmoreland v Parkinson,* 727 F.3d 719 (7th Cir 2013; *Re Safeway Stores v Twigger*

this to ensure environmental protection especially in the Niger Delta. However, it is important to add that courts are hesitant and restrained from piercing the corporate veil to hold the directors/executives liable unless the company is being used as a façade to enable the illegality.[108]

6.2. Payment of Compensation for Oil Spill Damage

> The Nigerian law provides that a spiller shall be liable for the damage from a spill for which he is responsible[109]
>
> It also provides for payment of fair and adequate compensation to anybody whose property is injuriously affected by oil exploration and production or to anybody in lawful occupation of the licenced or leased lands.[110] This includes compensation for damage by oil spills, as well as restoring/remediating the polluted environment[111]
>
> Additionally, the law also provides that compensation is not payable by the licensee when the damage to land is caused by the claimant's fault or the malicious acts of a third party[112]

The Nigerian law, however, did not expressly define what amounts to 'fair and adequate' compensation or 'reasonable compensation'[113] Currently, compensation in the Niger Delta is mostly negotiated. Although this is not against the law,[114] there is an obvious imbalance in bargaining powers between the powerful MNOCs and the local landowners and the oil spill victims. The oil companies have greater financial power and could hire more experienced and astute negotiators than the oil spill victim/s and thus would be able to get more favourable outcomes from the negotiation. Also of equal concern is that the current system of evaluating oil spill damage and compensation in the Niger Delta is not based on proper valuation of the oil spill damage caused.[115] The courts usually rely on the common law interpretation of terms leading to results that could hardly be described as adequate.[116]

[2010] EWCA Civ 1472; In Australia, *EPA v Foxman Environmental Development Services* [2015] NSWLEC 105; and *EPA v Foxman* (No 2), [2016] NSWLEC 120.

108 *VTB Capital plc v Nutritek International* Corp. [2013] UKSC 5, [2013] 2 WLR 398 in which the UK Supreme Court noted that the relevant actor is the person behind the company and not the company but was hesitant in piercing the corporate veil because it found that the company was not used as a façade for the illegal act – Lord Neuberger: 142.

109 EGASPIN (n 1) Part VIIIB, s 8(1).

110 PIA (n 56) s 101(1)(c)(ii), s 101(2)–(3); Oil Pipelines Act (1956), Cap. O7 LFN 2004, s 11(5).

111 EGASPIN (n 1) Part IX 4.6.2 (b) (c).

112 Oil Pipelines Act (n 110) s 11(5)(c).

113 NOSDRA (Est) Act (n 1) s 31(3).

114 The Nigerian law provides that settlement for damages and compensation shall be determined by direct negotiation between the operator/s and landowner/s – EGASPIN (n 1) Part VIIIB, s 8.3.1.

115 *Bodo v Shell* [2014] EWHC 1973 (TCC).

116 *SPDC Ltd v Chief Tiebo and Others* (2005) 4 NWLR (Pt 445) 657; (2005) 9 NWLR (Pt 931) 439; (2005) 3–4 S.C. 137 in which the Supreme Court affirmed as adequate the general damages of five million naira and cost of one million naira awarded by the trial court but reversed the award of special damages when the claimant was unable to prove that such special damages have been suffered.

While standardised compensation rates for oil spill damages do not exist globally, compensation should reflect the current market value of the damaged property and restore the person who has suffered the loss to the position in which he was before the loss or would have been but for the loss.[117] Indices applied internationally and acknowledged by NOSDRA in determining the level of compensation due to victims of oil spill damages[118] include: *damage to property* usually calculated in terms of the value of the property before and after the spill or the actual cost of repairing or replacing the property; *damage to natural resources* calculated with reference to the cost of remediating or replacing the lost or damaged natural resources, including interim losses; *compensation for the loss of subsistence use of the natural resources and other associated losses*, as well as *pure economic losses*[119] and *prospective and potential future losses* reasonably anticipated and issuing from the defendant's activity, as well as *interests accruable*.[120] Applying these in the Niger Delta will bring the quantum of compensation in that region on a par with what is obtainable internationally and meet the expectations of the polluter-pays principle. Presently, this does not appear to be the case. Compensation payable in the Niger Delta for oil pollution is still very small compared to what is obtainable in advanced jurisdictions. The largest out-of-court compensation settlement paid in relation to oil spill in Nigeria is £55 million ($83 million) paid by Shell for the 2008 operational oil spills in the Bodo community of Niger Delta.[121] This was for spilling an estimated 600,000 barrels of crude oil.[122] However, in 2006, when 200,000 gallons (about 4,762 barrels)[123] of oil was spilled from a BP-operated pipeline in Alaska, USA, BP was ordered to pay $25 million and to install a system-wide pipeline safety management system estimated at $60 million as part of court settlement.[124] BP complied, and by the end of 2008, the company had completely replaced the Prudhoe Bay oil pipelines and installed modern leak detection and anti-corrosion systems, all at the cost of about $500 million.[125] BP also pleaded guilty to criminal charges in relation to the spill, in 2007 and was

117 *Farah v Shell* [1995] 3 NWLR (Part 382) 148.

118 SDN and NOSDRA, 'Existing International Legal and Regulatory Frameworks for Oil Spill Compensation – Summary Advice' (16 July 2014) <https://www.stakeholderdemocracy.org/wp-content/uploads/2015/04/SUMMARY-ADVICE-International-Best-Practice.pdf> accessed 2 May 2022.

119 SDN and NOSDRA (n 118). This includes incomes/earnings.

120 *Farah v Shell* [1995] 3 NWLR (Part 382) 148.

121 Anne Look, 'Shell to Pay $83 Million for Nigerian Oil Spills' *VoA* (07 January 2015) <https://www.voanews.com/a/shell-to-pay-83-million-settlement-for-nigerian-oil-spills/2588534.html> accessed 24 September 2024.

122 Abigail Daisy Morgan, 'Long-Term Effects of Oil Spills in Bodo, Nigeria' *Aljazeera* (28 July 2017) <https://www.aljazeera.com/gallery/2017/7/28/long-term-effects-of-oil-spills-in-bodo-nigeria/> accessed 24 September 2024.

123 Unit Converter <https://www.unitconverters.net/volume/gallon-us-to-barrel-oil.htm> accessed 25 September 2024.

124 Associated Press, 'BP to Pay Out $25m for 200,000-Gallon Alaska Oil Spill in 2006' *Associated Press* (4 May 2011) <https://www.theguardian.com/environment/2011/may/04/bp-25m-north-slope-oil-spill> accessed 25 September 2024.

125 Associated Press (n 124).

ordered to pay $20 million including $1 million in criminal fines.[126] Regarding the environmental and economic damages done to the Gulf Coast States in the BP Deepwater Horizon oil spill at the Gulf of Mexico in 2010, a financial settlement of $18.7 billion was paid by BP.[127] This was for being 67 percent culpable because Transocean and Halliburton were held to be 30 percent and 3 percent liable, respectively.[128] Additionally on 15 November 2012, BP reached a plea agreement with the US Department of Justice (DoJ) and pleaded guilty to 14 criminal charges, including 11 counts of felony manslaughter and violations of the Clean Water and Migratory Bird Treaty Acts.[129] In the light of these civil and criminal penalties imposed on BP for spills in the US, the situation in Nigeria pales in comparison.

In addition to the inadequacy of compensation awarded for oil spills in the Niger Delta, section 11(5)(c) of Oil Pipelines Act,[130] provides that compensation is not payable by the licensee when the damage to land is caused by the claimant's fault or the malicious acts of a thirty party. This implies that payment of compensation for any injury to land or the environment resulting from spills caused by oil theft, pipeline vandalism/sabotage, illegal oil bunkering, etc. is excluded.[131] The MNOCs operating in the Niger Delta sometimes hide under this provision to evade payment of compensation for oil spills in the Niger Delta even without definitive proof of pipeline vandalism/sabotage.[132] This ended in January 2021 when the Hague Appeal Court ruled that the party alleging sabotage of the oil pipelines must prove it beyond all reasonable doubt, because pipeline sabotage is a criminal offence.[133] SPDC failed to discharge this burden and was consequently held liable for the damage resulting from oil leakages from its pipelines in Goi[134] and Oruma[135] communities in the Niger Delta. From 2010 to 2021, it was observed that a higher percentage of oil spill was recorded to have occurred as a result of sabotage than operational errors in each year except for 2011. This is highly consequential because it makes the affected communities and victim/s of such spill ineligible for compensation by

126 Associated Press (n 124).

127 Campbell Robertson, John Schwartz and Richard Perez Pena, 'BP to Pay $18.7 Billion for Deepwater Oil Spill' *NY Times* (2 July 2015) <https://www.nytimes.com/2015/07/03/us/bp-to-pay-gulf-coast-states-18–7-billion-for-deepwater-horizon-oil-spill.html#:~:text=NEW%20ORLEANS%20%E2%80%94%20An%20%2418.7%20billion,the%20nation's%20history%2C%20officials%20said> accessed 23 September 2024.

128 Richard Pillardy, 'Deepwater Horizon Oil Spill' <https://www.britannica.com/event/Deepwater-Horizon-oil-spill/Legal-action> accessed 23 September 2024.

129 US EPA, Administrative Agreement, In the matter of Bp plc and the Office of Administration and Resources Management, US EPA Case No 12–0295, 6.

130 Oil Pipelines Act (n 110).

131 G Etikerentse, *Nigerian Petroleum Law* (2nd edn, Dredew Publishers 2004) 165.

132 Amnesty International (n 11); JG Frynas, 'Legal Change in Africa: Evidence from Oil-Related Litigation in Nigeria' (1999) 43(2) J Afr Law 121, 128; *Shell v Isaiah* (1997) 6 NWLR (pt 508) 263.

133 *Oguru, Efanga and Milieudefensie v RDS and SPDC*, ECLI:NL:GHDHA:2021:132 <https://uitspraken.rechtspraak.nl/inziendocument?id=ECLI:NL:GHDHA:2021:132, para 5.9.

134 *Dooh and Milieudefensie v RDS and SPDC*, ECLI:NL: GHDHA:2021:133 <https://uitspraken.rechtspraak.nl/inziendocument?id=ECLI:NL:GHDHA:2021:133, paras 5.25–5.26.

135 *Oguru v Shell* (n 133) paras 5.27–5.28.

the oil company.[136] Given the fact that some spills may have been mislabelled as haven resulted from theft and pipeline sabotage, the burden of proof is well placed on the oil companies by the Hague Appeal Court. This ruling will likely result in improved surveillance of the oil pipelines and facilities by the oil companies, thus, reducing oil pipeline vandalism (malicious acts of third parties).

An operator must make effort to prevent oil pipeline sabotage and malicious acts of third parties or mitigate the harm where such interference has either occurred or is highly anticipated. He must, for instance, bury pipelines or make it difficult to access by strangers in high-risk areas where sabotage is anticipated. He must install a leak detection system to enable automatic shutdown during oil spillage. Where the operator fails to do these, it is recommended that his exclusion from payment of compensation for damages caused by sabotage spills be limited to damages caused before the leak was discovered and not with respect to those occasioned by on-going spills resulting from the operator's delays in containing and stopping it. However, where the operator is found to have acted with due care and has taken reasonable precautions against such predictable acts of strangers, it is suggested that such actions be taken into consideration in assessing a *reasonable* amount of compensation to the injured party.

Ensuring the security and safety of the oil pipelines and infrastructure against sabotage and vandalism is the responsibility of the owners of the pipelines and infrastructure *to wit.,* the oil companies. However, since the issue of security is a matter for the State in most countries including Nigeria, protecting the oil infrastructure should be the dual responsibility of the MNOCs and the government. This responsibility should not be placed on the community or the innocent landowner. Victims of oil spills must be *reasonably* compensated unless it is established that such victims were, in fact, responsible for the spill.

7. Conclusion

Evidence indicates that Shell and the other MNOCs do not comply with the Nigerian oil spill laws the way they do in advanced countries. Spills are not reported within 24 hours of the onset of oil spill and JIVs are not done on time. It was also discovered that the oil companies do not generally start oil spill clean-up within 24 hours of the onset of the spill as required by law; neither do they conduct oil clean-up operations in accordance with 'good international petroleum industry practice,' in the Niger Delta the same way they do in the US, UK, and EU.

Also, the volume and cause of spills in the Niger Delta are determined by very subjective processes during the JIVs unlike what happens in the UK where more accurate methods are used to estimate the volume of spills. Both the UK and the US have effective, pre-planned, well-coordinated oil spill contingency plans that could be activated at a moment's notice. But the oil spill contingency requirement in

136 Oil Pipelines Act (n 110) s 11(5)(c).

Nigeria, though comprehensive, could be better enforced to improve spill response and clean-up and reduce oil pollution in the Niger Delta.

Difficult operating environment (security issues and swampy terrain etc) notwithstanding, if the MNOCs improve on their pipeline maintenance protocol and integrity management; install leak detection systems in all their pipelines; improve surveillance of their pipelines and facilities to reduce or eliminate oil pipeline vandalism/sabotage; and replicate the principle behind the oil spill contingency plan in Alaska – an ever-ready response team that could be activated within a moment's notice – there is bound to be much reduction in the number and volume of spills in the Niger Delta.

3 Analysis of Shell's Oil Spill Environmental Performance Data

1. Introduction

Most major oil companies now provide yearly report of their environmental performance in sustainability reports as part of their corporate social responsibility. The Royal Dutch Shell (RDS/Shell) started reporting voluntarily on its environmental performance in 1997, in a bid to show transparency and its contributions to sustainable development.[1] This chapter analyses Shell's oil spill environmental performance data in Nigeria as presented in the RDS's Annual Sustainability Reports from 2010 to 2021.[2] It covers both the sabotage and operational spills in volume and numbers for the 12-year study period. Sabotage spills result from oil pipeline sabotage/vandalism for purposes of oil theft and illegal oil bunkering while operational spills result from technical problems or equipment malfunction during oil exploration and production operations. Records indicates that all sabotage- and theft-related spills have occurred in Nigeria except for two that occurred in 2015 and 2016 with minimal volumes.[3] So, the analysis in this chapter focused more on operational spills rather than sabotage spills. This is because operational spill is within the direct control of the operator. Additionally, out of over 70 countries in which Shell operates globally,[4] it provides a separate report on the Nigerian operational spills from the rest of the world. This is an indication that the Nigeria situation is peculiar and merits a separate analysis. In addition to the data from the Sustainability Report, figures from Shell Annual Report and the BP's Statistical Review of World Energy[5] covering the relevant 12 years are also used in the analysis. The chapter also reflects on the volume of crude oil production in Nigeria, and the quantity of spills associated with such level of production compared to that

1 'Royal Dutch Shell (RDS) Sustainability Reports' <https://www.shell.com/sustainability/sustainability-reporting-and-performance-data/sustainability-reports.html> accessed 9 February 2023.
2 RDS Sustainability Reports (n 1) 2010–2021.
3 RDS Sustainability Reports (n 1) 2017, 68.
4 RDS Sustainability Reports (n 1) 2016, 3.
5 'BP's Statistical Review of World Energy 2020' <https://www.bp.com/content/dam/bp/business-sites/en/global/corporate/pdfs/energy-economics/statistical-review/bp-stats-review-2020-full-report.pdf> accessed 9 February 2023.

DOI: 10.4324/9781003435150-3

from advanced jurisdictions (specifically the UK and the USA) with comparable levels of crude oil production.

Shell's oil spill environmental performance data in this chapter covers both sabotage and operational spills in volume and numbers for 12 years from 2010 to 2021. Data were obtained from the RDS's Annual Sustainability Reports, which present the information on crude oil and natural gas liquids production in thousand barrels/day (b/d). The production of SPDC, Shell's Nigerian subsidiary, was compared with the global production of crude oil and natural gas liquids to show the volume of crude oil production in Nigeria in relation to the global production. Also, the quantity of spills associated with the level of production in Nigeria is compared to that from advanced jurisdictions with comparable levels of crude oil production or the global production in general.

The use of the figures provided by Shell in its sustainability/annual reports for this research is not an admission that there may not be variations if, for instance, figures are made available from other sources such as the regulatory agencies, NGOs, or the oil-bearing communities, rather, the analysis is aimed at finding out how the data on sabotage and operational spills supplied by the RDS from its operations in Nigeria compare with those also supplied by RDS from its operations in advanced jurisdictions (where available) or the global figure in general. These data are on a 100% basis, for companies and joint ventures where Shell is the operator and can directly manage the data reported.[6]

One impediment, however, is that Shell does not use one unit of volume measurement in its reports. It provides volume data in thousand metric tonnes in its yearly sustainability report and volume of crude oil and natural gas liquid production in thousand barrels per day in its annual report. This makes it difficult to compare information in different reports by Shell. Maintaining one unit of volume measurement in reporting would improve clarity either in Shell's reports or that of any other oil company. In the present study, for consistency and clarity, comparisons are made within the data provided by Shell in the same report. It is also almost impossible to compare information among oil companies because of different units of measurement used and variations in the content of the crude oil being measured. For instance, although BP reports volume of crude oil production in thousand barrels per day, like Shell's system of measurement in its annual report, while Shell measures crude oil and natural gas liquids production, BP's measures include crude oil, shale oil, oil sands, and natural gas liquids (where this is recovered separately).

In the present analysis, attention is placed more on operational spills rather than sabotage spills because the former is under the direct control of the operator. Out of more than 70 countries in which Shell operates around the world,[7] the company singled out the Nigerian *operational spills* from the rest of the world. This shows the peculiar nature of the oil spill situation in Nigeria from Shell's operations and justifies the special attention given to it in this chapter.

6 RDS Sustainability Report (n 1) 2011, 37.
7 RDS Sustainability Report (n 1) 2016, 3.

2. Analysis of Sabotage Spills

There is no discernible trend in volume of sabotage spills in Nigeria within the 12-year study period.[8] It is neither consistently up nor down. However, the number of sabotage spills in nine out of the 12 years are above 100 per annum. This is very significant. Although oil pipeline sabotage is prevalent in the Niger Delta, having over one hundred sabotage spills per year in Shell pipelines *alone* is too much and may point to weakened security and inadequate surveillance and safeguard of the oil pipelines and facilities by the company and the Nigerian government.

A reduction in theft of crude oil was reportedly down from 37 thousand barrels a day in 2014 to 25 thousand barrels a day in 2015.[9] This was attributed in part to 'continued surveillance efforts, implementation of antitheft protection mechanisms on key equipment,' as well as increased security by the Nigerian government.[10] This proves that oil theft and sabotage-related spills are not beyond control. It simply required sustained efforts and amplification of the strategies that are already proven to be working. This reduction in the theft of crude oil corresponds to a drop in the number of sabotage spills from 139 in 2014 to 95 in 2015.[11] This was further reduced to 49 in 2016. Regrettably, though, the number rose steadily from 49 in 2016 to a whopping 156 in 2019 before reducing to 106 in 2021.[12] No reason was given in the sustainability report for this increase.[13] Could it be because there has been a decrease in surveillance and security, or have the thieves and saboteurs become more sophisticated? Without more information, it is difficult to draw any conclusions. But as suggested in *Bodo v Shell*,[14] it is the responsibility of Shell to protect its facilities and pipelines from sabotage or be held liable for damages issuing from sabotage spills.[15]

It should be noted that 2016 with the lower number of sabotage spills (49) came with a higher volume of such spills (3.9 thousand tonnes) in the same year while 2019 with a record high number of sabotage spills (156 spills) came with relatively low volume of such spills (2.3 thousand tonnes). Shell has not reported the reasons for these inconsistent fluctuations so it is difficult to know what caused them and the proper action to take or recommend for improvement. It is hoped that the smaller volume of spills compared to the number of sabotage spills indicates an improvement in spill response and containment time.

8 RDS Sustainability Report (n 1) 2010–2021, last updated 14 July 2023.

9 RDS Sustainability Report (n 1) 2015, 24.

10 RDS Sustainability Report (n 1), Matiu Sunmonu, the Chairman of Shell Companies in Nigeria in 2013, also alluded to these techniques; RDS Sustainability Report (n 1) 2013, 22.

11 RDS Sustainability Report (n 1), 2010–2021, last updated 14 July 2023.

12 RDS Sustainability Report (n 1).

13 Shell confirmed that the figures on the number of sabotage spills for 2018 and 2019 were updated and as published in its 2019 Annual Report following a review of the data; RDS Sustainability Report (n 1) 2019, 89.

14 *Bodo v Shell* [2014] EWHC 1973 (TCC).

15 *Bodo*, paras 78, 93.

Shell reported that all sabotage- and theft-related spills have occurred in Nigeria except in 2015 (one spill of 0.005 thousand tonnes) and 2016 (one spill of 0.001 thousand tonnes).[16] However, Shell did not disclose the country or countries in which these outliers, *de minimis* sabotage spills, occurred. If this information had been provided, then it would have been a good basis for comparing Shell's action or inaction regarding the control and prevention of such spills. This, in turn, would have provided insight into Shell's conduct on such spills compared to its conduct to sabotage spills in Nigeria. A search for reports of sabotage spills from Shell's operations in the UK, the USA, or any other jurisdiction did not produce further information.

The 2017 Shell Sustainability Report recorded that air and ground surveillance was continued and that antitheft mechanisms were installed on equipment and pipelines to ensure quick detection and response to spills with daily flights over the pipeline network to identify any new spill incidents or illegal activities.[17] This may have explained the reason why the volume of sabotage spills decreased from 3.9 thousand tonnes in 2016 to 1.4 thousand tonnes in 2017, indicating prompt response to spills and their control as soon as they were detected. Surprisingly though, the number of sabotage spills went up from 49 in 2016 progressively to 156 in 2019, making one question the effectiveness of all the techniques on the ground.

As a way of dealing with the endemic oil pipeline sabotage and sabotage spills in the Niger Delta, the Nigerian government introduced the Amnesty Programme in 2009 under which the militant groups that vandalise oil pipelines are trained to acquire various skills for gainful employment. The expectation was that this will reduce local resentment, improve security, and restore peace in the Niger Delta. However, available data indicate that this programme has not done much to reduce the number and volume of sabotage spills in the Niger Delta in any significant and consistent way. More must be done to make it difficult for the oil pipelines to be sabotaged such as improved surveillance, installation of up-to-date leak detection devices in all pipelines for prompt detection of spills and automatic shutdowns of oil flows, as well as fighting the corrupt oil syndicates. Replicating the principle of the Alaskan spill contingency plan in Nigeria with appropriate modifications to suit local conditions will also improve the present oil spill response time. In Alaska, USA, Shell is able to mount an effective oil spill response within 60 minutes, 24 hours a day, with dedicated on-site fleet, near-shore barges, and onshore response teams.[18] Similarly, the Niger Delta plan should have dedicated onshore response teams ready to mount effective oil spill response within 60 minutes, 24 hours a day and 'regularly trained to take part in large-scale joint exercises with other industry partners, government agencies, scientists and oil spill experts.'[19] Although Shell's report shows that the company is already doing some of these,

16 RDS Sustainability Report (n 1) 2017, 68.
17 RDS Sustainability Report (n 1) 30.
18 RDS Sustainability Report (n 1) 2014, 32.
19 RDS Sustainability Report (n 1).

a complete replica of the Alaskan plan in practice must be adopted. However, as the Alaskan terrain is quite different from that of Niger Delta coupled with the fact that most of the spills in the Niger Delta are onshore spills, the plan will be created with Niger Delta peculiarities in mind. Although there is no guarantee that it will eliminate the spills completely because of the high level of oil pipeline sabotage in the Niger Delta, at least the number and volume of spills will reduce.

3. Analysis of Operational Spills

Operational spills occur during the oil exploration and production operations and, consequently, more within the control of the operator than spills from pipeline vandalism. The following analysis attempts to compare Shell's operational spills in Nigeria with the global numbers and volume of operational spills. It also compares the level of crude oil production in Nigeria with that of the UK and the USA to see if that may offer justification for the high level of operational spills in Nigeria.

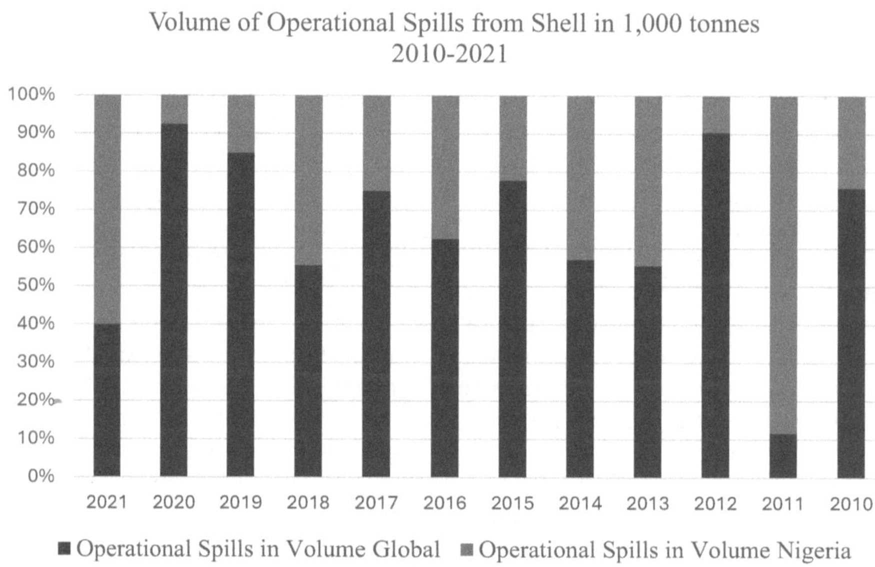

Figure 3.1 Volume of Operational Spills from Shell in 1,000 tonnes 2010–21.

All spill volumes are for spills over 100 kilograms. Due to the rounding of numbers, spill volumes for Nigeria and the rest of the world might not add up to the exact total volume of spills.

Volume of operational spills for Nigeria includes SPDC onshore operations and SNEPCo offshore operations. A single spill at the Bonga offshore field, Nigeria, amounted to 4.8 thousand tonnes in 2011. Around 80% of the volume of spill in 2011 was from this spill.

There was a spike in the volume of operational spills from 2.9 thousand tonnes in 2010 to 6.0 thousand tonnes in 2011. This was as a result of a single offshore operational spill of 4.8 thousand tonnes of oil at the Bonga field during a routine oil transfer from a floating platform to an oil tanker.[20] Although it was reported that 'action was swiftly taken to stop the spill,' much oil was discharged into the surrounding marine environment before containment.[21] Questions remain as to the adequacy of Shell's contingency plan prior to this operation.

The volume of operational spills started to decrease from 2012 and has remained at less than one thousand tonnes from 2013 to 2021. In its 2018 sustainability report, Shell stated that the reduction in operational spill is due to its focus on the appraisal, maintenance, and replacement of key sections of their pipelines and flowlines.[22] This reduction in operational spills from 2012 underscores the point that a significant number of oil spills in the Niger Delta result from aging pipelines and corrosion. While this reduction in volume of operational spill is commendable, it does not call for celebration if the volume of such spills remains in tonnes per year and the number remains in double digits as recorded in nine out of the 12-year study period. Since Shell operates in over 70 countries in the world, this makes the situation in the Niger Delta by far worse than other parts of the world in terms of the number of operational spills.

With cumulative global volume of operational spill totalling 15.95 thousand tonnes for the study period (2010–21), Nigeria gets 7.99 thousand tonnes (50.1%) while the rest of the world shares 7.96 thousand tonnes (49.9%).[23] This is a huge proportion for Nigeria considering that Shell operates in more than 70 countries.[24]

This is even more disproportionate since at least from 2017 (last five years of the study period), records indicate that Shell Nigeria has produced less than 9% of the global oil production from RDS while Shell oil production in the USA is two to three times the percentage average yearly quantity it produced in Nigeria during the same period.[25] In fact, for the last three years of the study period (2019–21) Shell USA produced up to three times the volume of crude oil and natural gas liquids that it produced in Nigeria.[26] Yet, there is no indication that the US has as many operational spills as in Nigeria.

The difference is even more stark when viewed in terms of the overall global crude oil and natural gas liquids production by countries. Data from the BP's Statistical Review of World Energy 2010 to 2021[27] indicate that Nigeria produced an average of only 2.38% of the global total in crude oil for that 12-year period while the United States produced an average of 13.96% – almost six times the production

20 RDS Sustainability Report (n 1) 2011, 30.
21 RDS Sustainability Report (n 1) 20, 30.
22 RDS Sustainability Report (n 1) 2018, 41. More than 1,300 kilometres of pipelines and flow lines were reportedly replaced.
23 See the Pie Chart on cumulative volume of operational spills in thousand tonnes and RDS Sustainability Report (n 1) 2010–2021, last updated 14 July 2023.
24 RDS Sustainability Report (n 1) 2016, 3.
25 See the Bar Chart on crude oil and natural gas liquids production from Shell subsidiaries in thousand bbls/day and Shell Annual Report, 2010–2021, updated 14 July 2023.
26 Shell Annual Report (n 25).
27 See the Bar Chart on percentage oil production in 1000 b/d from BP's Statistical Review of World Energy 2010–2021; and BP's Statistical Review of World Energy 2010–2021 (n 5).

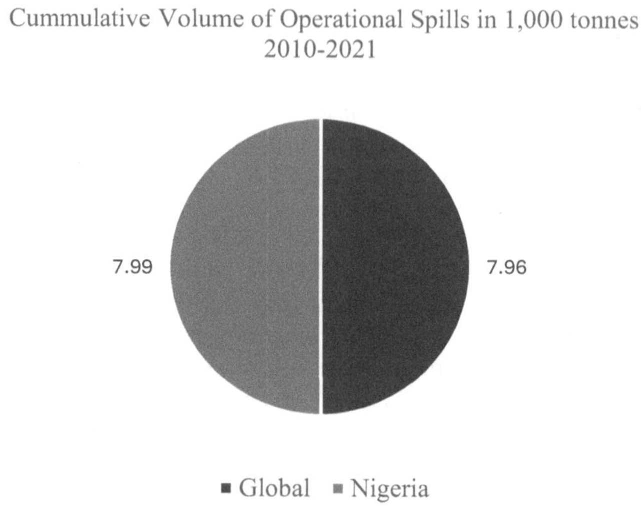

Figure 3.2 Cumulative Volume of Operational Spills in 1,000 tonnes 2010–21.

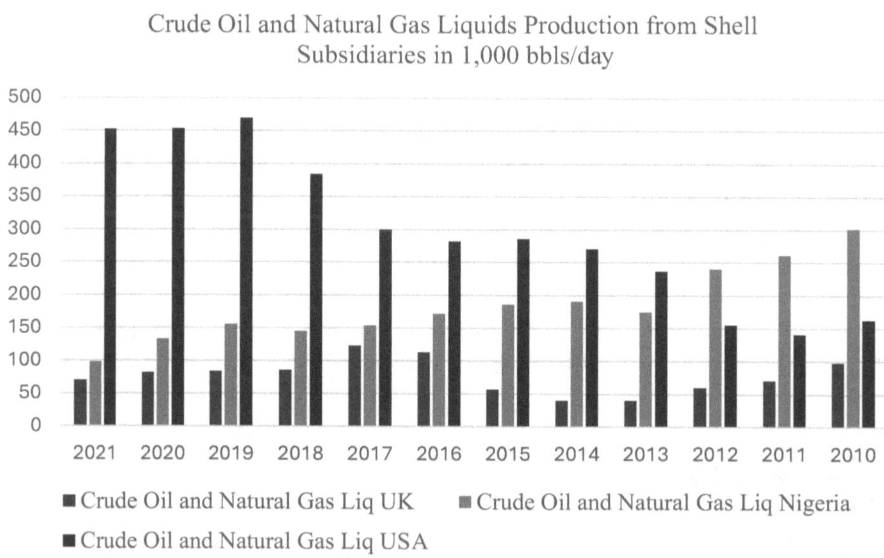

Figure 3.3 Crude Oil and Natural Gas Liquids Production from Shell Subsidiaries in 1,000 bbls/day.

These figures were obtained from SHELL ANNUAL REPORT for the respective years. *They appear under* 'Oil and Gas Production (available for sale)' in the yearly annual reports. *Where the figures were provided per annum, they were divided by 365 to get the daily production.*

in Nigeria.[28] Going by percentage production of oil, Nigeria should not have more operational spills than the USA. No existing data invalidates this conclusion. Shell's avowed corporate objective of meeting the energy needs of the society in ways that are 'economically, *environmentally* and socially *responsible*'[29] should apply to all jurisdictions in which it operates, including Nigeria.

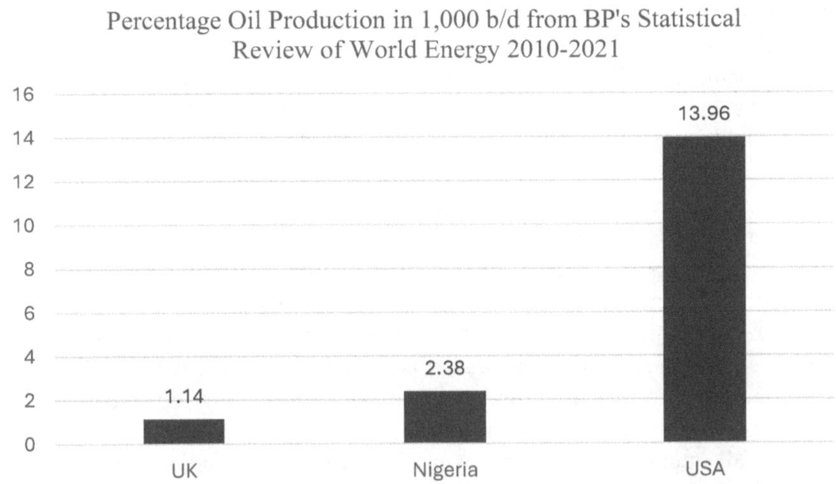

Figure 3.4 Percentage Oil Production in 1,000 b/d from BP's Statistical Review of World Energy 2010–21.

BP includes in its calculation crude oil, shale oil, oil sands, and natural gas liquids (NGLs – the liquid content of natural gas where this is recovered separately). However, it excludes liquid fuels from other sources such as biomass and derivatives of coal and natural gas.

Another explanation for the disproportionate volume of operational spills in Nigeria is probably because Shell's oil spill response in Nigeria is slow when compared to its response in the UK and the USA. Only a slow response to oil spills will result in such a disproportionately large volume of oil spills in Nigeria and lend credence to the claim of differential behaviour by Shell in Nigeria as opposed to the UK and the USA.

In terms of numbers, Shell's operational spills in Nigeria were found to be significantly worse, accounting for a yearly average of about 18.8% for the study period.[30] Again, this is very significant in terms of proportion because Shell operates in more than 70 countries all over the world – theoretically giving the other 69 countries about 1.2% yearly average in number of operational spills. Although the disproportionately large number of operational spills in Nigeria could arguably stem from weakened infrastructure due to continuous pipeline vandalism, it could

28 BP's Statistical Review of World Energy 2010–2021 (n 5).
29 RDS Sustainability Report (n 1) 2011, 'About Shell.'
30 RDS Sustainability Report (n 1) 2010–2021, last updated 14 July 2023.

also point to inadequate pipeline maintenance and integrity checks by the oil company in Nigeria. Records indicate that proper appraisal, maintenance, and timely replacement of worn-out pipelines and flowlines reduces the number of operational spills.[31] Untimely maintenance was recorded as the cause of the oil spill incident number 2017–1826306 involving the Shell Oil and Gas Bonny Storage Tank 9 in 2017. NOSDRA reported that the tank was out of service and five years overdue for repair, but this could not be done due to financial constraints.[32]

The *number* of operational spills in Nigeria rose from 32 in 2010 to 64 in 2011 representing 30.3% of the total global spills.[33] Shell explained that the reason for the spike was because they were putting more pipelines back into service.[34] This is questionable especially if the replacement was done with the competence and skill it requires. The number of spills, however, decreased significantly in 2012, and by 2021 it was down to nine. Although this is commendable, it does not call for celebration because it accounts for 22.0% of the global number of operational spills, which was 41 in 2021.[35] Nine of those spills occurring in Nigeria is still disproportionate since the remaining 32 are theoretically shared among 69 remaining countries in which Shell operates. Shell did not give the countries where these other 32 remaining spills happened, so it is difficult to make any form of comparison beyond the fact that the number occurring in Nigeria is too much. Unfortunately, these nine spills that occurred in Nigeria accounted for 60% of the global volume of all operational spills that year. This may be an indication that a much higher volume is spilt in Nigeria before containment. This means that Shell must have a better contingency plan for oil spill response to meet the peculiarities of Niger Delta; improve on its pipeline maintenance protocol and integrity management; and install leak detection systems in all their pipelines. There is a lot of room for improvement and Shell being the pioneer and arguably most experienced oil company in Nigeria[36] should set the pace for others to follow.

The preceding analysis of the 12-year study period gives material evidence of how skewed and out of proportion the number and volume of operational spills that occur from Shell's operation in the Niger Delta is, when compared with the rest of world. This is irrespective of the fact that the questionable credibility of the process and records of the joint investigation visits (JIV)[37] to sites of oil spills may have resulted in underestimation of the volume of spills. Overall, the analysis underscores

31 RDS Sustainability Report (n 1) 2018, 41.

32 'NOSDRA Report of the Joint Investigation Visit of the Oil Spill Incident Number 2017–1826306' <https://oilspillmonitor.ng/#/61884.2017_1826306 accessed 06 April 2021.

33 RDS Sustainability Report (n 1) 2010–2021, last updated 14 July 2023.

34 RDS Sustainability Report (n 1) 2011, 18.

35 RDS Sustainability Report (n 1) 2010–2021, last updated 14 July 2023.

36 RDS Sustainability Report (n 1) 2013.

37 Nigerian Oil Spill Monitor <https://oilspillmonitor.ng/ accessed 07 September 2024; The NOSDRA Oil Spill Monitor <https://nosdra.oilspillmonitor.ng/ accessed 07 September 2024.; Amnesty International and the Centre for Environment, Human Rights Development (CEHRD), 'Bad Information: Oil Spill Investigations in the Niger Delta' *Amnesty International* (7 November 2013) 7 <www.amnesty.org/en/documents/AFR44/028/2013/en/> accessed 07 September 2024.

Shell's differential behaviour with respect to oil spill response and clean-up in Nigeria and the advanced jurisdictions. To improve on the present figures, it is recommended that Shell improve on its pipeline maintenance protocol and integrity management; install leak detection systems in all its pipelines to enable automatic shutdown of oil flow; and replicate the principle behind the oil spill contingency plan in Alaska. This means having dedicated response teams with the capability to mount an effective oil spill response within 60 minutes, 24 hours a day. It also means that the response team should regularly take part in large-scale joint exercises with other industry partners, government agencies, and oil spill experts; and that the spill response plan should be regularly tested and updated.[38] When this is done, there will not only be fewer operational spills, but the volume of such spills will also significantly reduce.

4. Conclusion

This chapter analysed Shell's oil spill environmental performance data as presented in the RDS's Annual Sustainability Reports from 2010 to 2021. The outcome indicated that Shell Nigeria (the SPDC) generally gets a disproportionately high volume and number of operational spills when compared to the rest of the world. This accounts for 50.1% of the average global volume, and 18.8% of the average global number of operational spills within the 12-year study period (2010–21). This is huge given that the RDS operates in more than 70 countries globally. With this fact, although specific numbers and volumes of operational spills were not reported for the US and the UK in the RDS Sustainability Reports within the study period, it is safe to conclude that they get far fewer operational spills than Nigeria, both in number and volume. No existing data invalidates this conclusion.

It is noteworthy that Shell Nigeria has a lower yearly average production of oil when compared to the United States. From the data obtained from Shell Annual Report, within the 12-year study period (2010–21), Nigeria produced a yearly average of 13.3% of the global oil production while the US produced a yearly average of 21.5%.[39] Figures from the BP's Statistical Review of World Energy are even more glaring with Nigeria producing an average of 2.38% while the US produces an average of 13.96% (almost six times the production in Nigeria) of the global volume of oil within the study period. Yet Nigeria and not the US takes the lion's share in operational spills each year for the study period. Given the questionable credibility of the JIV process, the reported volume of spills in Nigeria may even be underestimated.

38 RDS Sustainability Report (n 1) 2014, 32.
39 Shell Annual Report, 2010–2021, updated 14 July 2023.

4 Managing Oil Spills in the Niger Delta

The Laws, Regulations, and Challenges*

1. Introduction

A cursory look at the Nigerian/NOSDRA oil spill monitor[1] shows how recurrent and pervasive oil spill is in the Niger Delta. The frequency and magnitude of oil spills in the region is so much that the data in the oil spill monitor is constantly changing, making any attempt to compile data on oil pollution almost an exercise in futility because such data go out of date almost as soon as they are published. In 2021 alone, there were 409 publicly available oil spill records[2] and between 2010 and 2021, there was a yearly average of 893 oil spills in the Niger Delta[3] with a total volume of about 504,743.94 barrels of spilt oil within the same period.[4] Although figures vary,[5] it is an undeniable fact that an unacceptable number and volume of oil spills have occurred and are still occurring in the Niger Delta today.[6]

Apart from how to manage and clean-up these freshly occurring oil spills, two big challenges that have persisted for almost as long as oil exploration and production in the Niger Delta are the security problems in the region and how to clean up pre-existing oil spills. Some of these spills have accumulated for decades[7] from

* An earlier version of this chapter was published in the Journal of Sustainable Development Law and Policy by Millicent Ele, 'Oil Spills in the Niger Delta: Does the Petroleum Industry Act 2021 Offer Guidance for Solving this Problem?' (2022) 13(1) J Sustain Dev Law Policy 130–61. This version is published with permission from the JSDLP.

1 NOSDRA Oil Spill Monitor <https://nosdra.oilspillmonitor.ng/> accessed 2 May 2022; Nigerian Oil Spill Monitor <https://oilspillmonitor.ng/> accessed 2 May 2022.

2 TABLE 1, Chapter 1 of this book.

3 TABLE 1, Chapter 1 of this book.

4 TABLE 1, Chapter 1 of this book.

5 For instance, it was reported that records on file provided by the Department of Petroleum Resources (DPR), Lagos, Nigeria in February 2016, indicated that a total of 773,727 barrels of oil were spilt in Nigeria between 1999 and 2014 alone (15 years) – Dickson E Omukoro, 'Environmental Regulations in Nigeria and Liability for Oil-Pollution Damage: Musings from Norway and the US (Alaska)' (2017) 8 Int Energy Law Rev 324–30, 324.

6 NOSDRA and Nigerian Oil Spill Monitor (n 1); Damilola Olawuyi, 'Legal and Sustainable Development Impacts of Major Oil Spills' (2013) 9(1) J Sustain Dev (Columbia University) 1–15.

7 United Nations Environment Programme (UNEP), 'Environmental Assessment of Ogoniland' (2011) 9 <https://www.unep.org/resources/report/environmental-assessment-ogoniland> accessed 06 July 2024.

DOI: 10.4324/9781003435150-4

multiple pipelines owned and managed by different operators. Lack of reliable spill data makes accurate determination and apportionment of clean-up liability very difficult. Additionally, it can also be argued that the previously government-owned Nigerian National Petroleum Corporation (NNPC) had a controlling interest in all Joint Ventures with the MNOCs in Nigeria[8] and therefore its progeny, the NNPC Limited, should be equally liable for the clean-up of any pre-existing oil spills to the same extent as the MNOCs. In this chapter, a legal framework for cleaning up these pre-exiting oil spills will be created with insights from the UK/EU laws on contaminated land, the US Comprehensive Environmental Response, Compensation, and Liability Act (CERCLA or the Superfund), and the UK regime on oil infrastructure decommissioning. This chapter will also review the applicable petroleum laws and policies, their implementation, and enforcement protocols and concurrently evaluates the relevant provisions of the Petroleum Industry Act (PIA), 2021.

In the light of this, the chapter is presented in five parts covering the introduction, the general statutory provisions, the problems of implementation and enforcement of petroleum laws in Nigeria, and the creation of a legal framework for cleaning up pre-existing (stale) oil spills in the Niger Delta, before the conclusion.

2. General Statutory Provisions

The major legislation currently governing the Nigerian petroleum industry is the Petroleum Industry Act (PIA) 2021.[9] The PIA did not expressly cover oil spills. So, the law on this issue remains any legislations, regulations and guidelines that survived the old Petroleum Act 1969.[10] This includes the Petroleum Act, Cap P10, LFN 2004; the Oil Pipelines Act, Cap O7, LFN 2004, the Environmental Guidelines and Standards for the Petroleum Industry in Nigeria (EGASPIN) 2018, and any subsidiary legislation in so far as it is consistent with this PIA.[11] Other petroleum laws applicable to the upstream petroleum operation in Nigeria are the Oil Pipelines Act, 1956[12] and the National Oil Spill Detection and Response Agency (NOSDRA) Establishment Act, 2006.[13]

The earlier laws require that petroleum operations be conducted in accordance with *good oil field practice* or the licence to operate would be revoked by the Minister of Petroleum Resources.[14] The PIA 2021 retained this provision by providing

8 Shell Sustainability Report, 2011, 18; The NNPC has now been converted to the NNPC Limited, an incorporated company free to manage its affairs without government control and oversight – PIA 2021, s. 53–65.

9 The PIA signed into law on 16 August 2021 replaced, for the most part, the old Petroleum Act 1969, Cap P10, LFN 2004.

10 PIA (n 8) s 311 – the Saving provisions.

11 PIA (n 8) s 311(1) (9). These subsidiary legislation include, Mineral Oils (Safety) Regulations (1997), Petroleum Regulations 1967, Petroleum (Drilling and Production) Regulations (1969) etc.

12 Updated by the Oil Pipelines Act, Cap. O7 LFN 2004.

13 NOSDRA (Est) Act, 2006 (as amended).

14 Petroleum Act (n 9) s 8(g); s 25(1)(a)(iii) of the First Schedule to the Petroleum Act 1969; Mineral Oils (safety) Regulations (n 11) s 7; the Petroleum (Drilling and Production) Regulations (n 11) s 25 and 37.

that the Minister may revoke a petroleum prospecting licence or petroleum mining lease where the applicable licensee/lessee fails to conduct petroleum operations in accordance with *good international petroleum industry practices*[15] or where he fails to comply with environmental obligations required by the applicable law, licence, or lease.[16] Despite this provision and its antecedents in Nigeria,[17] there has always been a reluctance to revoke a petroleum licence or lease in view of the strategic importance of petroleum to the Nigerian economy.

The term 'good oil field practice' in the old petroleum laws and regulations[18] in Nigeria appears synonymous with the term 'good international petroleum industry practices' in the PIA 2021. However, while the 1969 Petroleum Act, did not define the term 'good oil field practice,' the Mineral Oils (Safety) Regulations (1962), updated in 1997, considers the requirement satisfied if the petroleum operation conforms with any internationally recognised and accepted system or codes such as the American Petroleum Institute (API) codes or the codes of the Energy Institute (EI), London. These institutes publish internationally recognised codes of good oil field practice, but the codes generally prescribe specifications for oilfield hardware[19] and do not relate to environmental standards.[20] However, in the light of the massive environmental pollution that comes with oil exploration and production, their effects on human health, the ecosystem, and climate change, 'good oil field practice' must be redefined and interpreted to embody the concept of environmental protection and sustainability. The PIA 2021 filled this gap, and under it, the term *good international petroleum industry practices* means:

> Those uses and practices that are, at the time in question, generally accepted in the international petroleum industry as being good, safe, economical, environmentally sound, and efficient in petroleum operations and should reflect standards of service and technology that are either state-of-the-art or otherwise appropriate to the operations in question and should be applied using standards in all matters that are no less rigorous than those in use by petroleum companies in global operations.[21]

This definition embraced, for the first time, the concept of sound environmental practice in the oil and gas industry in Nigeria. It also indicates that the

15 PIA (n 8) s 96(1)(a).
16 PIA (n 8) s 96(1)(i).
17 Petroleum Act (n 9) s 8(g); s 25(1)(a)(iii) of the First Schedule to the Petroleum Act 1969; Mineral Oils (safety) Regulations (n 11) Pt II; the Petroleum (Drilling and Production) Regulations (n 11) ss 25 and 37.
18 Petroleum Act (n 9) s 8(g); s 25(1)(a)(iii) of the First Schedule to the Petroleum Act 1969; Mineral Oils (safety) Regulations (n 11) Pt II; the Petroleum (Drilling and Production) Regulations (n 11) ss 25 and 37.
19 Michael AG Bunter, 'World-wide Standards of Good Oilfield Practice . . . the Impact of the Blow-out, Deaths and Spills at the BP Macondo Well, the MC 252/1–01, US Gulf of Mexico' (2013) 11(2) Oil Gas Energy Law 3.
20 Bunter (n 19).
21 PIA (n 8) s 318.

standard of petroleum operation technology and services accepted in Nigeria must be 'state-of-the-art' and 'no less rigorous than those used by petroleum companies in global operations.' This imports the use of best available technology (BAT) as the requisite standard for petroleum services and operations in Nigeria. It also makes the Nigerian standard equivalent to the BAT standard used in Alaska, USA[22] where Shell and the other MNOCs also operate.

It is the responsibility of the operator under the Nigerian law to take all practicable steps and employ internationally accepted standards and practice to prevent oil spills,[23] The API codes provide that pipelines of higher specification should be used in high risk/high consequence areas where pipeline sabotage and vandalism are anticipated or foreseeable.[24] Since High Consequence Area has been defined to include highly populated and/or very sensitive area with very dynamic ecosystems,[25] it means that most parts of the Niger Delta qualify as *High Consequence Areas.* This also means that the MNOCs operating in this region must, therefore, satisfy this API requirement and incorporate high-level safety measures to protect against pipeline sabotage in the Niger Delta.[26] Granted that such sabotage-specific integrity management programmes and monitoring may not always protect against the sophistication[27] of oil thieves and vandals now operating in the Niger Delta, they will at least provide another layer of obstacles that will have to be overcome by oil pipeline saboteurs.

API has also developed standards for pipeline leak detection systems, emergency flow reduction devices, and automatic shutdowns for reducing or shutting down oil flows in cases of spills.[28] The use of these devices are however, not always implemented and effectively enforced in Nigeria, because spills have been known to continue for days or even weeks without being detected. For instance, in the 2005 oil spills near the Oruma community in the Niger Delta, the plaintiffs alleged that the oil spills started from the Shell Petroleum Development Corporation's (SPDC) underground pipeline on 26 June 2005 but could not be stopped until 7 July 2005, leaking an estimated 400 barrels of oil.[29] As a result, the Hague

22 Alaska Statute, AS 46.04.030(e) <https://dec.alaska.gov/spar/ppr/contingency-plans/bat> accessed 28 September 2024.

23 The Petroleum (Drilling and Production) Regulations (n 11) s 37.

24 API 1160 – Managing system integrity for *hazardous liquid* pipelines, defined in the US Code of Federal Regulation, Title 49 CFR 195.2.

25 49 CFR s 195.450 (USA).

26 Richard Steiner, 'Double Standard: Shell Practices in Nigeria Compared with International Standards to Prevent and Control Pipeline Oil Spills and the Deepwater Horizon Oil Spill' *Milieudefensie* (November 2010) 28 <https://www.foei.org/wp-content/uploads/2014/01/20101109-rapport-Double-Standard.pdf>; Amnesty International, 'Negligence in the Niger Delta: Decoding Shell and Eni's Poor Records on Oil Spills' *Amnesty International* (2018) 5, 19. <https://www.amnesty.org/en/documents/afr44/7970/2018/en/> accessed 28 September 2024.

27 Sophisticated equipment and ocean-going vessels are now used in oil theft in the Niger Delta.

28 Computational Pipeline Monitoring, API 1130, 2nd edn. 2002, codified under the US Code of Federal Regulation, 49 CFR s 195.444 <https://law.resource.org/pub/us/cfr/ibr/002/api.1130.2002.pdf> accessed 28 September 2024.

29 *Oguru, Efanga and Milieudefensie v RDS & SPDC*, ECLI: NL: GHDHA: 2015: 3588, para 1.1<https://uitspraken.rechtspraak.nl/inziendocument?id=ECLI:NL:GHDHA:2015:3588>accessed 28 September 2024.

Appeals Court ordered the Royal Dutch Shell (RDS) and the SPDC to install a 'state of the art' leak detection system in their pipelines in the Oruma community within one year of the judgment in *Oguru v Shell*[30] or face a fine of €100,000 (about GBP 87, 004 or US$121,522) for every day they fail to do so once the year is up.[31] This order will make Shell pipelines in Oruma of equivalent standard as those in Alaska, USA where oil spill prevention and response must be conducted with the BAT.[32] Today, an inbuilt mechanism capable of indicating the exact spot in the pipeline system that has been compromised is in existence.[33] So, an upgrade in the Nigerian oil pipelines will be in line with best international oil industry practices as required by the PIA.[34]

Shell and the other MNOCs have been known to act swiftly to contain and clean up oil spills when they occur in the UK and the USA. For instance, the actions of Shell in the Gannet Alpha platform oil spill in the UK North Sea in 2011,[35] Exxon in an Exxon-operated crude oil pipeline rupture in the Yellowstone River and floodplains of Montana, USA in 2011,[36] and BP during the Gulf oil spill in 2010. This massive oil spill was so thoroughly cleaned up by BP within four months so that President Barack Obama (then President of the USA) was able to have a demonstration swim in the beach waters after the clean-up just to show the waters were safe.[37] Yet, for more than 13 years after the Bodo operational oil spill of 2008 in the Niger delta, Shell has yet to fully clean-up and remediate the environment polluted by the spill. Admittedly, there were additional spills over the years occasioned by oil pipeline sabotage and oil theft, and general security problems in the Niger Delta occasionally preventing access to clean-up sites. However, just like any other business risk, operators must be seen to be constantly trying to overcome this risk if they continue to engage in oil exploration and production in the Niger Delta.

The Nigerian law requires the licensee/operator to take all practicable precautions to prevent oil spill, and where it occurs to immediately control and contain it,

30 *Oguru, Efanga and Milieudefensie v RDS and SPDC*, ECLI:NL:GHDHA:2021:132, para 6.43, on 29 January 2021 <https://uitspraken.rechtspraak.nl/inziendocument?id=ECLI:NL:GHDHA:2021:132> accessed 28 September 2024.

31 *Oguru* (n 30).

32 Alaska Statute, AS 46.04.030(e) (n 22).

33 *Oguru v Shell* (n 30) para 6.14.

34 PIA (n 8) s 318.

35 Fiona Harvey, 'Oil Spill Investigation begins as Shell Plugs North Sea Leak' *The Guardian* (22 August 2011) <https://www.theguardian.com/environment/2011/aug/22/shell-north-sea-oil-leak> accessed 2 May 2022.

36 Janet McGurty and Matt Daily, 'Exxon Mobil Shuts Louisiana Oil Pipeline After Leak' *Reuters Business News* (30 April 2012) <https://www.reuters.com/article/us-exxon-spill/exxon-mobil-shuts-louisiana-oil-pipeline-after-leak-idusbre83t0k120120430> accessed 2 May 2022.

37 Suzanne Goldenberg, 'BP Oil Spill: Barack Obama Dives into Safety Debate with Gulf of Mexico Swim' *The Guardian* (15 August 2010) <https://www.theguardian.com/environment/2010/aug/15/barack-obama-swim-gulf-florida> accessed 2 May 2022.

irrespective of cause[38] or even when the source is unknown.[39] This imports strict liability and the licensee/lessee is strictly liable in tort for any oil spill from its facility.[40] This liability is also extended to the parent company where it controls and supervises the activities of the subsidiary. In *Okpabi v Shell*,[41] it was suggested that the *de facto* management of part of a subsidiary's activities satisfies this requirement for 'control,' though the subsidiary may still maintain *de jure* control of its activities. Also, a duty of care could be imposed on a defendant/operator, where the defendant created a dangerous situation that could be abused by a third party, resulting in damages to the plaintiff.[42] Under this head, oil exploration and production could be viewed as dangerous activities with likelihood of damage to the pipelines by third parties resulting in oil spills. Based on this, a general duty of care should be imposed on the operator to prevent sabotage of its oil pipeline or oil facility by third parties[43] or at least minimise its occurrence by improved surveillance and also mitigate harm by installing appropriate leak detection and automatic shutdown devices.[44] Furthermore, consistent with the common law negligence liability, this duty of care imposed on the subsidiary company is extended to the parent company. According to the UK Supreme Court,

> the general principles which determine whether A (a parent company) owes a duty of care to C (a third party) in respect of the harmful activities of B (a subsidiary company) are neither novel nor controversial[45] but well-established in common law negligence liability.[46]

In such cases, a duty of care should be imposed on the defendants without the need to go into the *Caparo test* analysis.[47]

> The *Caparo test*[48] states that the tort of negligence is committed when the defendant that owes a duty of care, breaches that duty resulting in damage

38 Petroleum (Drilling and Production) Regulations (n 11) s 25; Environmental Guidelines and Standards for the Petroleum Industry in Nigeria (EGASPIN), 2018, Part VIII B 1.1.1; Lawrence Atsegbua, Vincent Akpotaire and Folarin Dimowo, *Environmental Law in Nigeria: Theory and Practice* (2nd edn, Ambik Press 2010) 32.

39 EGASPIN (n 38) Part VIII B 4.1.

40 *Ryland v Fletcher* (1866) L.R.1 Ex 265; (1868) L. R. 1 H. L. 330. The strict liability rule established in this case is applicable to the petroleum industry because the use of land for petroleum operation is a non-natural use – *Umudje v Shell Petroleum Development Co. of Nigeria Ltd* (1975) 11 SC 155.

41 *Okpabi & Others v RDS & Another* [2021] UKSC 3, para 147.

42 *Smith v Littlewoods Organization Ltd* UKHL 18 [1987] AC 241; [1987] 2 WLR 480; [1987] 1 All ER 710, per Lord Goff; *Akpan and Milieudefensie v RDS plc and SPDC Nig. Ltd*, C/09/337050/HA ZA 09–1580, 30 January 2013, paras 4.24.

43 *Bodo v Shell* [2014] EWHC 1973 (TCC) para 93.

44 *Oguru v Shell* (n 30) paras 6.17–6.25; *Okpabi v Shell* [2021] (n 41) para 145.

45 *Vedanta Resources plc and other v Lungowe and Others* [2019] UKSC 20, paras 49–54.

46 *Vedanta v Lungowe* (n 45) para 56; *Robinson v Chief Constable of West Yorkshire Police*, [2018] UKSC 4, para 26.

47 *Vedanta v Lungowe* (n 45) paras 49–56.

48 Established in *Caparo Industries plc v Dickman* (1990) 2 AC 605 and based on the House of Lord's ruling in *Donoghue v Stevenson* (1932) SC (HL) 31.

> to the plaintiff. The three criteria on which the determination of duty of care were based, as established in the *Caparo case*, are as follows: i) the foreseeability of the defendant that the plaintiff would suffer damage; ii) the proximity between the plaintiff and the defendant; iii) whether it is fair, just, and reasonable to assume that a duty of care exists in a specific situation.

Where the case relates to oil spills due to poor oil pipeline maintenance, the court has imposed a duty of care on the owners of the pipeline (the parent company and its subsidiary)[49] without going into the Caparo test analysis and ordered the installation of leak detection systems.[50] However, although a general duty of care could be imposed on all MNOCs operating in the relevant area, there may be challenges in properly quantifying damages and apportioning liability especially when the spills are from multiple operators, have been in existence for many years, and are without reliable spill records.

It is argued that in the Niger Delta, damages to plaintiffs from sabotage spill is foreseeable, and so, there exists a general duty of care to prevent or limit such spills by taking additional and preventive measures, otherwise, the operator would be held liable.[51] In *Bodo v Shell*,[52] the court suggested that it is the responsibility of the licensee (Shell) to take reasonable steps to adequately protect their facilities, installations, and pipelines from sabotage, vandalism, and theft or be held liable for damages issuing from such preventable acts. But section 11(5)(c) of the Oil Pipelines Act seems to absolve the oil companies of this responsibility because it excludes payment of compensation by the licensee when the damage to land is due to the claimant's fault or *the malicious acts of a thirty party* (emphasis added). This means that claimants cannot be compensated for any injury to land or the environment resulting from spills caused by acts of theft, sabotage, illegal oil bunkering, etc., because they could be categorised as 'malicious acts of third parties.'[53] This provision, therefore, affords the licensees the convenience of claiming that the majority of the oil spills in the Niger Delta is due to pipeline sabotage and vandalism.[54] Examples abound of cases in which SPDC had advanced sabotage as a defence but was unable to prove it beyond all reasonable doubt as required by section 135(1) of the Evidence Act, 2011. They include *SPDC v Ohaka*,[55] *SPDC v Enoch*,[56] *SPDC v Firibeb*,[57] *SPDC v* Edamkue,[58] and *Shell v Isaiah*.[59] In a crowd-sourcing research about oil spills in the Niger Delta published by Amnesty

49 *Oguru v Shell* (n 30) paras 6.17–6.26.
50 *Oguru v Shell* (n 30) para 43.
51 *Oguru v Shell* (n 30); *Akpan v Shell* (n 42) paras 4.39 and 4.41.
52 *Bodo v Shell* (n 43).
53 Oil Pipelines Act (n 12) s 11(5)(c).
54 *SPDC (Nig) Ltd v Otoko* (1990) 6 NWLR (Part 159) 693.
55 *SPDC v Ohaka* (2008) 8 CLRN 94.
56 *SPDC v Enoch* (1992) 8 NWLR (Pt 259) 335.
57 *SPDC v Firibeb*, Suit No CA/PH/168/2007.
58 *SPDC v Edamkue and others* (2009) 14 NWLR (Pt 1160) 1; (2009) 6–7 S.C. 74.
59 *SPDC v Isaiah* [1997] 6 NWLR 236.

International in 2018, it was noted that at least 89 spills may have been wrongly attributed to sabotage or theft by Shell and Eni.[60] For these reasons, section 11(5)(c) of the Oil Pipelines Act should be expunged or modified to accommodate relief for the victims of sabotage spills.

But the days of alleging sabotage without adequate proof are over following the Hague Appeals Court ruling in January 2021. Henceforth, where the operator alleges sabotage, he must prove it beyond all reasonable doubt or be held liable for damages including payment of compensation.[61] Additional liabilities with corresponding legal and equitable remedies for the victims of oil spills could also be imposed through actions in common law torts[62] because the application of section 11(5)(c) of the Oil Pipelines Act does not exclude these. Also, the Petroleum Production and Distribution (Anti Sabotage) Act 1975[63] enacted in Nigeria to mitigate the negative effects of oil pipeline sabotage made oil pipeline sabotage and oil bunkering a criminal offense punishable by death or up to 21 years imprisonment.[64] While the death penalty is not advocated, a 21-year imprisonment is considered high enough to have a deterrent effect. However, this is not the case in the Niger Delta because acts of sabotage and oil theft remain rife in the region partly because no one has ever been convicted for that offence.[65] There is thus a clear deficiency in the implementation and enforcement of the laws on oil spill control and clean-up in Nigeria. The next segment will address this, starting with the adequacy of trained workforce (the regulators) and resources for the implementation and enforcement of the oil spill laws and regulation.

3. The Implementation and Enforcement of Petroleum Laws in Nigeria

3.1. The Regulators

Before August 2021, the two major regulatory bodies in the oil and gas industry in Nigeria were the Department of Petroleum Resources (DPR) – which is the technical arm of the Ministry of Petroleum Resources – and the NOSDRA under the Federal Ministry of Environment.

The DPR was statutorily responsible for regulating all petroleum operations in Nigeria. The bulk of its functions relate to compliance monitoring and enforcement of the petroleum laws, regulations, and guidelines in Nigeria.[66] The Minister

60 Amnesty International, 'Negligence in the Niger Delta' (n 26) 7. In that research, Shell and Eni's poor record on oil spills in the Niger Delta was made plain by analysing thousands of oil spill documents and photographs made public by the two companies.

61 *Oguru v Shell* (n 30) paras 5.3–5.10.

62 *Oguru v Shell* (n 30) paras 3.22–3.24. There is ample evidence in support of this e.g., *SPDC v Edamkue* (n 58); *SPDC (Nig.) Ltd v Anaro* (2015) 12 NWLR (Pt 1472) 122; JELR 52884 (SC).

63 Petroleum Production and Distribution (Anti Sabotage) Act, Cap P12, LFN 2004.

64 Petroleum Production and Distribution (Anti Sabotage) Act, s 1.

65 Omukoro, 'Environmental Regulations in Nigeria' (n 5).

66 Roles of DPR – Upstream <https://www.nuprc.gov.ng/upstream/> accessed 2 May 2022.

of Petroleum Resources was the head of the DPR and the chairman of the NNPC.[67] There is an intrinsic conflict of interest in this arrangement because the minister who oversees the regulator, DPR, also heads the oil revenue generating body, the NNPC. This changed when the PIA 2021 was signed into law on 16 August 2021. Under this Act, the Nigerian Upstream Regulatory Commission (the Commission)[68] replaced the DPR, and the NNPC was turned into an incorporated company, NNPC Limited.[69] The functions of the Commission were clearly delineated and separate from that of the NNPC Limited, thus avoiding the institutional overlaps and conflict of interests that were the hallmarks of the old law. The NNPC Limited can generate and manage its cash flow independent of the government. Also, any government ministry, agency, or department exercising any power or function or taking any action that may impact on the upstream petroleum operations shall consult with the Commission before taking any such action or before issuing any regulation, guideline, enforcement order, or directive.[70] This provision for consultation was designed to produce harmonious operations and to reduce overlaps and conflicts of functions among the relevant government agencies and departments to a minimum.

NOSDRA was established in 2006 as the lead agency responsible for the detection of and response to all oil spillages in Nigeria.[71] It coordinates and implements the National Oil Spill Contingency Plan (NOSCP) for Nigeria, as required under the International Convention on Oil Pollution Preparedness and Response Cooperation, (OPRC).[72] Oil spill detection and response, formally a function of the DPR, was assigned to NOSDRA probably because of the endemic nature of this petroleum pollution in the Niger delta. Other variants of oil and gas pollution, such as gas flaring, drill cuttings, seismic surveys, and effluent discharges from oil refineries etc. are still managed and regulated by the DPR (now the Commission).

The objectives of NOSDRA include ensuring a safe, timely, and effective response to major oil spills; establishing the mechanism to monitor and assist or where expedient direct the response and clean-up of the impacted sites to the best practical extent.[73] The agency is equally responsible for surveillance and detection of oil spills in the petroleum sector and for the enforcement of existing environmental legislation relating to oil spills in the Niger Delta.[74]

67 Nigeria National Petroleum Corporation (NNPC) Act, Cap N123, LFN 2004 ss 10 & 11; G Etikerentse, *Nigerian Petroleum Law* (2nd ed., Dredew Publishers 2004) 21.

68 PIA (n 8) ss 4–28.

69 PIA (n 8) Chapter 1, Part V, ss 53–65.

70 PIA (n 8) s 25(1).

71 NOSDRA Act (n 11) ss 1 & 5.

72 NOSDRA Act (n 11) s 5; OPRC 1990, art 3; Eghosa Osa Ekhator, 'Environmental Protection in the Oil and Gas Industry in Nigeria: The Roles of Governmental Agencies' [2013] Int Energy Law Rev 196, 198.

73 NOSDRA Act (n 11) s 5.

74 NOSDRA Act (n 11) s 6.

3.2. The Ineffective Implementation and Enforcement of Petroleum Laws in the Niger Delta

Oil pollution in the Niger Delta is an ongoing process despite laws and regulations put in place to check it and despite the agencies established for the implementation of these laws. It has been observed that the laws are not only ineffective[75] but their implementation and enforcement are equally deficient and ineffective.[76] This ineffectiveness in enforcement was mainly credited to overlaps and conflicts of interest among regulatory agencies and lack of capacity. The former has largely been eliminated by the PIA 2021, but the lack of capacity subsists due to inadequate finances, which impacts training, logistics, availability of resources, and qualified workforce[77] Because the DPR and NOSDRA to a great degree, lack the resources (both human and material) to do the job effectively and enforce the law, they often rely on the oil company they ought to regulate for assistance.[78] This is a recipe for regulatory capture,[79] which undermines the supervisory authority of the agencies over the oil industry. As a result, the industry is not held fully accountable for their actions. Self-regulation has not worked either, because it is neither genuine nor enforceable.[80] Also, the joint venture partnership between the Nigerian government and the MNOCs (prior to the PIA 2021) did not help issues.

In the UK, the industry tries as much as possible to minimise, mitigate, or prevent accidental oil and chemical spills by addressing the plant, process, and people elements.[81] In the Niger Delta, on the other hand, the poor maintenance of oil pipelines and facilities, the disproportionately large number and volume of operational spills, as well as the near total exclusivity of sabotage spills points in the opposite direction.[82] Also, the experience in Nigeria is that penalties in fines are

75 Akinseye Akinteye, 'Adjudicating the Impact of Oil Spills in Nigeria: The Need for Black Benches in Oil Producing States' (2018) 16(1) Oil Gas Energy Law 2.

76 Akinteye (n 75) 4–5; Barisere Rachel Konne, 'Inadequate Monitoring and Enforcement in the Nigerian Oil Industry: The Case of Shell and Ogoniland' (2014) 47(1) Cornell Int Law J 181, 192; DS Olawuyi, *The Principles of Nigerian Environmental Law* (Rev edn, Afe Babalola University Press 2015) 32, 207.

77 IL Worika, U Etemire and PS Tamuno, 'Oil Politics and the Application of Environmental Laws to the Pollution of the Niger Delta: Current Challenges and Prospects' (2019) 17(1) Oil Gas Energy Law 1, 14–15; Akinteye (n 75) 5; UNEP (n 7) 12.

78 DE Omukoro, 'Environmental Degradation in Nigeria: Regulatory Agencies, Conflict of Interest and the Use of Unfettered Discretion' (2017) 15(1) Oil Gas Energy Law 18–19; Damilola Olawuyi and Zibima Tubondenyefa, 'Review of the Environmental Guidelines and Standards for the Petroleum Industry in Nigeria' <https://docs.wixstatic.com/ugd/60b422_74da66d41dfa41b2963c73772cffafd1.pdf>.

79 Regulatory capture is the process by which the regulatory agencies are dominated by the industries they are charged with regulating with the result that an agency charged with acting in the public interest, instead, acts in ways that benefit the industry it is supposed to be regulating. Olawuyi and Tubondenyefa (n 78).

80 Eghosa O Ekhator, 'Regulating the Activities of Oil Multinationals in Nigeria: A Case for Self-Regulation?' (2016) 60 J Afr Law 1.

81 Oil and Gas UK (OGUK) Environmental Report, 2019, 42.

82 Chapter 3 of this book on the analysis of Shell's oil spill environmental performance data.

low[83] and as a result, they do not provide enough deterrence or incentive for the oil companies to prevent or mitigate the oil spills or to clean it up thoroughly when it occurs.[84] Additionally, there are not many successful oil pollution litigations in Nigeria as a result of strong defence and opposition by the MNOCs and the onerous evidentiary burden on the litigant to prove that the oil company had been negligent in their operations.[85] Most cases are, likewise, dismissed on technical grounds[86] or inordinately delayed.[87]

Following the Bonga oil spill of about 4.8 thousand tonnes of crude oil in 2011, NOSDRA levied the sum of $3.6 billion on Shell Nigeria Exploration and Production Company (SNEPCo) owned exclusively by RDS.[88] This was pursuant to NOSDRA's powers under the Oil Spill Recovery, Clean-up, Remediation and Damage Assessment Regulations (OSDAR),[89] a NOSDRA regulation made under the authority of section 26 of the NOSDRA Act (2006). Shell contested this fine and refused to pay it.[90] This will not happen in advanced jurisdiction such as the UK and the USA after a spill of that magnitude. The diligence with which Shell handled their Gannet Alpha spill in the UK North Sea the same year (2011) supports this assertion. And that was a comparatively smaller spill of about 200 tonnes. Shell quickly stemmed the spill, cleaned it up, and paid the applicable fines with apologies. The company even went further than the requirements of the law to conduct a comprehensive review of their North Sea pipeline system and applied the result throughout their UK operations – clearly an attempt to prevent or reduce the chances of reoccurrence.[91]

From the preceding analysis, deficiencies in the laws as well as their ineffective implementation and enforcement are contributory to oil spills in the Niger Delta. Other legal and regulatory issues of concern are the enormous ministerial discretions granted by the laws and regulations and the security problems in the Niger Delta. These are discussed in the following section.

83 EGASPIN (n 38) Part IX 4.6.2 (a)-(c); NOSDRA Act (n 11) s 6(2)(3). See chapter 2 of this book on oil spill liability, sanctions, and payment of compensation.

84 Konne (n 76) 196; *Agbara et al v Shell Petroleum et al*, Suit No: FHC/ASB/CS/231/2001.

85 *Ogale v Shell* (1997) 1 NWLR (pt 480) 148.

86 *Chinda & 5 others v Shell-BP Petroleum Development Company* [1974], 2 RSLR 1; *Ogiale v Shell* (1997) 1 NWLR (Part 408) 148.

87 *Agbara et al v Shell Petroleum et al* (n 84). This case, which started in 2001, was resolved in 2010, but the judgement debt remains unsettled; see also *SPDC Ltd v Ambah* (1999) 3 NWLR Pt 593 12, an oil pollution case that lasted nearly 20 years in the Courts.

88 RDS Sustainability Report, 2013, 23.

89 Federal Republic of Nigeria Official Gazette No 68, Vol 98, 17 July 2011, ss 25–27.

90 *Shell Nigeria Exploration and Production Company (SNEPCo) v NOSDRA*, unreported, delivered 24 May 2018.

91 Adam Barnett, 'Shell's £22,500 Fine for North Sea Oil Spill Slammed as "Paltry" by Campaigners' *Independent News* (24 November 2015) <https://www.independent.co.uk/environment/shells-22500-fine-for-north-sea-oil-spill-slammed-as-paltry-by-campaigners-a6747536.html> accessed 2 May 2022.

3.3. Ministerial Discretions

The Minister of Petroleum Resources has a lot of discretionary powers under the Nigerian petroleum laws to enable him to perform his duties with necessary flexibility. For instance, the regulations are replete with phrases such as 'approved by the Director of Petroleum Resources' or 'acceptable to the Minister of Petroleum Resources.'[92] The Minister also has the power under the law to revoke any oil prospecting licence or oil-mining lease if *in his opinion* the licensee/lessee is not conducting operations in accordance with good oil field practice.[93] Hundreds of spills (big and small) occur in the Niger Delta every year[94] and they are either not cleaned up at all or are poorly cleaned up by the oil companies.[95] However, there is no evidence of revocation of licence by the minister based on this violation or on grounds of the consequent environmental damage.[96] This is probably because oil is the mainstay of the Nigerian economy, accounting for about 80% of the government revenue and 90–95% of Nigeria's export earnings.[97] It's production must, therefore, not be stopped. So, the use of these discretionary measures for oil pollution control in the Niger Delta appear to be underutilised and ineffective. But they could also be abused if unfettered. To forestall this possibility, the PIA 2021 puts the necessary guardrails and restrictions on the ministerial discretion by providing that the minister can only revoke a licence or lease based on a written recommendation of the Nigerian Upstream Regulatory Commission.[98] It trimmed the powers of the Minister – assigning most of them to the Commission.[99] This is to provide for checks and balances. Also, the Commission (and no longer the Minister) now oversee the strict implementation of environmental policies, laws, regulations, and standards as they relate to oil and gas operations in Nigeria.[100]

3.4. Standard Setting

The regulatory and governmental function of standard setting and enforcement have been widely discussed by scholars and it is a fundamental basis for performance assessment of environmental concerns.[101] The Commission (formally the

92 Mineral Oils (Safety) Regulations (n 11); Petroleum (Drilling and Production) Regulations (n 11) (made pursuant to the Petroleum Act (n 9) ss 25, 37, 39–41, 49, 52–54 & 61 etc.

93 Mineral Oils (safety) Regulations (n 11); the Petroleum (Drilling and Production) Regulations (n 11) s 37.

94 TABLE 1, Chapter 1.

95 Nigerian Oil Spill Monitor (n 1); UNEP (n 7) 150.

96 Konne (n 76) 196.

97 Worika, Etemire and Tamuno (n 77) 4; Olawuyi (n 76) 173–74; United Nations Development Programme, 'Niger Delta Human Development Report' (2006) 9.

98 PIA (n 8) s 10(g), s 96(1)(a).

99 PIA (n 8) ss 4–28.

100 PIA (n 8) s 6(h)(i).

101 Robert Baldwin, Martin Cave and Martin Lodge, *Understanding Regulation: Theory, Strategy, and Practice* (2nd edn., OUP 2014) 2; Philip Ejoor Agbonifo, 'Rist Management and Regulatory Failure in the Oil and Gas Industry in Nigeria: Reflections on the Impact of Environmental

DPR) is responsible for setting environmental standards and issuing guidelines.[102] It must set and require a high standard of operation and environmental practice by the oil companies. Such standards must be in accordance with good international petroleum industry practice[103] and no less rigorous than those in use by petroleum companies in global operations. It must also monitor, regulate, and enforce them properly.[104] Some degree of conflict of functions may exist in this regard between the Commission and the NOSDRA, still responsible for oil spill management and control. It remains to be seen how the courts will interpret this regulatory provision and navigate the potential challenges.

Using fines and compensations as examples, the NOSDRA Act did not impose significant fines on oil spillers, and neither did it place an obligation for them to pay compensation to the victims of oil spills.[105] Section 6 of the Act provides that an oil spiller shall report the spill to the agency within 24 hours of the onset of the spill or pay N500,000:00 (about £232 ($304))[106] for each day in default.[107] He is also required to clean up and remediate the impacted site, *to all practical extent* or attract a further fine of one million naira[108] (about £465 ($608).[109] In real terms, these fines are paltry and unlikely to produce a deterrent effect. Fines for environmental offences are much higher in the UK and could run into millions of pounds[110] and also in the USA.[111] So, fines in Nigeria are overdue for an upwards review.[112] It is also recommended that the requirement to clean up and remediate the impacted sites *to all practical extent* be interpreted to involve the use of best available technology (BAT) for the process. This is the standard used in Alaska, USA[113] and Nigerian law requires the use of comparable equivalence.[114]

The issue of standard setting also touches on compensation for oil pollution damages and how it is quantified in Nigeria. The NOSDRA Act simply enjoins the agency to ensure that appropriate remedial action is taken for the restoration

---

Degradation in the Niger Delta Region' (2016) 9(4) J Sustain Dev 1–10; Sarah Light, 'The Law of the Corporation as Environmental Law' (2019) 71 Stanford Law Rev 137, 153.

102 PIA (n 8) s 10(d)(f).

103 PIA (n 8) s 318.

104 PIA (n 8) s 7(c).

105 Payment of compensation is provided for under the Petroleum Act (n 9) s 37 of the First Schedule; Petroleum (Drilling and Production) Regulation (n 11) s 23; Oil Pipelines Act (n 12) ss 6(3) & 11(5); and EGASPIN (n 38) Part IX 4.6.2 (b) (c).

106 Currency Converter online <http://www.convertmymoney.com/> accessed 10 September 2024.

107 NOSDRA Act (n 11) s 6(2).

108 NOSDRA Act (n 11) s 6(3).

109 Currency Converter online (n 106).

110 *R v Thames Water Utilities Ltd* [2015] EWCA Crim 960; UK Oil and Gas Authority's Financial Penalty Guidance, 2017, s 14.

111 Oil Pollution Act 1990 (as amended in 2000), s 4301 (a)–(c). Oil Pollution Act Review <https://archive.epa.gov/emergencies/content/lawsregs/web/html/opaover.html> accessed 10 September 2024.

112 Chapter 2 of this work – The paragraph on Oil Spill Sanctions.

113 Alaska Statute, AS 46.04.030(e) (n 22).

114 PIA (n 8) s 318 on the requirement for the oil companies in Nigeria to maintain good international petroleum industry practice.

and *compensation of the environment* (emphasis added).[115] Restoration of the environment is clear, but 'compensation of the environment' (and not the victims) is ambiguous, and so far no court has had the opportunity to interpret or elucidate this. However, one could argue that since it is now possible to grant a river a legal personality as a living entity with all the corresponding rights, duties, and liabilities of a legal person,[116] including the right to sue those who harm it,[117] it could successfully be argued that the environment could equally be recognised as having a legal personality imbued with the rights to be compensated if harmed, and the ability to sue for that compensation. Besides, since the purpose of compensation in tort law is to put the victim/claimant back to the position he would have been in, had the tort not occurred (the baseline condition), for the environment, one would argue in line with the provisions of the EU Environmental Liability Directive, that compensation of the environment would include not only the restoration of the environment to its pre-pollution event condition but also compensating for the 'interim losses.' This means losses that result from the fact that the damaged environment/natural resources and/or services are not able to perform their ecological functions or provide services to other natural resources or species pending recovery.[118] Such compensation may also be determined by factoring in additional improvements to protect natural habitats and species or water either at the damaged site or at an alternative site until the primary or complementary measures have taken effect.[119] This will compensate for growth in the environment – which must have been hindered by the pollution – and thus ensure that the polluter fully pays for the complete restoration of the environment in line with the polluter-pays principle.

3.5. Funding for Environmental Management

Prior to the enactment of the PIA 2021, the Joint Venture (JV) partners[120] funded the JV according to their ownership interest[121] with co-venturers providing their pro-rated share of funds for business operations and management.[122] The government, which owns the majority shares in the oil business, must, therefore, contribute its share of funds for oil pollution clean-up and environmental management. Hitherto, the government is not always able to do this, and this inability to meet its cash calls

115 NOSDRA Act (n 11) s 19(1)(d).

116 The Te Awa Tupua (Whanganui River Claims Settlement) Act 2017 (New Zealand).

117 M Tanasescu, 'Rights of Nature, Legal Personality, and Indigenous Philosophies' (2020) 9(3) Trans Environ Law 429–53; Toni Collins and Shea Esterling 'Fluid Personality: Indigenous Rights and the Te Awa Tupua (Whanganui River Claims Settlement) Act 2017 in Aotearoa New Zealand' (2019) 20(1) Melbourne J Int Law 1–24.

118 Environmental Liability Directive (ELD) – EU Directive 2004/35, on environmental liability regarding the prevention and remedying of environmental damage [2004] OJ L143/56, art 14(1) <https://eur-lex.europa.eu/legal-content/EN/TXT/PDF/?uri=CELEX:02004L0035–20190626&qid=1568193390794&from=EN> accessed 22 February 2025. Annex II, para 1(d) and para 1.1.3.

119 Environmental Liability Directive (n 118).

120 The Nigerian government and the MNOCs operating in Nigeria.

121 Shell Sustainability Report, 2011, 18.

122 Shell Sustainability Report (n 121).

significantly reduces available funds for business management and environmental compliance.[123] This could be part of the reason for poor oil pipeline maintenance, and the consequent oil spills in the Niger Delta. Shell has been known to insist that if a court-imposed fine and judgement for environmental infraction must be paid, the government must contribute its own share.[124] With the enactment of the PIA 2021, it is envisaged that the newly formed, self-financing, and commercially driven NNPC Limited will be able to generate enough funds to meet its cash obligations and consequently provide enough funds for oil pipeline maintenance and oil pollution control and clean-up in the Niger Delta.

The PIA 2021 specifically provided a mechanism of funding for environmental management and remediation of environmental damage. It mandates the establishment of an environmental remediation fund by the Commission and directs that the licensee/lessee pay a prescribed financial contribution into the environmental remediation fund for the rehabilitation or management of negative environmental impacts occasioned by the licence or lease.[125] The Act made such financial contribution a condition precedent for the grant of the licence.[126] However, it did not go far enough to provide for sources of additional funding where the available fund is insufficient to meet the environmental remediation costs.[127] In such a case, it is recommended, in line with the UK Petroleum Act 1998, that the parent company of the immediate polluter, all former licensees/lessees, and all persons, companies, and entities *associated with*[128] the immediate polluter be held liable to provide the additional funds and resources needed to meet the clean-up and remediation costs, particularly where they have been found to play any role in the management or control of the immediate polluter.[129]

The phrase 'associated with' has so far not been interpreted by the courts. It is suggested that the courts should interpret it broadly enough to include any company that has an equity interest (other than the security for a loan) in the polluter company.[130] This will broaden the liability group and ensure that funds are made available for the remediation of the environment. Further insights could also

123 Richard Steiner (n 26) 40–42. A specific example could be seen in the crude oil seepage at Shell's Bonny Oil and Gas Terminal Storage Tank 9 on 25 March 2017. The tank has been out of service and reportedly due for repair for the past five years but due to financial constraints, that could not be done. NOSDRA Report of the joint investigation visit of the oil spill incident number 2017–1826306 <https://oilspillmonitor.ng/#/61884.2017_1826306> accessed 2 May 2022.

124 *Chief Pere Ajuwa & Others v Shell Petroleum Development Company Nig. Ltd* (2011) 18 NWLR (Pt 1279). In this case, the Federal High Court imposed a judgement of $1.5 billion on Shell. Shell argued that if the payment was due at all, the federal government should contribute its prorated portion of the sanction since the government owns the controlling interest in the Joint Venture.

125 PIA (n 8) s 103.

126 PIA (n 8) s 103(1).

127 Millicent N Ele, 'Cleaning up the Oil Spill Mess in the Niger Delta with Insights from the Contaminated Land Regimes in the UK and the US' (2021) 7(1) Int Energy Law Rev 134.

128 UK Petroleum Act 1998, s 30.

129 In *Okpabi v RDS*, the UK Supreme Court seemed to suggest that the management of part of a subsidiary's activities by the parent company, satisfies this requirement for 'control' – *Okpabi v Shell* [2021] (n 41) para 147.

130 UK Petroleum Act 1998, ss 30(1)(e) and 30(2)(c) on the imposition of decommissioning liability.

be gained from the Queensland, Australia Chain of Responsibility Act (CoRA) 2016,[131] which imposes responsibility on companies and *related persons/entities* accountable for the environmental harm, to bear the cost of rehabilitating the relevant sites.[132] 'Related persons' or 'related entities' could include all persons, companies, and entities *associated with* the company that is carrying out the relevant activity, for example, the immediate polluter. These could be holding companies; persons with a 'relevant connection' to the immediate polluter; *associated entities*; and persons that have the capacity to influence the extent of the company's environmental compliance. They could also be persons capable of acquiring 'significant financial benefit'[133] from the relevant activities of the company.[134] A 'relevant connection' may exist where a person is capable of significantly benefiting financially or has received a significant financial benefit from a company's relevant activities or is (has been) in a 'position to influence'[135] the company's conduct in relation to the way in which – or extent to which – the company complies with its obligations under the Environmental Protection Act (EPA).[136]

A person in a 'position to influence' may be an officer of the company such as a director or a shadow director acting in an unofficial capacity for the company.[137] It is submitted that the phrase *associated with (or associated entities)* should be interpreted in the same way as *related entities* under the CoRA. This means that like the CoRA, it should simply go where the money has gone and target any person, company, or entity who stands to profit from the relevant company's activities and thereby contributed to the pollution of the environment that needs to be cleaned or remediated.

Targeting corporate executives and holding the directing minds of the corporation personally liable have been found to produce more effective deterrence where the company breaches its environmental duties if such executives are in a position to make or influence corporate decisions on the illegal act.[138] In New South Wales (NSW), Australia, the law provides for the *'special executive liability,'*[139] which makes it legal, subject to certain exceptions, to prosecute directors and

131 Environmental Protection (*Chain of Responsibility*) Amendment *Act* 2016 (Qld).

132 Environmental Protection (*Chain of Responsibility*) Amendment Act 2016, *Guidelines* on Environmental Protection Order to 'related persons' under Chapter 7, Part 5, Division 2 of the Environmental Protection Act 1994 (hereinafter The Guideline to the Chain of Responsibility Act).

133 Factors to be considered in determining what amounts to significant financial benefit are provided for under the Guideline to the Chain of Responsibility Act (n 132) para 4.1.1.

134 The Guideline to the Chain of Responsibility Act (n 132) para 1.0.

135 A person in a 'position to influence' may be an officer of the company such as a director or a shadow director acting in an unofficial capacity for the company. The Guideline to the Chain of Responsibility Act (n 132) para 4.1.2.

136 Section 363AB (2)–(4) of the EPA. The Guideline to the Chain of Responsibility Act (n 132) para 4.1.

137 The Guideline to the Chain of Responsibility Act (n 132) para 4.1.2.

138 Queensland *Environmental Protection Act 1994* (Qld) Australia, s 493. The EPA 1994 was amended by the Chain of Responsibility Amendment Act (CoRA) 2016 to broaden the circumstances in which an environmental protection order (EPO) can be issued by the Department of Environment and Science (DES).

139 Protection of the Environment Operations Act (PEOA) 1998 (NSW) s 169.

management personnel for corporate infractions irrespective of whether or not the company has been prosecuted or convicted.[140] This was applied in *EPA v Foxman Environmental Development Services*[141] and underscores the court's willingness to pierce the corporate veil and go after directors and those concerned with the management of a company for environmental offences committed by the company. It is recommended that, likewise, company executives should be held personally accountable and prosecuted in Nigeria for the misconducts of the company and any breach of environmental law including oil spills in the Niger Delta in appropriate cases. Although success may not have been guaranteed, at least an attempt should have been made to incorporate this into the PIA 2021. With respect to oil spills and other forms of oil pollution in the Niger Delta, this will have a big deterrent effect for the executives of Shell and the other MNOCs operating in the Niger Delta as well as the executives of the NNPC Limited. It is also in line with the decision of the UK Supreme Court to the effect that the relevant actor is the person behind the company and not the company.[142]

Whatever the ultimate interpretation the court may eventually give to the phrase *associated with*, it would make the entities liable for the pollution very broad. Applying this to oil spills will equally broaden the liability group and ensure that the clean-up funds either for freshly spilt or for pre-existing oil spills will be provided for adequately. The PIA 2021 should have gone this extra mile.

3.6. The Polluter-pays Principle in Nigeria

The polluter-pays principle simply implies that the person(s) or entities that caused the pollution should bear its cost both in terms of clean-up costs and compensation for damages. In Nigeria, this legal principle is not explicitly provided for, in any legislation. Although, the courts generally hold polluters liable for their action under the torts of negligence,[143] nuisance,[144] and the strict liability rule in *Ryland v Fletcher,*[145] they do not necessarily do this as environmental matters involving the polluter-pays principle. However, the EGASPIN imposed on the polluter (the spiller) the responsibility to restore and remediate the polluted environment to its original state[146] and this provision would seem to import the notion of the polluter-pays principle.

On a general note, the polluter-pays principle has not been effectively enforced in Nigeria due to weak institutions, poorly funded, poorly staffed, and poorly

140 Protection of the Environment Operations Act (n 139) ss 143(1) and 144(1); The state of Victoria, in Australia has similar provisions with minor difference – *Environmental Protection Act 1970* (Vic) s 66B.

141 *EPA v Foxman Environmental Development Services; EPA v Botany Building Recyclers Pty Ltd; EPA v Foxman (No 2)*, [2016] NSWLEC 120.

142 *VTB Capital plc v Nutritek International Corp*, [2013] UKSC 5, [2013] 2 WLR 398 (Lord Neuberger) [142].

143 *S.P.D.C. (Nig.) Ltd. v Tiegbo VII* (2005) 9 NWLR (Pt 931) 439 (2005) 3–4 S.C 137; *Chief Pere Ajuwa & Others v SPDC* (n 124); *SPDC v Abel Isaiah and others* (2001) 11 NWLR (Pt 723) 168.

144 *Amos and Ors v Shell BP Petroleum Development Company of Nigeria* (1977) 6 S.C. 9.

145 *Ryland v Fletcher* (n 40).

146 EGASPIN (n 38) Part VIII B, s 2.11.1; Part IX 4.6.2 (c).

equipped agencies.[147] The Niger Delta environment steeped with oil pollution lends credence to this assertion. It is envisaged that when the principle is properly implemented in Nigeria, it will incentivise the oil companies (polluters and potential polluters) to adopt measures and develop practices to minimise the risks of environmental damage so that their exposure to financial liabilities is reduced.[148]

Section 103 of the PIA 2021 on financial contribution for remediation of environmental damage could be interpreted to import the notion of the polluter-pays principle in a very broad way. As already observed, it did not go far enough but it could offer the courts a good ground to order proper assessment of the environmental damage, delineate the responsible polluter(s), and stipulate what happens where the remediation funds are insufficient to fully pay for the remediation. The previous analysis and recommendations for sources of additional funding would equally apply here.

3.7. The Security Problems in the Niger Delta

Government inefficiency in implementing and enforcing existing environmental laws contributes to oil pollution in the Niger Delta.[149] The law requires the oil companies to conduct petroleum operation in accordance with 'good international petroleum industry practices'[150] but the enforcement is weak and ineffective.[151] As a result, oil companies are relatively relaxed with respect to their obligations on oil spill response and clean-up and in addressing the impact of spills on the environment.[152] This enrages the affected communities who in turn sabotage oil pipelines and facilities. This generally leads to more oil spills into the environment, loss of revenue both for the government and the oil companies, and general security problems in the region.

As part of the solution for cleaning up oil spills in the Niger Delta, UNEP recommended that an Environmental Restoration Fund for Ogoniland be set up with USD 1 billion to be contributed by the oil company and the government.[153] In response to this recommendation, the Nigerian government launched the clean-up Ogoniland programme in June 2016.[154] The agency for the implementation of this clean-up programme – the Hydrocarbon Pollution Remediation Project

147 Atsegbua, Akpotaire and Dimowo (n 38) 60.
148 ELD (n 118) preamble 2.
149 Engobo Emeseh, 'Limitations of Law in Promoting Synergy between Environment and Development, Policies in Developing Countries: A Case Study of the Petroleum Industry in Nigeria' (2006) 24(4) J Energy Nat Resourc Law 574.
150 PIA (n 8) s 96(1)(a); the Petroleum (Drilling and Production) Regulations (n 11) s 37.
151 Atsegbua, Akpotaire and Dimowo (n 38) 60.
152 Amnesty International, 'Shell in Nigeria Briefing: Shell: Own UP, Pay Up and Clean Up' *Amnesty International* (2012) <http://www.amnesty.org.uk/sites/default/files/shell_briefing_2012_lores_0.pdf> accessed 2 May 2022.
153 UNEP (n 7) 15.
154 UNEP, 'Nigeria Launches $1 Billion Ogoniland Clean-up and Restoration Programme' *Europa* (2 June 2016) <https://europa.eu/capacity4dev/unep/blog/nigeria-launches-1-billion-ogoniland-clean-and-restoration-programme> accessed 2 May 2022.

(HYPREP) has been set up[155] and is enjoined to determine the scope, means, and modalities of remediation of soil and groundwater contamination in the impacted communities, enhance local capacity for better environmental management and sustainable development, promote peace and security in the impacted communities, and strengthen governance, transparency, and accountability in the region.[156] It remains to be seen how far this agency will go in discharging these set objectives.

The issues discussed under this segment demonstrate that the implementation and enforcement of oil spill laws in Nigeria are ineffective in part due to lack of capacity of the agencies, huge ministerial discretion, improper standard setting, as well as the security problems in the Niger Delta. The next segment will tackle the challenges of pre-existing oil spills in the Niger Delta.

4. Clean-up Liability for Pre-existing Oil Spills in the Niger Delta

4.1. The Challenges

The Niger Delta is literally steeped in pre-existing oil spills. Some of these spills have accumulated in parts of the Niger Delta for over 40 years[157] defying every attempt to effectively clean them up. Estimating that it may take 25–30 years to clean up,[158] the UNEP recommended setting up an Environmental Restoration Fund first, for Ogoniland with contributions from the oil companies and the government.[159] In response to this recommendation, in June 2016, the Nigerian government launched $1 billion Ogoniland Clean-up and Restoration Programme.[160] Although the agency for the implementation of this programme – the Hydrocarbon Pollution Remediation Project (HYPREP) – has been set up,[161] clean-up has been slow with limited success.[162] Lack of capacity, inadequate infrastructure, funding challenges, and bureaucracy have been mooted as clogs on the wheel of progress for the programme.[163] Since Ogoniland is 1/70 of the Niger Delta,[164] it will take tremendous effort in terms of technical, financial, and human resources to clean up the entire Niger Delta.

In the light of the aforementioned challenges, the next segment will attempt to create a legal framework for cleaning up the pre-existing oil spills in the Niger

155 *HYPREP* was established under the Federal Ministry of Environment as published in the Federal Government gazette No 176, Vol 103 of December 2016 <https://hyprep.gov.ng/> accessed 20 August 2023.

156 *HYPREP*, Federal Ministry of Environment (n 155).

157 UNEP (n 7) 9.

158 UNEP (n 7) 12, 211.

159 UNEP (n 7) 15.

160 UNEP (n 7) 15.

161 *HYPREP* was established under the Federal Ministry of Environment as published in the Federal Government Gazette No 176 Vol 103 of December 2016. <https://hyprep.gov.ng/ accessed 06 July 2024.

162 K Sam, N Zabbey and AP Onyna, 'Implementing Contaminated Land Remediation in Nigeria: Insights from the Ogoni Remediation Project' (2022) 115 Land Use Policy 1–12, 1.

163 Sam, Zabbey and Onyna (n 162).

164 Niger delta covers an area of 70,000 Km^2 and Ogoniland is about 1000 km^2 – UNEP (n 7) 20, 22.

Delta by drawing insights from the UK/EU laws on contaminated land, the US Comprehensive Environmental Response, Compensation, and Liability Act (CERCLA or the Superfund), and the UK regime on oil infrastructure decommissioning.

4.2. *Creating a Legal Framework for Cleaning up the Pre-existing (Stale) Oil Spills in the Niger Delta*

The management and remediation of oil contaminated land in Nigeria is provided for under the Petroleum (Drilling and Production) Regulations, 1969,[165] the Oil Pipelines Act 1956,[166] the Petroleum Refining Regulations, 1974,[167] the NOSDRA Establishment Act 2006,[168] and the Environmental Guidelines and Standards for Petroleum Industries in Nigeria (EGASPIN)[169] The Petroleum Industry Act (PIA) 2021 retains the provisions of these statutes and guidelines where they are not inconsistent with the Act.[170] Additionally, the PIA provides for financial contributions for remediation of environmental damage,[171] although it did not go far enough to provide sources of additional funding where the contributed fund is insufficient to meet the environmental remediation costs.

Frequent oil spills still go on in the Niger Delta and because they are either not cleaned up (particularly spills from oil pipeline sabotage) or cleaned up improperly, they remain as soil contaminants and eventually become stale oil spills. The lack of a lasting solution to the clean-up of stale oil spills in the region suggests that more must be done in terms of statutory provisions, implementations, and enforcement of laws to prevent and/or correct this situation in Nigeria. An earlier work by Ele[172] indicated that valuable insights for doing this could be obtained from the contaminated land regimes in the UK,[173] the EU Environmental Liability Directive (ELD),[174] the US Comprehensive Environmental Response, Compensation and Liability Act (CERCLA or the Superfund),[175] and the UK regime on oil infrastructure decommissioning.[176] Each of these laws brings their unique perspective to the prevention of environmental damage and imposition of clean-up liabilities.

165 Petroleum (Drilling and Production) Regulations (n 11) s 37(a)(e). This regulation survives the PIA (2021) – PIA (n 8) s 311(9)(c).
166 Oil Pipelines Act (n 12) ss 17(4) and 33(c); PIA (n 8) s 311(9)(c).
167 Petroleum Refining Regulations 1974 ss 38 and 43(3); PIA (n 8) s, 311(9)(c).
168 NOSDRA (Est) Act 2006 ss 6 and 7.
169 EGASPIN (n 38) Part VIII-G, s 1.1.1.
170 PIA (n 8) s 317-Transitional and savings provisions.
171 PIA (n 8) s 103.
172 Ele (n 127) 129–40.
173 The Environmental Protection Act (EPA) 1990, Part 2A. However, because environmental protection is a matter for the devolved assemblies in the UK, there is a separate Contaminated Land Statutory Guidance for each of the regions (England, Wales, and Scotland). The Act and the relevant Guidance delegate the primary regulatory and enforcement role to the relevant local authorities (local or city councils) for England, Wales, and Scotland and explain how they should implement the regime on contaminated land.
174 EU ELD (n 118) This Directive ensures, among other things, that there are enough funds to prevent and remedy environmental damage and to cover clean-up liability.
175 CERCLA 42 U.S.C. s 9601–9675.
176 The UK Petroleum Act (1998), Pt IV.

Under the EU ELD, an operator whose activity has caused the environmental damage or the imminent threat of such damage will bear the cost of restoring and remedying the damaged environment or the cost of preventing the threat of such damage from coming to fruition.[177] This was intended to induce operators to adopt measures and develop practices that would minimise the risks of environmental damage and reduce their exposure to financial liabilities.[178] So, apart from compensation for the environmental damage due to the pollution, the Directive was also meant to have a deterrent effect on potential polluters, incentivising them to prevent environmental damage in their operations. Under Annex I of the Directive, any damage with a proven effect on human health must be classified as *significant damage*. Annex II sets out a common framework to be followed in determining the most appropriate measures to adopt to ensure proper remediation of the environmental damage. Van Den Broek noted that the ELD approach as presented in Annex II resembles the methods for assessment of damages under the US CERCLA 1980.[179] One of the main benefits of the Directive is that funds are set aside from the assets of the operator and are readily available to the competent authority for use in remediating the contaminated land as soon as the pollution occurs. It is recommended that this idea be built into the Nigerian contaminated land regime either in the PIA when it is up for review or in subsequent regulations, to help in dealing with the issue of the stale oil spills in the Niger Delta.

CERCLA is designed to identify and clean-up abandoned, contaminated waste sites such as abandoned mines and old industrial sites in the United States. It should be noted that this legislation does not cover liability for damages caused by the generation, processing, release, or threatened release of petroleum (crude oil, liquefied natural gas, etc.)[180] However, the toxic contents of abandoned mines and old industrial sites that are cleaned up under the CERCLA could be likened to pre-existing oil spills in the Niger Delta. CERCLA's liability attaches to a broad class of parties (both individuals and corporations) known as potentially responsible parties (PRPs).[181] These are generally associated with the generation and disposal[182] of the toxic wastes. In the Niger Delta, the oil companies (whether MNOCs or indigenous oil companies) could be likened to CERCLA PRPs since they are involved in oil exploration and production that potentially 'generate' oil pollution. Like CERCLA PRPs, they are, therefore, liable for the cost of cleaning up the oil pollution and for paying associated damages (both in the past and present) resulting from the contamination. This liability attaches just by acquiring the asset whether the PRP/oil company have participated in the pollution activities or not. Liability is strict

177 ELD (n 118) arts 8(1) and 2(16).

178 ELD (n 118) para 2 of the Preamble.

179 GM van den Broek, 'Environmental Liability and Nature Protection Areas: Will the EU Environmental Liability Directive Actually Lead to the Restoration of Damaged Natural Resources?' (2009) 5(1) Utrecht Law Rev 117, 125–26.

180 CERCLA, s 101(14), 42 U.S.C. s 9601(14) (1988). Pollution liability from this source is covered under the US Oil Pollution Act, 1990 (OPA) – see, US Oil Pollution Act (OPA 1990) 33 U.S.C.A. ss 2701 *et seq.*, amended in December 2000 (OPA 1990–33 U.S.C. s 4202(b) (2000)).

181 CERCLA, s 107(a)(1), 42 USC s 9607(a)(1)–(4) (2000).

182 Under CERCLA, 'disposal' is broadly defined to include any discharge, deposit, dumping, spilling, release, leaking etc. CERCLA, s 101(29).

for all PRPs under the CERCLA irrespective of fault or the degree of contribution to the pollution.[183] Liability is also joint and several. However, where a plaintiff obtains full judgment against one of the defendants, such a defendant could sue the other jointly and severally liable defendants to recover their prorated share of the judgement. Also, a party/PRP can sue another PRP under section 107(a) to recover or be reimbursed for its own expenses associated with cleaning up contaminated sites.[184] Where orphan sites[185] are involved, Kilbert suggested that claims under ss. 107 and 113[186] should be governed by the adoption of 'uniform scope of liability' for all responsible parties under which orphan sites are 'allocated among all viable responsible parties, both plaintiffs and defendants, pursuant to equitable factors.'[187] However, this may likely increase enforcement cost for the regulators and amount to imprudent use of scares resources. In Nigeria, perhaps, a pollution clean-up fund as recommended by UNEP and provided for under the EGASPIN[188] for cleaning up mystery spills could be used to cover clean-up costs for orphan sites, which arguably may have resulted from mystery spills.

Claims for damages to natural resources are broader under the CERCLA than the ELD.[189] This covers total response and clean-up costs and all natural resource damage claims,[190] which may include compensation to the public for injury to the public resource and lost functionality of a natural resource caused by a release of a petroleum product or hazardous substance. The polluter is also liable for full restoration of such natural resources and associated services lost due to such release.[191] Liability burden under the CERCLA is also heavier than that under the ELD.[192] CERCLA defences and challenges are strictly interpreted and narrowly applied, making it difficult for a PRP to avoid liability.[193]

One distinct characteristic of CERCLA is that it is retroactive in application. Neither the Nigerian law nor the ELD has this feature. CERCLA applies to incidents that occurred before its enactment in 1980[194] and to previous owners and/or operators of a site at the time of the contamination even if this happened before 1980 and even if they have sold the asset and have relinquished control over a long time. If they could be traced, they would be made to bear the clean-up liability or reimburse the state for the clean-up costs. This makes the CERCLA the ideal contaminated land regime for cleaning up the pre-existing oil spills in the Niger Delta.

183 CERCLA, ss 107(a).
184 *United States v Atlantic Research Corp.*, 551 U.S. 128 (2007).
185 Sites whose responsible parties are dead, insolvent, or defunct.
186 CERCLA, ss 107 and 113 deal with contributions for clean-up cost recovery.
187 Kenneth K Kilbert, 'Neither Joint nor Several: Orphan Shares and Private CERCLA Action' (2011) 41 Envtl Law 1045, 1045, 1092.
188 EGASPIN (n 38) Pt VIIIB s 4(1).
189 Directive 2004/35 art 2(12) compared to CERCLA 42 *USC s* 9601(16), 42 USC s 9607(a).
190 CERCLA 42 USC s 9607.
191 CERCLA – 42 *USC s* 9601(16) and US, Oil Pollution Act (OPA 1990) – 33 *USC* s 2706(d).
192 Bio Intelligence Service, 'Study on the implementation Effectiveness of the Environmental Liability Directive (ELD) and Related Financial security issues, Final Report' (DG ENV November 2009) 50–51.
193 Ele (n 127) 136.
194 Ele (n 127).

The UK Petroleum Act (1998), Pt IV, provides for the decommissioning[195] and abandonment of offshore oil and gas installations. Section 29 of this legislation is unique because it gives the Secretary of State for Business, Energy, and Industrial Strategy (BEIS)[196] the power to make a wide array of entities with an equity interest in a particular petroleum installation jointly and severally liable for all decommissioning costs of that installation simply by giving them notice to that effect.[197] The ambit of s.29 notice is very wide[198] and failure of any s.29 notice holder to comply with the notice requirements and implement decommissioning amounts to an offence.[199] Nigeria has no equivalent provision as s.29 in any legislation.

However, where a party is desirous of selling an oil asset, the Secretary of State could relieve him of his decommissioning liabilities by withdrawing the s.29 notice, if the party acquiring the asset has the ability, both technical and financial, to meet the decommissioning responsibilities.[200] But the Secretary of State retains the power under s.34 to call back a party previously relieved of his decommissioning responsibilities to assume such responsibilities again. Under the PIA 2021, a licensee/lessee formally discharged of decommissioning responsibility by the Commission due to sale cannot be called back if the current owner of the asset took up the decommissioning responsibility with the approval of the Commission when the asset was transferred.[201] This is much narrower than the call-back power under s.34 of the UK Petroleum Act, 1998 and could result in the non-decommissioning of some oil installations. This could very well happen if the current asset owner is a small indigenous oil company created as a Special Purpose Vehicle (SPV) specifically for the purpose of acquiring the mature, 'near end of life' oil fields/asset(s) and without the capacity to carry out the decommissioning process. No clear provision was made in the laws to cover what happens if SPVs are no longer in existence after the usual short investment duration. It is recommended that the seller/MNOC should not be relieved of the decommissioning liability easily. And by analogy, regarding the clean-up of the stale oil spills, the seller/MNOCs should not be let off the hook either.

In the UK, despite the Maximising Economic Recovery strategy,[202] which encourages smaller oil companies to acquired mature oil assets in the UK Continental Shelf from oil majors, to get the deal approved, the sale purchase agreement must be structured in such a way that the decommissioning liability remains entirely with the seller/oil major for better assurances to the government that the

195 Decommissioning is the safe dismantling and removal of the oil and gas installations at the end of operational lifespan of an oil well.

196 The UK BEIS is the Nigerian equivalent of the Department of Petroleum Resources (Now named the Nigerian Upstream Regulatory Commission under the PIA (n 8)). In 2023, UK BEIS was split to form the Department for Business and Trade (DBT), the Department for Energy Security and Net Zero (DESNZ), and the Department for Science, Innovation and Technology (DSIT).

197 UK Petroleum Act, 1998, ss 36 and s 37(1).

198 UK Petroleum Act (n 197) s 30(3).

199 UK Petroleum Act (n 197) ss 30(4), 37(2) and 40.

200 UK Petroleum Act (n 197) s 38.

201 PIA (n 8) s 232(13).

202 The 'Maximising Economic Recovery' (MER) strategy was implemented by the UK Oil and Gas Authority (OGA) in 2016 <https://assets.publishing.service.gov.uk/media/5a7f2175ed915d74e622892d/MER_UK_Strategy_FINAL.pdf> accessed 06 July 2024.

decommissioning would be done. A real-life scenario happened in 2018 when Serica Energy acquired interests in the Bruce, Keith and Rhum fields, from BP and TotalEnergies E&P UK. The decommissioning liability remains with seller/oil majors.[203] Borrowing from this, it is recommended that the clean-up liability (much like the decommissioning liability) always remain with seller/oil majors in the Niger Delta although this may end up being a concern to investors and an impediment to oil asset divestments in the region. Such clean-up responsibility could also be extended to the private equity entity that sponsored the SPVs by piercing the corporate veil to make them responsible for the cost of clean-up of the stale oil spills or the decommissioning of the oil and gas installations associated with the asset, the purchase of which they sponsored and profited from.

Under the UK Petroleum Act, 1998, decommissioning liability is imposed on a person or company *associated with* a company that owns any interest (other than the security for a loan) in the infrastructure to be decommissioned.[204] This makes the entities liable for decommissioning very broad, and when combined with the call-back provision of s.34 of the UK Petroleum Act 1998, it makes 'any former licensee/lessee potentially liable for decommissioning until it is done.'[205] These should be adopted in the Niger Delta with respect to the clean-up responsibility for stale oil spills. However, an operator cannot be held liable for the decommissioning of oil asset infrastructure that was not in existence when he possessed interest in the relevant property.[206]

In relation to pre-existing oil spills in the Niger Delta, former licensee/oil companies or entities *associated with* the polluted asset or that have an equity interest in such asset should remain potentially liable for its clean-up until it is done. However, operators will not be liable for cleaning up oil spills that occurred after they had sold their interest in the property. Although the NNPC has now been converted to the NNPC Limited,[207] which is an incorporated company free to manage its affairs without government control and oversight, the government still owns 100 percent of the NNPCL shares.[208] Also, the company and its subsidiaries acquired the bulk of the assets, interest and liabilities of the NNPC, and the ones not acquired are retained by to the government.[209] This means that as part of its liability, the NNPCL would be obligated to take up and finance any clean-up of pre-existing oil spills for which NNPC was liable.[210]

203 Serica Energy plc (Serica Energy UK Ltd) 'Acquisition of BHP interests in Bruce and Keith' (*London* 5 November 2018) <https://www.serica-energy.com/downloads/releases/Acquisition%20BHP%20Interests%20181105.pdf> accessed 22 July 2024.

204 UK Petroleum Act, 1998, s 30(1)(e) and (2)(c).

205 Ele (n 127) 138.

206 *Apache UK Investment Ltd v Esso Exploration and Production UK Ltd* [2021] EWHC 1283 (Comm); [2021] 4 W.L.R. 85.

207 PIA (n 8) ss 52–65.

208 PIA (n 8) s 53(2)(3).

209 PIA (n 8) s 54(1)(2), Mary Izuaka 'NNPC Limited Ends Operations as Government Corporation' *Premium Times* (18 February 2023) <https://www.premiumtimesng.com/news/top-news/582778-nnpc-limited-ends-operations-as-govt-corporation.html?tztc=1> accessed 12 July 2024.

210 It should be noted that the Nigerian government through the old NNPC has a controlling interest in the joint venture with the MNOCs and is technically in a joint and several liability relationship

Pre-existing oil spills could also be likened to residual infrastructure left after decommissioning. The BEIS Guidance Note 2018 imposes liability for residual infrastructure on all s.29 notice holders, and this liability remains with them in perpetuity.[211] The PIA 2021 has similar provision on liability for damages which may result where the installation is partly removed.[212] It made such residual liability remain with the licensee/lessee.[213] This could be directly interposed in stale oil spill situations where oil residue that can still cause unacceptable risks to human health and the environment, remains after clean-up. Liability issuing from such residue should be made to remain in perpetuity with the licensee/lessee and all associated companies at that time.[214] Financial security arrangements are encouraged both for oil infrastructure decommissioning[215] and the cleaning up of oil spills.[216]

5. Conclusion

This chapter examined the legal and regulatory dimensions of the problem of oil spills in Nigeria in the light of their implications on corporate behaviour. It identifies and discusses the problems and lapses in the existing laws and policies and the weaknesses in their implementation and enforcement. The chapter further examines the effectiveness of the polluter-pays principle in Nigeria, the improper standard setting, and the insufficient funding for environmental management. Security problems in the Niger Delta were also examined as one of the issues leading to increase in oil pipeline sabotage and spills.

As demonstrated in this chapter, the regulatory agencies are ill-equipped both in technical and human resources to effectively regulate the oil industry, the polluter-pays principle is not properly and effectively implemented, and the security problems in the Niger Delta compound rather than help issues. In the end, poorly developed laws and weak institutions continue to result in weak implementation and enforcement protocols, which exacerbate the problem of oil spills in the Niger Delta.

The problem of pre-existing (stale) oil spills is huge in the Niger Delta. UNEP observed that some have accumulated for decades from multiple pipelines owned and managed by different operators and that lack of reliable spill data makes accurate determination and apportionment of clean-up liability very difficult. Insights were sought from the UK/EU laws on contaminated land, the US Comprehensive Environmental Response, Compensation and Liability Act (CERCLA), and the UK laws on oil infrastructure decommissioning to create a legal framework and reformed legal regime for solving this problem in Nigeria.

---

with them. This means that the NNPC could technically be a clean-up duty holder and could be held responsible for the clean-up of the spills.

211 BEIS Guidance Notes 2018 para17(1).

212 PIA (n 8) s 232(6)(d).

213 PIA (n 8).

214 Ele (n 127) 138.

215 E.g., Decommissioning Security Agreements (DSA) trusts to ensure that money is guaranteed to be available for decommissioning in case a party responsible for decommissioning becomes insolvent. Such monies are not accessible to creditors under insolvency legislation – see, UK Petroleum Act, 1998, s 38; PIA (n 8) s 233(1).

216 EGASPIN (n 38) Pt VIIIB s 4(1); UNEP, Environmental Assessment of Ogoniland (n 7) 15.

The PIA 2021 aims to resolve some of the issues. For instance, it defined 'good international petroleum industry practice' to embrace for the first time the concept of sound environmental practice in the Nigerian oil and gas industry and made provisions for funding environmental management. It commercialised the NNPC, turning it into an incorporated, limited liability company, the NNPC Limited, thus eliminating the conflicts of interest between the DPR (now the Commission) and NNPC. The NNPC Limited is also self-financing and able to make and manage its funds. It is hoped that the company would henceforth be able to meet its cash call obligations for business management and environmental compliance and ultimately meet up with the polluter-pays principle in oil pollution matters in the Niger Delta.

The PIA equally curtailed the enormous ministerial powers and discretion given to the Minister of Petroleum Resources – assigning most of them to the Commission to ensure separation of duties and provide checks and balances. Therefore, the PIA 2021 made good attempts to improve the management of oil pollution in the Niger Delta, but it did not go far enough in providing for adequate funding for environmental management. In particular, it did not provide for sources of additional funding where the available funds are inadequate to meet the environmental remediation costs. To fill this gap, several reforms are essential.

First, it is important to ensure that the parent company of the immediate polluter and all persons, companies, and entities *associated with* the immediate polluter be held liable to provide the additional funds and resources needed to meet the clean-up and remediation costs, particularly where they have been found to play any role in the management or control of the immediate polluter. This way, the liabilities for funding environmental management will be reasonably and equitably distributed among a broad range of persons, companies, and entities *associated with* the immediate polluter.

Second, drawing insight from the UK Petroleum Act, 1998 and the Queensland Australia Chain of Responsibility Act (CoRA) 2016, the phrase *associated with* should be interpreted to include any person, company, or entity that has an equity interest (other than the security for a loan) in the polluter company; could profit significantly from the polluter company's activities; or could influence its environmental compliance decisions at the relevant site. In fact, the phrase *associated with (or associated entities)* should be interpreted in the same way as *related entities* under the CoRA, making the imposition of liability to 'follow the money' and target any person, company, or entity who stand to profit from the relevant company's activities and who contributed to the pollution of the environment that needs to be cleaned or remediated. This will broaden the liability group and ensure that the clean-up funds for oil spills will be provided for adequately.

Third, like the *special executive liability* of New South Wales, Australia, the Nigerian law should target corporate executives and hold the directing minds of the corporation personally liable where the company breaches its environmental duties if such executives have made or are in a position to make or influence corporate decisions on the illegal act. For effective deterrence, the courts should pierce the corporate veil and go after directors and those concerned with the management of a company for environmental offences committed by the company, including oil spills in the Niger Delta in appropriate cases. Incorporating these provisions into the PIA 2021 would go a long way to improve it, both in content and effectiveness.

5 Regulatory Capture, Revolving Doors, and the Multinational Oil Companies in the Niger Delta

1. Introduction

Regulatory capture has been described as the process by which the regulatory agencies are dominated by the industries or interests they are charged with regulating, through the deliberate intent and actions of those industries.[1] The result is that an agency, charged with acting in the public interest, fails to do so but instead acts in ways that benefit the regulated entity. In other words, the regulated entity or the industry controls the regulatory institution or agency that is supposed to oversee it, causing the latter to depart from the performance of its mandate and to serve the private rather than public interest.[2] Capture has also been described in term of the power relationship between the agency and the regulated entities.[3] An agency is presumed to be captured when the regulated entity has substantial power over it, such that the agency regularly adopts regulatory policies favoured by the regulated entities in contravention of its mandate and ostensibly neglects to protect the public interest.[4]

Carpenter and Moss define regulatory capture as:

> the result or process by which regulation, in law or application, is *consistently or repeatedly* directed away from the public interest and toward the interest of the regulated industry, by the *intent and action* of the industry itself.[5]

1 Daniel Carpenter and David A Moss, 'Introduction' in Daniel Carpenter and David A Moss (eds) *Preventing Regulatory Capture: Special Interest Influence and How to Prevent It* (CUP 2014) 13; Laurence Tai, 'Regulatory Capture and Quality' (2017) 37(3) J Public Policy 261.

2 Michelle E Portman, 'Regulatory Capture by Default: Offshore Exploratory Drilling for Oil and Gas' (2014) 65 Energy Policy 37, 38; Warren Bernauer, 'Regulatory Capture and Extractive Hegemony: The Relevance of Nicos Paulantzas' Theory of the State to Contemporary Environmental Politics in Canada' (2020) 13(2) Hum Geogr 160, 162.

3 Sidney A Shapiro, 'The Complexity of Regulatory Capture: Diagnosis, Causality, and Remediation' (2012) 17(1) Roger Williams Univ Law Rev 221, 223.

4 Shapiro (n 3) 223–25.

5 Carpenter and Moss (n 1).

DOI: 10.4324/9781003435150-5

According to them, and flowing from the foregoing definition, regulatory capture could be established by:

1. Describing what is in the *public interest* and defending it.
2. Explaining how the regulation has been shifted away (policy shift) from the public interest towards the regulated (special) entity.
3. Describing how the regulated industry (or special interest group) *actively and knowingly* pushed the regulation away from the public interest to satisfy the requirement for *'action and intent'* and showing that the regulated entity have possibly caused an appreciable part of the shift.[6]

This shows that it is not enough merely to prove that the regulated industry benefits from the regulation.[7] One must describe how they *actively and knowingly* pushed the regulation away from the public interest. These requirements make diagnosing and measuring regulatory capture more empirical and with a heavy evidentiary burden to meet. This is more so because most of the information required for this proof may be neither accessible nor documented making it very challenging to prove the intent and actions of the industry.[8] This high evidentiary requirement may lead to underdiagnosis of capture by allowing some potential capture situations to slip through the net unchecked. To forestall this, the application of precautionary principle emphasises caution and a protective approach to avoid or diminish the harm. It is, therefore, suggested that the *consistent and repeated action* of the industry or special interest group to direct the regulation away from the public interest towards the interest of the regulated entity be a signpost of impending capture leading to the need to put checks in place to stop it.

Regulatory capture has been found to be prevalent in the energy sector and was implicated in the 2010 BP Macondo well blowout and massive oil spill at the Gulf of Mexico.[9] The Mineral Management Service (MMS), the agency responsible for the US oil and gas industry, allegedly failed to prevent the BP oil spill because the oil industry largely controlled the decision-making power of the agency.[10] As a result, the agency failed to stipulate the steps to be taken to deal with the safety concerns observed in the BP operations, negligently signing off on the BP's defective plans, and basically leaving the industry to determine what to do.[11] In Nigeria, NOSDRA was established by the government to manage oil spill response and clean-up in the Niger Delta and thus regulate the activities of the oil companies with respect to that. The question is whether the seeming lack of control of the NOSDRA over the multinational oil companies (MNOCs) in terms of the management of oil pollution can be attributed to a *degree* of regulatory capture.

6 Carpenter and Moss (n 1) 15.
7 Carpenter and Moss (n 1).
8 Carpenter and Moss (n 1) 16.
9 Portman (n 2); Shapiro (n 3) 227–28.
10 Shapiro (n 3) 223.
11 Portman (n 2).

This chapter would attempt to answer this question using the analysis of a Joint Investigation Visit (JIV) to an oil spill site as a case study.

2. Causes of Regulatory Capture

It has been observed that regulatory capture can occur if there is ambiguity and absence of clear agency jurisdiction about the environmental protection standards to be adhered to.[12] It can also occur where outdated regulation creates a regulatory vacuum and a situation vulnerable to capture.[13] Such vulnerability could also be created where the group in favour of stronger environmental regulation for public interest have been weakened by the group that favour deregulation for the benefit of the industry[14] and where there is strong collaboration between the industry and government aided by regulatory uncertainty.[15] This was the case in the Deepwater Horizon oil spill (the BP Macondo well blowout) at the Gulf of Mexico in 2010.

Information asymmetry is also seen as a possible cause of regulatory capture.[16] This occurs where the information that the regulatory agencies (and legislators) receive via lobbyists, emails, phone calls, comments during the notice and comment period of rulemaking, as well as judicial reviews, come more from the regulated entities, thus making it more likely for the agencies to adopt industry-favoured policies.[17] It has been noted that more lobbyists that want to influence agency policies work for industry and trade associations rather than the public interest or non-profit and citizens' groups.[18] They participate more in rulemaking procedures by filing more comments and petitions for reconsideration, notice of appeals, etc. This control and dominance over the information that gets to the agencies increases the likelihood that the regulators would adopt the position that favours the industry[19] and ultimately leads to capture. Thus, information asymmetry could be a pathway to regulatory capture. In the Niger Delta, weaknesses in the existing regulatory frameworks, weak monitoring and enforcement of regulations, overlaps in regulatory functions by multiple agencies often resulting in jurisdictional confusion, as well as widespread corruption among public officers may be enablers of regulatory capture by the industry.

3. Mitigation and Prevention of Regulatory Capture

Regulatory capture in the oil industry could be prevented or at least reduced by introducing and implementing clear and rigorous regulations coupled with

12 Portman (n 2) 37.
13 Portman (n 2) 37.
14 Portman (n 2) 39, 43–44.
15 Portman (n 2) 46.
16 Shapiro (n 3) 222, 234–41.
17 Shapiro (n 3).
18 Shapiro (n 3) 234, 237.
19 Shapiro (n 3) 222, 234–38; Nnona, 'Group Interests in Nigeria's Companies and Allied Matters Act: A History of Subterranean Regulatory Capture' (2018) 11 Afr J Legal Stud 201, 210–30.

the application of the precautionary principles.[20] The Macondo well blowout in 2010 highlights the increased need for environmental precaution in regulating the oil and gas industry. Regulatory transparency has also been suggested as a way of solving the problem of regulatory capture.[21] This would afford the public a window into the regulatory activities of the agency and alert them to potential captures.[22] According to Shapiro, this could be done by blocking or reducing revolving doors and establishing stronger rules of ethics, among others.[23]

Although it is difficult or almost impossible to eliminate corporate and regulated-industry influence on regulatory agencies and policy makers, they can be moderated. In his examination of complementary strategies to government regulation Neil Gunningham and co-authors considered the circumstances in which businesses, commercial and non-commercial third-parties such as public interest groups, insurance companies, banks, and other lending institutions, etc. could be used as proxy or 'surrogate regulators' to complement a government regulator or regulatory agency.[24] These third-party substitute regulators could be harnessed to either prevent regulatory capture in the first place or make them unsuccessful especially in pollution and environmental non-compliance issues. The use of these proxy regulators as a means of curbing regulatory capture merits further exploration.

3.1. Insurance Institutions

It is normal business practice for insurers to thoroughly examine the environmental qualifications and licences of clients before approval of coverage and the amount of premiums to be paid. Higher premiums are usually charged to poor environmental performers to reflect higher risks they pose to the insurance company by their activities. It is believed that this would normally incentivise the operators to improve their environmental credentials even though the company may have captured the regulatory authority. Insurers can also set their own standard and require the installation of certain risk-reduction technology, as a condition for coverage. They could retain the right to monitor the site to ensure that relevant safety measures are in place and well maintained, otherwise the policy would be cancelled, not renewed, or renewed at a higher premium.[25] Differentiated premiums proportionate to risks is a good way to incentivise positive corporate environmental behaviour in the oil industry and an antidote to corporate impunity that may be associated with regulatory capture.

20 Portman (n 2) 37.
21 Shapiro (n 3) 249, 257.
22 Shapiro (n 3).
23 Shapiro (n 3) 253–55.
24 Neil Gunningham, Martin Phillipson and Peter Grabosky, 'Harnessing Third Parties as Surrogate Regulators: Achieving Environmental Outcomes by Alternative Means' (1999) 8(4) Business Strategy Environ 211.
25 Colin Mackie, 'The Regulatory Potential of Financial Security to Reduce Environmental Risk' (2014) 26(2) J Environ Law 189, 197; Gunningham, Phillipson and Grabosky (n 24) 217.

3.2. Banks and Other Lending Institutions

Banks and other lending institutions generally require an environmental audit of their corporate clients to get full information about their environmental practice before advancing a loan.[26] This helps them to assess the risks involved in a particular loan transaction and also ascertain the environmental status of the assets they accept as security for the loan. It also helps them to avoid liability and unnecessary litigation for loan recovery in the event the collateral ends up being under par.[27] Where a client's operation is of questionable environmental practice and too much of a financial risk, banks would generally be restrained in advancing a loan to such a client. Such denials would incentivise the client to improve on its environmental footprint and in this regard, banks and lending institutions act as substitute or surrogate regulators and influence their client's environmental behaviour even if the government regulatory agency is potentially captured by the industry.

3.3. Public Interest (Citizen-) groups

Public Interest (citizen-) groups have become very relevant in the environmental regulatory process especially in developed countries where environmental awareness is more widespread. They help to pressure the government and the industry through advocacy and litigation to perform their environmental functions and meet their environmental obligations. They educate the public, providing relevant information through public events and activism. This has been known to incentivise consumers to demand that goods are certified as sustainably produced and incentivise communities to demand that compliance documents and accident plans are regularly reviewed and updated. By so doing, they act as environmental watchdogs and help in the implementation of environmental policies even though the agency actions may have been stifled by regulatory capture.[28]

3.4. Environmentally Conscious Consumers

Where there is minimal differential in price, some consumers would readily choose to buy merchandise produced in an environmentally sustainable manner.[29] However, environmental consumer behaviour is significantly influenced by the consumer's environmental knowledge and perceived environmental consequences.[30] This means that the more environmentally knowledgeable a consumer is, the more likely he would make the decision to reject non-green products. Corporate consumers and

26 Gunningham, Phillipson and Grabosky (n 24) 217.
27 Gunningham, Phillipson and Grabosky (n 24).
28 Gunningham, Phillipson and Grabosky (n 24) 213.
29 Gunningham, Phillipson and Grabosky (n 24) 214.
30 Pradeep Kautish and Rajesh Sharma, 'Determinants of Pro-environmental Behaviour and Environmentally Conscious Consumer Behaviour: An Empirical Investigation from Emerging Market' (2020) 3(1) Business Strategy Dev 112–12.

government procurement agents, particularly those from the developed countries, are also gradually rejecting goods that do not meet adequate environmental standards.[31] As a result, companies that have captured the regulatory process and continue to produce in an environmentally unsustainable way would soon realise they are losing market share and would need to change course.

3.5. ESG Investors

Socially conscious investors often use environmental, social and governance (ESG) standards for companies to screen potential investments. This involves considerations of a company's environmental footprints, including, for instance, its policies on climate change, how it manages employee relationships, customer care, suppliers, and the communities where it operates. It also examines its corporate leadership, internal controls, audits, executive pay, and shareholder rights. All these considerations enable ESG investors to invest in socially responsible companies and reject the others. Companies that have captured the regulatory process and are not compliant to ESG standards would soon start to lose market share and would ultimately be forced to review their policies towards becoming more compliant.

The activities of the aforementioned 'surrogate' regulator groups could be used to mitigate or prevent regulatory capture (consciously or unconsciously) where the responsible agency is not performing its functions optimally due to regulatory capture or for any other reason.

4. Case Study of a Joint Investigation Visit (JIV) and the Potential Regulatory Capture of the National Oil Spill Detection and Response Agency (NOSDRA) in the Niger Delta

The Nigerian law provides that oil spills should be reported to the NOSDRA and the Nigerian Upstream Petroleum Regulatory Commission (the Commission)[32] within 24 hours of the onset of the spill.[33] Where the spill is large and/or sensitive, an immediate notification shall be made to the designated office by telephone.[34] Similar provisions exist in the USA and the UK. In the US, the EPA requires that the operator *reports immediately* any oil spill incident,[35] and in the UK, telephone notifications of onset of spills must be made *immediately* within one hour

31 Gunningham, Phillipson and Grabosky (n 24) 215.

32 Formally the Department of Petroleum Resources (DPR).

33 The National Oil Spill Detection and Response Agency (NOSDRA) (Establishment) Act, 2006, s.6(2). Hereinafter, NOSDRA Act 2006; The Environmental Guidelines and Standards for the Petroleum Industry in Nigeria (EGASPIN) 2018, Part VIII-B, s 6(1)(i). EGASPIN Appendix VIII-5B shows the JIV Form.

34 EGASPIN (n 33) Pt II, s 5.6.2. Similar provisions exist in the USA where the EPA under s 311(j)(1)(C) of the Clean Water Act as amended by the Oil Pollution Act of 1990; 40 CFR s 110(1)–(3) requires that the operator report immediately any oil spill incident. Also, in the UK.

35 US Clean Water Act, s. 311(j)(1)(C) as amended by the Oil Pollution Act of 1990; 40 CFR s 110(1)–(3).

in accordance with the BEIS[36] Petroleum Operations Notice (PON)1 Guidance.[37] While evidence of non-compliance with the oil spill reporting requirement could hardly be sited in the USA and the UK, the Nigerian Oil Spill Monitor is replete with evidence of non-compliance both in the spill incident notification and in the time within which the requisite joint spillage investigation visit (JIV) to the site of an oil spill is conducted as shown through the JIV forms and reports posted in the site.[38] While this cannot per se be linked to regulatory capture, the specific incident analysed later could be used to illustrate evidence of potential regulatory capture.

In Nigeria, the law provides that a joint investigation team[39] be activated by the Operator within 24 hours of spill notification to conduct a Joint Investigation Visit (JIV) to determine the cause, and assess the degree of impact.[40] The JIV team jointly investigates the spill, noting, in the JIV Form, inter alia: the spiller/company, the incident details (date, time, etc.), the site details, circumstances around spill point such as the visual observation of the hole/leak point position (for possible pipeline corrosion or vandalism), cause of spill and estimated quantity spilled, the impacted area/s, and whether photographs and maps are available. At the end, all the members of the team sign the JIV report,[41] and this document generally forms the basis of any legal proceedings or compensation claims.[42]

The data from the JIV on each oil spill and the analysis from the oil companies are used to populate the Nigerian Oil Spill Monitor.[43] This is a dynamic and constantly populated oil spill database created and maintained by NOSDRA since 2006.[44] It gives the public access to up-to-date official data on oil spills in the Niger Delta. From this, the frequency of spills from each oil company can be determined

36 BEIS is the UK Department of Business, Energy, and Industrial Strategy. In 2023, it was split to form the Department of Business and Trade (DBT), the Department of Energy Security and Net Zero (DESNZ), and the Department for Science, Innovation and Technology (DSIT).

37 BEIS Department, 'Guidance Notes for Preparing Oil Pollution Emergency Plans (OPEPs)' Rev 7, June 2022, Appendix D (Oil Spill Reporting Arrangements) 61–62 <https://assets.publishing.service.gov.uk/media/62a9992ad3bf7f036cb7a22e/OPEP_Guidance_-_Rev_7_-_June_2022.pdf> accessed 26 November 2023.

38 Nigerian Oil Spill Monitor <https://oilspillmonitor.ng/ accessed> 11 December 2024.

39 This team shall comprise representatives of the licensee/operator/spiller/oil company, the community, and the appropriate government agency mainly the DPR, pre-2006 or the NOSDRA from 2006, the Ministry of Environment and the Local Government Council. EGASPIN 2018 (n 33) Pt II, s 5.6.3, and Appendix VIII-5B (16). Representatives of a coalition of principal NGOs in the Niger Delta – The National Coalition on Gas Flaring and Oil Spills in the Niger Delta (NACGOND) – are now also invited to join the JIV team as observers – Shell Sustainability Report, 2014, p 37.

40 EGASPIN 2018 (n 33) Pt II, s 5.6.3. Neither the US nor the UK have joint investigation visit to oil spill sites.

41 *Akpan and Milieudefensie v RDS plc and SPDC Nig. Ltd*, C/09/337050/HA ZA 09–1580, 30 January 2013, paras 2.7 & 4.20.

42 Amnesty International and the Centre for Environment, Human Rights Development (CEHRD), 'Bad Information: Oil Spill Investigations in the Niger Delta' *Amnesty International* (7 November 2013) 14, 33 <www.amnesty.org/en/documents/AFR44/028/2013/en/> accessed 11 December 2024.

43 Nigerian Oil Spill Monitor (n 38); Michael Watts and Anna Zalik, 'Consistently Unreliable: Oil Spill Data and Transparency Discourse' (2020) 7 Extractive Indus Soc 790, 792.

44 Nigerian Oil Spill Monitor (n 38).

and how the companies accomplish their legal responsibilities with respect to oil spills and the environment. It is, however, questionable how reliable this data is since NOSDRA largely 'relies on the voluntary engagement and support of oil companies for the provision of the data, logistics, *quantity estimates*, soil/water samples, and to carry out clean-up operations.'[45] The oil companies (the potentially liable party) are left virtually in control of the JIV process – initiating, organising, and leading the process.[46] Thus, they are largely in control of the process that determine the basis of their liability e.g., the cause and volume of spill, the affected area, as well as the degree of impact. Non-approved JIVs allegedly get to be signed because of this practice and so the figures in the oil spill monitor are, to that extent, arguably compromised.[47] For this reason, it is plausible to argue that the figures presented in this database may likely be underestimated at least in terms of volume of spills and some other indices dependent on technical procedure and lead provided by the oil companies.[48] So, a major impediment to the quality and reliability of the JIV process is the fact that the regulatory agencies do not always have the necessary equipment, resources, and expertise to take charge of the process. The NOSDRA is poorly funded[49] and often depends on the industry to provide equipment and necessary resources for the JIV process. This allows the industry to control and dominate the JIV process, thus rendering the agencies vulnerable to regulatory capture.

The result is that an agency, charged with acting in the public interest, fails to do so but instead, acts in ways that benefit the regulated entity. For instance, records show that where immediate containment and clean-up of oil spills are attempted, they are not adequately completed but are nevertheless certified by the regulators to have been completed.[50] During its environmental assessment of Ogoniland, the United Nations Environment Programme (UNEP) noted that ten out of 15 sites that the Shell Petroleum Development Company (SPDC) records show as having been completely remediated still have pollution levels exceeding the SPDC and

45 Nigerian Oil Spill Monitor (n 38) (About the Nigerian Oil Spill Monitor).

46 Amnesty International and CEHRD (n 42) 15–17.

47 Amnesty International and CEHRD (n 42); NACGOND, 2014. NACGOND JIV policy brief: oil spills in the Niger Delta – reflections and concerns on JIV and community interests. Port Harcourt, National Coalition on Gas Flaring and Oil Spills in the Niger Delta (NACGOND).

48 For instance, for detailed analysis of soil, water, and groundwater contamination, natural resource damage, etc., NOSDRA admitted that the information provided by the oil companies is often not complete and that the work environment is replete with security and logistical difficulties – Nigerian Oil Spill Monitor (n 38).

49 Amnesty International and CEHRD (n 42) 39.

50 IUCN-NDP, 'Sustainable Remediation and Rehabilitation of Biodiversity and Habitats of Oil Spill Sites in the Niger Delta' – A Report by the IUCN-Niger Delta Panel (IUCN-NDP) to the Shell Development of Nigeria Ltd (January 2013) 4 <https://portals.iucn.org/library/sites/library/files/documents/2013–061.pdf> accessed 11 December 2024; Terisa E Turner, 'The Land is Dead' Women's Rights as Human Rights: The Case of the Ogbodo Shell Petroleum Spill in Rivers State Nigeria June-July 2001 (July 2001) <http://www.terisaturner.com/ogbodospill.pdf> accessed 11 December 2024.

government remediation thresholds.[51] While this in itself does not equate to regulatory capture, the actions clearly favour the oil companies and were not in public interest.

4.1. Shell's Control of the JIV Process Smacks of Potential Regulatory Capture

A distinct case study is illustrated by the JIV invitation letter[52] that Shell wrote to NOSDRA inviting the agency to a joint spillage investigation of an oil spill incident (No: 2017–1826306), that occurred on 25 March 2017 from a facility under Shell's control. Shell was completely in charge of the JIV process as evidenced by the letter.[53]

The letter dated 6 April 2017 officially notified NOSDRA of an oil spill incident that occurred at Tank 9 on 25 March 2017. The law requires companies to notify the agency of any spill incident within 24 hours of the onset of the spill.[54] By making the report of an oil spill incident that occurred on 25 of March 2017 through this letter dated 6 April 2017, Shell reported the incident 12 days late. The letter was, in fact, received and stamped by NOSDRA on 20 April 2017, 26 days after the onset of the spill, and much later than the scheduled date for the JIV, which was 13 April. It must be noted that Shell (the operator of the affected facility) ought to notify the NOSDRA of the onset of the spill within 24 hours and activate a Joint Spillage Investigation (JSI) team within 24 hours of spill notification to conduct a Joint Investigation Visit.[55]

In the letter, Shell requests that NOSDRA nominate its staff to accompany Shell's team for the visit to the spill site. The company scheduled the JIV to take place on Friday, 13 April 2017, with pick up time at 0700hrs. This indicates that Shell unilaterally schedules the JIV and dictates the tone of the process.

Additionally, an attempt to match the letter with the NOSDRA JIV form completed after the JIV and the SPDC JIV Report of the Incident[56] reveals greater inconsistency. While the SPDC JIV report of the incident appears to have more information, the date in which the incident was reported to the agency and the description of the spill-point environment were missing in that report.[57] The

51 United Nations Environment Programme (UNEP), 'Environmental Assessment of Ogoniland' (2011) 9–10, 12, 87, 111, 122 <https://postconflict.unep.ch/publications/OEA/UNEP_OEA.pdf> accessed 2 May 2022.

52 SPDC Invitation Letter to NOSDRA, Nigerian Oil Spill Monitor, Incident Number 1826306 <https://oilspillmonitor.ng/#/61884.2017_1826306> accessed 21 February 2025.

53 NOSDRA and Nigerian Oil Spill Monitor (n 52).

54 NOSDRA Act (n 33) s 6(2); EGASPIN (n 33) Appendix VIII B2.

55 NOSDRA Act (n 33) s.6(2); EGASPIN (n 33) Part VIII-B, s.6(1)(i).

56 Filled NOSDRA JIV Form, and SPDC JIV Report, Nigerian Oil Spill Monitor Incident Number 1826306 <https://oilspillmonitor.ng/#/61884.2017_1826306> accessed 24 December 2024.

57 The agency was officially notified of the oil spill on 6 April 2017; See, SPDC Invitation letter to NOSDRA <https://oilspillmonitor.ng/#/61884.2017_1826306> accessed 23 February 2025. The

NOSDRA report also did not record the date in which the incident was reported[58] as well as the date of first investigation.[59] The two documents were signed on the same day (13 April 2017, the supposed date of the JIV) by the same representative from NOSDRA, the State Ministry of Environment, the Community, and asset owner/Shell.

A somewhat more detailed report was written by the NOSDRA rep and signed on 16 April 2017.[60] The rep reported that the cause of spill was equipment failure and that 'the impact was heavy.'[61] The volume of the spilt oil was recorded as approximately 570 barrels, covering a total land area of 1.02 HA. Also, according to the report, Tank 9 has been out of service and was due for rehabilitation for the past five years but due to financial constraint that could not be done.

Although the JIV was on 13 April 2017 according to the reports by the NOSDRA rep, the NOSDRA, and the asset owner, SPDC, it was paradoxically before 20 April 2017, the date on which NOSDRA received the letter from Shell notifying it of the spill incident and the scheduled date for the JIV.

Following the receipt of the letter, on 24 April 2017, the Personnel Executive Secretary (PES) directed that the investigation of the incident be assigned to a NOSDRA rep and on 26 April 2017, a NOSDRA rep, KA, was assigned to investigate the incident. But from all available documents, this investigation was already done on 13 April 2017 and signed by all participants including KA (the NOSDRA rep) who according to the letter was assigned to the job on 26 April 2017. This means that the NOSDRA rep took part in the JIV (on 13 April 2017) and wrote his report (dated 16 April 2016) even before he was officially assigned to do the job on 26 April 2017. There is clearly substantial incoherence about the timeline of this JIV process, and this makes the accuracy of its documentation questionable. This is not an isolated incident. There is hardly a JIV form or report that is complete and devoid of error in the forms and reports published in the Oil Spill Monitor.[62] Most forms are carelessly filled with key information missing or clearly wrong and some of the JIV were conducted far beyond the time stipulated under the law.[63] A lot of reasons could be contributing to this,[64] one of which could be deliberate attempt by the industry (Shell) to bend the agency towards the acceptance of its corporate will as the preceding account amply shows. Regrettably, the JIV and the report that results from it are relied on in determining the cause and volume of spill; the size

---

Leak/Seepage was from the Tank Foundation Shoulder and the Annular Plates; NOSDRA report of the JIV of the incident.

58 This was because the incident was not reported before the JIV. See, SPDC Invitation letter to NOSDRA.

59 The first investigation was made on 7 April 2017, and the agency was not invited – SPDC's Report 1 <https://oilspillmonitor.ng/#/61884.2017_1826306> accessed 24 December 2024.

60 NOSDRA JIV Report, Nigerian Oil Spill Monitor Incident Number 1826306, 25 March 2017 <https://oilspillmonitor.ng/#/61884.2017_1826306> accessed 11 December 2024.

61 Heavy impact may be subject to further interpretation.

62 Sample JIV Forms and Reports, Nigerian Oil Spill Monitor (n 38).

63 Nigerian Oil Spill Monitor (n 38).

64 These may include lack of commitment by agency personnel, negligence, corruption, etc.

and nature of the impacted area; damage assessment and ultimately the basis of any litigation; and the extent of compensation.

The question, then, is whether the preceding account evidences or amounts to regulatory capture? To answer this question, the starting point would be to establish whether the JIV process is in the public interest. To the extent that that process is to investigate an oil spill to determine the cause, volume, and degree of impact of the spill for purposes of proper clean up and remediation of the impacted area, it is in the public interest. This is because the public has a right to a safe, clean, healthy, and sustainable environment.[65] Second, it is the function of NOSDRA to conduct the assessment of damage caused by an oil spillage for the purpose of proper clean-up.[66] That this should be properly and independently done without undue influence by the industry is also in the public interest. Although the JIV must be done by a team that includes the oil company, ceding the control to Shell as was evidenced by the invitation letter and the associated conduct and reporting of the JIV, weakens the agency and appears to shift the regulation away from the public interest towards the regulated entity – Shell.

The commanding tone of the letter appears routine and smacks of an institutionalised practice and a sort of corporate 'takeover' of the regulatory process against public interest. It not only usurps the power of the agency but pushes the regulation away from the public interest and denies them of the right to a clean, safe, and sustainable environment. The agency appears weak and willing to go along with Shell in the process and ultimately against the public interest. This is clearly indicative of a potential regulatory capture although other factors like poor agency funding, lack of technical and human resources, or even corruption may be contributory. The next paragraph attempts to discuss revolving doors and its effects, if any, on regulatory capture.

5. Revolving Doors and Regulatory Capture

Revolving doors is the shuttling of individuals between public and private employment.[67] It dulls the line between the regulator and the regulated and works in favour of the individual and the company but against the public interest (just like regulatory capture). It could be 'revolving in' – moving from the private to the public sector e.g., moving from Shell to the NNPC – or 'revolving out' – being the reverse e.g., moving from the NNPC to Shell. A more subtle one occurs where there is 'revolving in without moving.'[68] In this case, the private sector surreptitiously enters public office and the policymaking process for their benefit and to the detriment of the public and the environment. A good example of this was demonstrated

65 UN Council on HR, 48th Session (A/HRC/48/L.23/Rev.1), 5 October 2021.

66 NOSDRA Act (n 33) s 19(1)(h); s 19(3)(d).

67 Monica Pons-Hernandez, 'Power(ful) Connections: Exploring the Revolving Doors Phenomenon as a Form of State Corporate Crime' (2022) 30 Crit Criminol 305.

68 Pons-Hernandez (n 67) 316.

by how private interest groups within Nigeria's commercial sector infiltrated and captured the law-making process during the formative years of the Company and Allied Matters Act (CAMA) 1990 and influenced the outcome of the CAMA for the benefit of the industry and to the detriment of the public interest.[69] The practice of revolving without moving is so widespread that if corporations are not wedged or controlled, lasting success in energy and climate change policies will remain a mirage and the environment and public health will suffer for it. Currently, there is no sign that the excesses of corporations in this light are being seriously addressed in international climate agreements or the Nigerian petroleum industry. According to Whyte, 'It is impossible to avert ecocide if corporations remain in control.'[70]

The revolving doors practice is strengthened by close collaboration between the government and the corporations.[71] Although revolving doors per se is not a crime, the practice could be linked to corruption, influence peddling, and regulatory capture. As a result, it has been suggested that the definition of revolving doors be broadened to make it a crime.[72] Employing the case study of the Spanish government and the fossil fuel industry, Pons Hernandez explored the revolving doors phenomenon as a form of state-corporate crime with a mutually reinforcing interaction between the state policy-makers and the corporations. Corporations manipulate the state into taking actions favourable to the industry but against public interest.[73] As noted by Rebecca Katz, citing the case of Dow Chemical corporation and the US government dating back to WWII, this mutually rewarding symbiotic association between the state and the corporation often makes it difficult to hold the corporations accountable for their environmentally harmful activities that amount to crimes.[74]

The revolving doors between public officials and the energy and fossil fuel industry has a negative effect on climate and energy policy and slows down the transition to renewable energy.[75] Individuals that revolve out generally sell access into public offices for lucrative government contracts, permits, or licences. Fossil fuel corporations and their lobbies are allegedly influencing energy policymaking at the European Commission through traditional revolving doors practice and are involved in policy development.[76] For instance, in Spain, Law 54/1997 of 27 November 1997 liberalised the electricity sector by setting up two private companies to assume the previously public functions. Two politicians who were among

69 Nnona (n 19) 210–30.

70 D Whyte, *Ecocide: Kill the Corporation Before it Kills Us* (Manchester University Press 2020) 111.

71 EA Bradshaw, "Obviously, We're All Oil Industry': The Criminogenic Structure of the Offshore Oil Industry' (2015) 19(3) Theor Criminol 376–95; D Whyte, 'Regimes of Permission and State-Corporate Crime' (2014) 3(2) State Crime J 237.

72 Pons-Hernandez (n 65).

73 Pons-Hernandez (n 65).

74 Rebecca S Katz, 'The Corporate Crimes of Dow Chemical and the Failure to Regulate Environmental Pollution' (2010) 18 Crit Crim 295, 305.

75 Pons-Hernandez (n 65) 307.

76 Fossil Free Politics, 'Stop the Revolving Door: Fossil Fuel Policy Influencers' (2021) <https://www.fossilfreepolitics.org/news-resources/stop-revolving-doors.html> accessed 18 January 2024.

the legislators for this law ended up revolving out to work for the two companies that benefited from the law.[77] This is a classic revolving doors scenario preceded by what seems like a carefully engineered regulatory capture. First, the industry infiltrates and 'controls' the government law-making process[78] and ensures that the resulting policies, rules, and regulations favour industry interest and for the most part work against public interest. The outcome of the Nigerian PIA 2021 in a certain respect reeks of this sort of influence by the MNOCs operating in the Niger Delta.[79]

6. Conclusion

This chapter discusses regulatory capture and oil pollution in the Niger Delta through that theoretical lens. It discusses the causes of regulatory capture and how it could be mitigated and prevented. It then focussed on the possible capture of the Nigerian agency in charge of oil spill detection and response (the NOSDRA) by Shell. This was evidenced by a case study of a joint spillage investigation in which the agency by all account appeared subdued by Shell. Revolving doors as a possible enabler of regulatory capture was also examined.

In the end, the fact that oil companies operating in the Niger Delta have *de facto* control over the process of joint spillage investigation raises serious concerns. Although it may be debatable whether this amounts to regulatory capture, it is undeniable that allowing the oil companies to have control of the process, the outcome of which would form the basis of their liability, would never work in the public interest and the public's right to a safe, clean, healthy, and sustainable environment.

77 Pons-Hernandez (n 65) 309. See also, O Reyes, 'Revolving Doors in Spanish Climate and Energy Policy' in M Huter and others, *Revolving doors and the Fossil Fuel Industry: Time to Tackle Conflicts of Interest in Climate Policy-Making* (Greens/EFA Group in the European Parliament, May 2018) 108–17 <https://www.greens-efa.eu/files/assets/docs/report_of_revolving_doors_digital_-min.pdf> accessed 18 January 2024.

78 Nnona (n 19) 210–30.

79 For instance the PIA 2021, ss 235(3) and 318 appear to give the Settlor (oil company) the authority to determine which community qualifies as Host community for purposes of benefiting from the Host Community Development Trust Fund (HCD Trust); s 257(2)(3) saddles the host community with the obligation to guard oil pipelines and facilities within their community against acts of pipeline sabotage and vandalism and denies them their entitlement under the HCD Trust if they fail to discharge this wrongfully imposed duty.

6 Litigating Nigerian Oil Spill Cases in the US, the UK, and the Netherlands

1. Introduction and Background

Civil litigation in national courts is generally used to enforce transnational corporate environmental responsibility. In oil spill matters, this would include the responsibility to clean up the spills, restore the environment, and compensate the victims of the oil spill. Compensation claims are generally made by individuals or groups that have been affected by the oil spill through litigation based on common law torts[1] of negligence, nuisance, trespass, and strict liability. However, to obtain justice and appropriate remedies, litigants need to have access to the courts, reasonable expectations of fair and speedy resolution of the matter, and funds to cover the cost of litigation. Although the Nigeria Constitution guarantees access to court[2] and a fair hearing within a reasonable time by a court,[3] and international treaties and agreements provide for access to justice,[4] courts are not easily accessible in Nigeria for oil pollution and environmental matters. This is because mines and minerals including oil fields, oil mining, etc. are within the exclusive jurisdiction of the federal government,[5] and oil pollution matters can only be adjudicated at the Federal High Court (FHC).[6] This has a restrictive effect on access to court because the FHCs originally created to handle few matters relating to federal revenue[7] are only

1 Some of these have been codified in statutes.

2 Constitution of Federal Republic of Nigeria, 1999 (as amended) s 17(2)(e).

3 Constitution of Nigeria (n 2) s 36. Also, the African Charter on Human and Peoples' Rights (Ratification and Enforcement) Act, Cap A9 (19 January 1981 but adopted and commenced in Nigeria on the 17th of March 1983, codified in LFN 2004) s 7, provides for the right to fair hearing.

4 The Rio Declaration on Environment and Development adopted by the UN Conference on Environment and Development 'Earth Summit' in Rio de Janeiro, Brazil, 3–14 June 1992, U.N. Doc. A/CONF.151/26 (Vol. I), Principle 10; and the UN Agenda for Sustainable Development adopted by the UNGA on 25 September 2015, 'effective 1 January 2016' (A/RES/70/1). UN SDGs, Goal 16 https://sdgs.un.org/goals accessed 30 November 2023; The Aarhus Convention 1998, art 9 also provides for access to justice. However, although it entered into force on 30 October 2001, as at the time of this writing in December 2024, Nigeria is not a signatory to it.

5 Constitution of Nigeria (n 2) Second Schedule, Part I, Item 39.

6 Constitution of Nigeria (n 2) s 251(1)(n); *SPDC Ltd v Abel Isaiah and Others* (2001) 11 NWLR (Pt 723) 168.

7 Revenue Court Act (Nigeria) 1973, s 7.

DOI: 10.4324/9781003435150-6

located in state capitals and therefore are much fewer than State High Courts in Nigeria. With the expansion of their role to include oil pollution matters,[8] the cases filed in these courts increased immensely.[9] This results in court congestion and delays, practically limiting access to justice in oil pollution matters.[10] For this reason, the establishment of Environmental Courts and Tribunals (ECT) has been suggested to improve access to justice in environmental matters[11] and to reduce delays in the adjudicatory process.[12] While Akinseye Akinteye suggested a designation of oil pollution division within the FHC to resolve oil pollution matters[13] others advocated for the establishment of specialised adjudicatory bodies for all environmental matters.[14] Whatever form this may take in Nigeria would be determined by availability of funds and legislative agreement within the Nigerian National Assembly.

Delay in the court proceedings presents challenges in terms of time and additional costs.[15] Some cases have been known to last for decades.[16] Such delays and associated time and cost can discourage the litigant from going to court, or they

8 Constitution of Nigeria (n 2) s 251(1)(n); *SPDC Nig. Ltd* v *Abel Isaiah and others* (n 6).

9 Engobo Emeseh, 'Mainstreaming Enforcement for the Victims of Environmental Pollution: Towards Effective Allocation of Legislative Competence under a Federal Constitution' (2012) 14(3) Environ Law Rev 185, 198.

10 Fabian Ajogwu and Oscar Nliam, *Petroleum Law, and Sustainable Development* (Centre for Commercial Law Development, Ceenai Multimedia Ltd. 2014) 150; EP Amechi, 'Strengthening Environmental Public Interest Litigation through Citizen Suits in Nigeria: Learning from the South African Environmental Jurisprudential Development' (2015) 23(3) Afr J Int Compar Law 383.

11 Don C Smith, 'Environmental Courts and Tribunals: Changing Environmental and Natural Resources Law around the Globe' (2018) 36(2) J Energy Nat Resourc Law 137–40.

12 Akinseye Akinteye, 'Adjudicating the Impact of Oil Spills in Nigeria: The Need for Black Benches in Oil Producing States' (2018) 16(1) Oil Gas Energy Law 1, 12; Brian Preston, 'Operating an Environment Court: The Experience of the Land and Environment Court of New South Wales' (2012) 29 Pace Environ Law Rev 46.

13 Akinteye and Preston (n 12) 1–22.

14 Evan Hamman, Reece Walters and Rowena Maguire, 'Environmental Crime and Specialist Courts: The Case for a "One-Stop (Judicial) Shop" in Queensland' (2015) 27 Curr Iss Crim Just 59; George Pring and Catherine Pring, 'Environmental Courts & Tribunals: A Guide for Policy Makers' (2016) United Nations Environment Programme. <https://wedocs.unep.org/bitstream/handle/20.500.11822/10001/environmental-courtstribunals.pdf?sequence=1&isAllowed=y> accessed 21 January 2024;G Pring and C Pring, *Greening Justice: Creating and Improving Environmental Courts and Tribunals* (The Access Initiative, World Resources Institute 2009) <https://www.eufje.org/images/DocDivers/Rapport%20Pring.pdf> accessed 21 January 2024.

15 *SPDC v Otoko* (1990) 6 NWLR (Part 159) 693; *Ogiale v Shell* (1997) 1 NWLR (Part 408) 148; *Shell v Enoch* (1992) 8 NWLR 335.

16 *Agbara et al v Shell Petroleum et al*, Suit No: FHC/ASB/CS/231/2001; this case, which started in 2001, could not be resolved until 2010. Even at that the execution of the judgement of N5, 407,777,246.00 (then equivalent to about £33 million) awarded to the plaintiffs in damages was challenged by Shell up to the Supreme Court. An attempt to execute the judgement in the UK under the AJA 1920 in 2019 also failed, Agbara *& ors v Shell & ors* [2019] EWHC 3340 (QB). *Anare & Others v SPDC* (Unreported) Suit No HCB/35/89 of 27 May 1997, with the final decision delivered by the Supreme Court in June 2015. *SPDC v Anare* (2015) LPELR-24750(SC); *SPDC Ltd v Ambah* (1999) 3 NWLR Pt 593, 12, an oil pollution case that lasted 19 (nearly 20) years in the Courts; and *Bakare v African Continental Bank* [1986] 3 NWLR (Pt 26) 47, 59.

may have difficulty securing legal services of experienced attorneys and expert witnesses. On the contrary, oil companies can hire and retain experienced attorneys and high-ranking expert witnesses.[17] Although expert opinions are not necessarily dictated by those paying for them, in litigation a company would naturally hire an expert whose point of view tends to favour the company's position. In this case, the plaintiff may lose the case or end up with the award of general damages since an expert witness is needed for special damages. They may also be frustrated into abandoning the case midstream[18] or accept out of court settlement even if they are under par to the actual measure of damages. Injunctive relief to stop ongoing production is also rarely granted by the Nigerian courts[19] because oil is the mainstay of the Nigerian economy, accounting for about 80% of the government revenue and 90–95% of Nigeria's export earnings.[20]

The non-profit organisations and public interest groups that generally step in to help indigent clients and communities to litigate their case are often held back for lack of *locus standi*[21] (or the requirement of 'sufficient interest').[22] However, this trend has changed significantly because NGOs are now allowed to bring action in the public interest where environmental degradation infringes or threatens any of the fundamental rights guaranteed under the Nigerian Constitution, and the African Charter[23] Oil pollution cases that survive dismissal on technical grounds or for want of *locus standi* and make it to trial in Nigeria are usually brought under common law and statutory torts.

17 *Seismograph services limited v Onokpasa* [1972] 1 All NLR 343; *Seismograph services limited v Akporuovo* [1974] 1 All NLR 95.

18 *SPDC v Ambah* (1997) 66 LRCN 390; Emeseh (n 9) 189.

19 Ajogwu and Nliam (n 10) 28–29; KSA Ebeku, 'Judicial Attitudes to Redress for Oil-Related Environmental Damage in Nigeria' (2003) 12(2) Rev Euro Compar Int Environ Law 199; Susan Wolf and Neil Stanley, 'The Administration and Enforcement of Environmental Law' in *Wolf and Stanley on Environmental Law* (5th edn, Routledge 2011).

20 IL Worika, U Etemire and PS Tamuno, 'Oil Politics and the Application of Environmental Laws to the Pollution of the Niger Delta: Current Challenges and Prospects' (2019) 17(1) Oil Gas Energy Law 1, 4; DS Olawuyi, *The Principles of Nigerian Environmental Law* (Rev edn, Afe Babalola University Press 2015) 173–74; United Nations Development Programme, 'Niger Delta Human Development Report' (2006) 9.

21 More on this later in this chapter.

22 *Abraham Adesanya v President of the Federal Republic of Nigeria & Anor* (1981) All NLR 1; *Akpan and Milieudefensie v RDS plc and SPDC Nig. Ltd*, C/09/337050/HA ZA 09–1580, 30 January 2013, paras 4.24; EA Taiwo, 'Enforcement of Fundamental Rights and the Standing Rules under the Nigerian Constitution: A Need for a More Liberal Provision' (2009) 9 Afr Hum Rights Law J 546, 553.

23 The African Charter (n 3) art 7; *Centre for Oil Pollution Watch v Nigerian National Petroleum Corporation* (2019) 5 NWLR (Pt 1666) 518.

2. The Common Law and Statutory Torts in the Nigerian Oil and Gas Industry

Environmental damage actions for oil spill compensation claims in Nigeria generally come in the form of civil tort claims based on the torts of negligence, trespass, nuisance, and strict liability (founded on the rule in *Rylands v Fletcher*).

2.1. The Tort of Negligence

The tort of negligence is committed when the defendant who owes a legal duty of care to the plaintiff breaches that duty, resulting in foreseeable damages to the plaintiff.[24] The burden of proof rests on the plaintiff[25] who must prove that the defendant (spiller) owes him a duty of care; that he is in breach of that duty; and that the breach has caused foreseeable damage to him, the plaintiff.[26] Discharging this high evidentiary burden, however, could be challenging to the plaintiff, but when he does, the remedies available to him may come in form of award of damages and/or injunction.[27]

To succeed, the plaintiff can rely on the equitable doctrine of *res ipsa loquitor* (the thing speaks for itself), which raises the presumption of negligence against the defendant. Under this doctrine, the plaintiff must prove that what caused the damage was under the management and control of the defendant and that the harm would not have occurred in the ordinary course of events, unless there was negligence. But the defendant can rebut this presumption of negligence by providing evidence to show how the damage would have occurred without negligence.[28] Where the defendant is able to rebut the presumption, the burden of proof shifts back to the plaintiff to prove breach of legal duty of care. This can be daunting to the plaintiff who may end up losing his case despite suffering damages from the defendant's operations or frustrated by high cost of litigation.[29]

Recent cases, however, have shown progress in oil spill negligence issues. In *Okpabi and ors v RDS plc and SPDC*,[30] thousands of Nigerian farmers and fishermen sued RDS, a UK-domiciled parent company and its Nigerian subsidiary SPDC in the UK Courts for negligence arising from decades of oil spills from SPDC's pipelines. The spills contaminated land, waterways, and fishponds in the Ogale and Bille communities of the Niger Delta.[31] The plaintiffs claimed that RDS owed them

24 *Donoghue v Stevenson* (1932) UKHL 100; SC (HL) 31; AC 562, All ER Rep 1; James Goudkamp and Donal Nolan, *Winfield and Jolowicz on Tort* (20th edn, Sweet & Maxwell 2020).

25 J Walton, Roger Cooper and Simon E Wood, *Charlesworth & Percy on Negligence* (15th edn., Sweet & Maxwell 2023).

26 Lawrence Atsegbua, Vincent Akpotaire and Folarin Dimowo, *Environmental Law in Nigeria – Theory and Practice* (2nd edn, Ambik Press 2010) 44.

27 Atsegbua, Akpotaire and Dimowo (n 26).

28 *NEPA v Role* (2000) 7 NWLR (Pt 663) 69.

29 *Shell v Enoch* (n 15).

30 *Okpabi and Others v RDS plc and SPDC (Nig) Ltd,* 2017 EWHC 89 (TCC).

31 *Okpabi v Shell* [2017] (n 30).

a duty of care either because it controlled SPDC's operation of the oil pipelines and infrastructure or because it had assumed a direct responsibility to protect them (the claimants) from the environmental damage caused by the oil spills.[32]

The Court of First Instance concluded that there was no arguable case that RDS owed the claimants a duty of care and that, in the absence of RDS, the English court has no jurisdiction to try SPDC, a foreign subsidiary. The claimants appealed, and the Court of Appeal in its judgement relied on the *Caparo test.*[33] This test was founded on the House of Lords ruling in *Donoghue v Stevenson,*[34] to the effect that the tort of negligence is committed when the defendant breaches a duty of care that results in damage to the plaintiff.

The Caparo test established three criteria for determining duty of care. These are:

1. The foreseeability of the defendant that the plaintiff would suffer damage
2. The proximity between the plaintiff and the defendant
3. Whether it is fair, just, and reasonable to assume that a duty of care exists in a specific situation

Applying this test, the Court of Appeal (with Sales LJ dissenting) dismissed the appeal holding that RDS could not be held responsible for oil pollution caused by SPDC, because there was insufficient evidence to prove that RDS had enough control over SPDC to establish the necessary degree of proximity with the claimants and that it would not be fair, just, and reasonable to impose a duty of care on RDS.[35] In his dissenting judgement, however, Sales LJ was of the view that a good arguable case that deserves to proceed to trial has been made by the claimants against RDS and that the claimants are entitled to treat the parent company as an anchor defendant for the purposes of a potential suit against SPDC.[36]

The plaintiffs/appellants appealed and the Supreme Court followed its decision in *Vedanta Resources plc and another (Appellants) v Lungowe and others (Respondents).*[37] In that case, which was also concerned with a UK parent company's accountability for the actions of its foreign subsidiary in a developing country, Zambia, the Court ruled that it was incorrect for the Appeal Court to analyse the case (*Vedanta case*) in line with the threefold test established in the *Caparo case* because 'the tortious liability of parent companies in relation to the activities of their subsidiaries is well established.'[38] It does not present a distinct category of

32 *Okpabi v Shell* [2017] (n 30) para 90; *Okpabi and Others v RDS and SPDC* [2018] EWCA Civ 191, para 47.
33 *Caparo Industries plc v Dickman* (1990) 2 AC 605.
34 *Donoghue v Stevenson* (n 24).
35 *Okpabi v Shell* [2018] (n 32) para 132; Canadian case – *Yaiguaje v Chevron Corporation* (2018) ONCA472.
36 *Okpabi v Shell* [2018] (n 32) para 134.
37 *Vedanta Resources plc & Or v Lungowe & Ors* [2019] UKSC 20.
38 *Vedanta v Lungowe* (n 37) para 56.

liability in common law negligence;[39] neither does it present a novel or controversial legal issue.[40] According to the Supreme Court in *Robinson v Chief Constable of West Yorkshire Police,*[41]

> [T]here are many situations in which it has been clearly established that a duty of care is or is not owed: for example, by motorists to other road users, by manufacturers to consumers, by employers to their employees, and by doctors to their patients. . . . Where the existence or non-existence of a duty of care has been established, a consideration of justice and reasonableness forms part of the basis on which the law has arrived at the relevant principles. It is therefore unnecessary and inappropriate to reconsider whether the existence of the duty is fair, just, and reasonable.[42]

This means that the test for negligence established in *Caparo Industries plc v Dickman* only applies to new and controversial legal issues and not to already established cases relating to the tortious liability of parent companies in relation to the activities of their subsidiaries. However, the *Vedanta Court* acknowledged that the parent company's ownership of the subsidiary may provide it with the opportunity to take control of the management of the operations of the subsidiary but it does not impose any duty upon the parent to do so.[43] Therefore, how and to what extent the parent company availed itself of that opportunity is a question of fact[44] to be established through discovery and access to the documents internal to each of the defendant companies.[45] Considering all the arguments presented, the Supreme Court in the *Vedanta* case ruled that there was sufficient material in support of the view that the claimants' case was arguable[46] and should proceed to trial. Following this decision (and in line with the dissenting judgement of Sales, LJ of the Appeal Court in *Okpabi case*),[47] the UK Supreme Court on 12 February 2021[48] overruled the Court of Appeal and decided the *Okpabi case* in favour of the plaintiffs/appellants.[49] According to the Court, how the organisational structure of RDS worked in practice and the extent of control that RDS (the CEO and the ExCo) has on

39 *Vedanta v Lungowe* (n 37) paras 49–51.
40 *Vedanta v Lungowe* (n 37) paras 50–54; The Supreme Court followed this reasoning in *Okpabi and Others v RDS plc and SPDC (Nig) Ltd* [2021] UKSC 3, paras 149–51.
41 *Robinson v Chief Constable of Yorkshire Police* [2018] UKSC 4.
42 *Robinson v Chief Constable of Yorkshire Police* (n 41) para 26.
43 *Vedanta v Lungowe* (n 37) para 49.
44 *Vedanta v Lungowe* (n 37) paras 44, 49 and 53.
45 *Vedanta v Lungowe* (n 37) paras 44, 57 and 61. The Supreme Court adopted this reasoning in *Okpabi v Shell* [2021] (n 40) paras 130–32.
46 *Vedanta v Lungowe* (n 37) paras 57–62.
47 *Okpabi v Shell* [2018] (n 32) paras 172–73.
48 *Okpabi v Shell* [2021] (n 40).
49 *Okpabi v Shell* [2021] (n 40) para 159.

decisions made by SPDC are very much in dispute; they warrant proper disclosure[50] and clearly raise triable issues.[51]

This is a wonderful development in the negligence liability of parent multinational oil companies for the torts of their subsidiaries in developing countries. Such progress has equally been registered in parallel litigations in the Netherlands (an EU member State) brought by Friends of the Earth on behalf of separate Nigerian communities. In January 2021, the Hague Appeals Court in *Oguru v Shell and* two other parallel cases[52] found Shell liable for the oil pollution of two Nigerian communities.[53] The implications of these decisions are very significant in the light of Shell's plan to sell its onshore oilfield and assets in Nigeria and move offshore. The liability to clean-up the oil pollution in the region, remediate the environment, and compensate the victims of the oil pollution must be clearly determined.

2.2. *The Tort of Trespass to Land*

The tort of trespass to land could be committed as a result of an unjustified interference caused by the defendant's action upon the plaintiff's land, e.g., oil spill from a defendant's ruptured pipeline into the plaintiff's land resulting in damage or unauthorised dumping of waste by the defendant on the plaintiff's land.[54] In such cases, the owner of the land or a person in lawful possession of the land could sue for trespass to land.[55] The tort of trespass to land could be actionable per se. This means that the plaintiff need not prove fault, negligence, or intention on the part of the defendant to succeed. As soon as the defendant's acts of interference are established, the court will proceed to determine damages and an order of clean-up and restoration of the land.

2.3. *The Tort of Nuisance*

Nuisance results when the defendant's actions cause irritation, inconvenience, or annoyance to the plaintiff. In nuisance cases, the court must decide whether the

50 *Okpabi v Shell* [2021] (n 40) paras 130–32.

51 *Okpabi v Shell* [2021] (n 40) paras 94–100, 158–60. The trial is anticipated to start in 2024/25 – Legal Briefing Note – *Ogale & Bille Communities v Shell plc* <https://www.leighday.co.uk/media/3wzjpauj/bille-and-ogale-legal-briefing.pdf> accessed 18 October 2024.

52 *Oguru, Efanga and Milieudefensie v RDS and SPDC*, ECLI:NL:GHDHA:2021:132 <https://uitspraken.rechtspraak.nl/inziendocument?id=ECLI:NL:GHDHA:2021:132>; *Dooh and Milieudefensie v RDS and SPDC*, ECLI:NL: GHDHA:2021:133 <https://uitspraken.rechtspraak.nl/inziendocument?id=ECLI:NL:GHDHA:2021:133>; *Akpan v and Milieudefensie RDS and SPDC*, ECLI: NL: GHDHA: 2021:134 <https://uitspraken.rechtspraak.nl/inziendocument?id=ECLI:NL:GHDHA:2021:134> accessed 9 February 2023.

53 *Oguru v Shell* (n 52): More discussion on this in Part III of this chapter.

54 Atsegbua, Akpotaire and Dimowo (n 26); G Kodilinye and O Aluko, *The Nigerian Law of Tort* (2nd ed., Spectrum Law Publishing 1999) 182.

55 Thomas W Merrill, 'Trespass, Nuisance, and the Costs of Determining Property Rights' (1985) 14 J Legal Stud 13–48.

defendant's activity has unreasonably interfered with the claimant's use and enjoyment of his property or whether it is detrimental to the plaintiff's health, comfort, and convenience.[56] It may be private nuisance,[57] public (or common) nuisance,[58] or both. In Nigeria, public nuisance is regarded as a crime.[59] It may include, for instance, oil pollution cases in which oil spills pollute communal lands and waterways or cases of gas flaring polluting the air, causing black soot and respiratory problems to the inhabitants. Initially, only the Attorney General of the Federation or the State (depending on where the nuisance occurred) or the government through the regulatory agencies can institute actions for public nuisance against the tortfeasor.[60] These actions are generally very rare in Nigeria, probably because of the government's involvement in the Joint Ventures (JVs) and Joint Operating Agreements (JOAs) for oil exploration and production and the associated conflict of interest. Such action will almost amount to personal indictment by the government. An individual can sue with the leave of the Attorney General of the Federation or the State if he can show that the harm suffered by him is over and above that suffered by other members of the public.[61] However, with the decision in *Adediran v Interland transport Ltd,*[62] the consent of the Attorney General is no longer required. Also, the non-profit organisations and NGOs that were generally prevented from suing for lack of *locus standi* (or the requirement of 'sufficient interest') in the matter[63] can now sue on their own behalf for environmental protection and on behalf of the group they represent. This is particularly true where environmental degradation infringes or threatens any of the fundamental rights guaranteed under the Nigerian Constitution and the African Charter.[64]

2.4. *The Strict Liability Rule in the Nigerian Oil and Gas Industry*

The strict liability rule as enunciated by the House of Lords in *Ryland v Fletcher*[65] seems to be the most readily applicable in claims for oil pollution damage in

56 Goudkamp and Nolan (n 24).

57 *Abiola v Ijeoma* (1970) 2 All NLR 768. Private nuisance is an unlawful interference with a person's use and enjoyment of his land or some rights in connection with it.

58 This is when the defendant's conduct/activity interferes with the public's enjoyment of a common right. *Amos and Ors v Shell BP Petroleum Development Company of Nigeria* (1977) 6 S.C. 9.

59 Criminal Code Act, Cap. 77 Laws of the Federation of Nigeria 1990, s 234(f).

60 *Internland Transport Ltd. v Adediran & Ors* (1986) 2 NWLR (Pt 20) 78, 87.

61 *Ipadeola and Anor. v Oshowole and Anor* (1987) 1 SC 376 at 393; *Adediran & Others v Interland transport Ltd* (1991) 9 NWLR (pt 214) 155; *Centre for Oil Pollution Watch v NNPC* (2013) 15 NWLR (Pt 1378) 556.

62 *Adediran & Others v Interland transport Ltd* (n 61).

63 *Centre for Oil Pollution Watch v NNPC* (2013) (n 61); *Akpan and Milieudefensie v Shell* in which Milieudefensie was ruled not to have standing because the oil spill in Nigeria did not affect them directly.

64 The African Charter (n 3) arts 7 & 24. *Centre for Oil Pollution Watch v NNPC* (2019) (n 23).

65 *Ryland v Fletcher* (1866) L.R.1 Ex. 265; (1888) L. R. 1 H. L. 330.

Nigeria. It requires no proof of negligence but infers it from the facts of the case.[66] The defendant is strictly liable for his actions (and that of his agents) irrespective of fault, intent, or negligence. The plaintiff only needs to prove that the defendant's land has been put to *a non-natural use*;[67] that there has been an *escape* from that land of anything likely to cause mischief; and that the plaintiff has suffered damages because of it. Such strict liability rule is notably applicable to liability for damages resulting from environmental pollution in countries like Germany and Norway.[68]

The Nigerian Court has broad discretion in determining what amounts to a *non-natural use* of land.[69] In *S.P.D.C. v Anaro,*[70] the Court of Appeal affirmed the finding of the trial court in holding that the rule in *Ryland v Fletcher* was applicable to the spillage of crude oil accumulated in the appellant's land.[71] The court thus confirmed the use of land for oil exploration and production as a non-natural use. The rule in *Ryland v Fletcher* is still good law in Nigeria and has, in fact, been codified in the Environmental Guidelines and Standards for the Petroleum Industry in Nigeria (EGASPIN) to apply to the clean-up of mystery spills.[72] However, certain exceptions apply. These include when the damage is caused by the plaintiff's default or where he consents to the discharge. The rule also does not apply where the escape is caused by act of God, the *unpredictable* act of a third party, or the act of a statutory authority. Oil pipeline vandalism, which results in numerous oil spills in the Niger Delta, are categorised under the 'acts of third party' and have been successfully used by the multinational oil companies (MNOCs) in Nigeria to avoid liability. In *Shell v Otoko,*[73] Shell alleged oil pipeline sabotage, and the trial court disagreed with the defence. On appeal, however, one of the plaintiff's witnesses testified that the defendant did nothing more to stop the spill apart from corking the manifold. This led the court to conclude that a third party must have removed a screw or bolt in the first place, which then results in the oil spill.

However, recent decisions have emphasised that pipeline vandalism/sabotage is a criminal offence in Nigeria.[74] Therefore, anyone who alleges it must prove beyond all reasonable doubt[75] that the particular spillage complained of was the

66 *Umudje v Shell Petroleum Development Co. of Nigeria Ltd* (1975) 11 SC 155.

67 *Rickards v Lothian* (1913) AC 263. In this case, Lord Moulton at p 280 defined non-natural use of land as 'some special use bringing with it increased damages to others and must not merely be the ordinary use of the land or such a use as is proper for the general benefit of the community.'

68 Norwegian Petroleum Act, 1996, Chapter 7, s 7–3; Atsegbua, Akpotaire and Dimowo (n 26) 267.

69 Goudkamp and Nolan (n 24).

70 *SPDC Nig Ltd v Anaro* (2015) 12 NWLR (PT 1472) 122 (SC).

71 *Umudje v SPDC* (n 66).

72 Environmental Guidelines and Standards for Petroleum Industries in Nigeria (EGASPIN) 2018, Part VIII B 4.1.

73 *Shell v Otoko* (n 15).

74 The Special Tribunal (Miscellaneous) Act, 1984, s 3(7)(a) & (b); Petroleum Production and Distribution (Anti Sabotage) Act, Cap P12, LFN 2004, s 1.

75 Evidence Act 2011, s 135(a).

result of pipeline sabotage and without the company's negligence.[76] Also, where oil pipeline sabotage is rife and foreseeable, it is arguably *predictable* and so ought not to succeed under 'the *unpredictable* act of a third party' exception to the rule.

2.5. The Statutory Torts in the Nigerian Oil and Gas Industry

Statutory torts in the Nigerian oil and gas industry are created in statutes by legislation. They include:

1. The Oil Pipelines Act, 1956 (Cap. O7 LFN 2004).
2. The Petroleum Industry Act (PIA) 2021 (replacing the Petroleum Act, 1969) with the surviving regulations and guidelines made under the old Petroleum Act 1969.[77]
3. The NOSDRA (Est.) Act, 2006.

However, the primary provision on environmental protection is the Constitution of the Federal Republic of Nigeria, 1999 (as amended). Section 20 of the Constitution created for the first time a fundamental obligation for environmental protection by enjoining the State to protect and improve the environment and safeguard the water, air and land, forest and wildlife of Nigeria. But section 6(6)(c) of the Constitution specifically made issues under Chapter II, covering the Fundamental Objectives and Directive Principles of State Policy (sections 13–23), non-justiciable. This is an impediment to environmental litigation in Nigeria because it means that the obligations covered under section 20 are not enforceable against the government in a court of law in Nigeria. In other words, the government cannot be compelled to take actions to protect and improve the environment. As a result, legal analysts have recommended that section 6(6)(c) of the Constitution be repealed to make chapter II enforceable by individuals.[78] In *Attorney General of Ondo State v Attorney General of the Federation,*[79] the Nigerian Supreme Court created a pathway of a sort for doing this by holding that the provisions of Chapter II of the Nigerian Constitution could be justiciable when the National Assembly enacts enabling (or implementing) legislation on them. This 2002 decision was followed in 2003 by another Supreme Court decision in *Attorney General of Lagos State v AG Federation.*[80] Therefore, via this channel, environmental rights (e.g., right to clean environment) as provided under section 20 of the 1999 Constitution could be justiciable in Nigeria.

76 *Oguru v Shell* [2021] (n 52) para 5.9; *Dooh v Shell* [2021] (n 52); and *Akpan v Shell* [2021] (n 52).
77 Mineral Oils (Safety) Regulations (1997), Petroleum Regulations 1967, Petroleum (Drilling and Production), Regulations (1969) etc.; the EGASPIN, 2018 (n 72).
78 Atsegbua, Akpotaire and Dimowo (n 26) 49.
79 *AG Ondo State v AG Federation* (2002) FWLR Part III, 1972; (2002) 6 SCNJ 1.
80 *AG Lagos State v AG Federation* (2003) 12 NWLR (Pt 833) 1.

In *Gbemre v SPDC, Nig. Ltd,*[81] the plaintiff/respondent sued SPDC, the NNPC, and the Attorney General of the Federation over the continuous flaring of petroleum associated gas for decades in their community. In its ruling, the court gave effect to the environmental rights provided under section 20 of the 1999 Constitution by combining the fundamental rights to life and dignity of the human person guaranteed under the Nigerian Constitution[82] with the rights to life and health under the African Charter on Human and Peoples Rights.[83] Without demanding proof of a *causal link* between the gas flaring and the alleged effects on the complainant community and the environment, the court held that the constitutionally guaranteed right to life inevitably *includes the right to a clean, poison-free, pollution-free and healthy environment*[84] and that the defendant's actions in continuing to flare gas in the course of their petroleum operations in the applicant's community are a violation of these rights.[85] This was a ground-breaking decision and a complete departure from the previously rigid attitude of Nigerian Courts in similar cases.[86] This is also the first case in Nigeria to interpret the right to life guaranteed under the 1999 Constitution to include the right to a clean and healthy environment. Although the *Gbemre* case was merely a High Court case, it was expected to pave the way for similar cases to follow. But this judicial trend was neither developed nor encouraged in Nigeria although it was consistent with the global trend of making the right to a clean environment a constitutional right often via a broad interpretation of the constitutionally guaranteed right to life.[87] This trend is notably dubbed the human rights approach to environmental protection.[88] The United Nations in 2021 appear to support this by declaring access to a clean environment, a human right.[89] Recent climate change cases have also shown that human right norms may form a basis for private litigation against governments. This is exemplified by the

81 *Gbemre v Shell Petroleum Development Company Nigeria Limited and Others* [2005] AHRLR 151 (NgHC 2005) <http://www.chr.up.ac.za/index.php> accessed 24 March 2021.

82 Constitution of Nigeria (n 2) ss 33(1) & 34(1).

83 The African Charter (n 3) arts 4, 16 & 24.

84 *The Social and Economic Rights Action Centre (SERAC) and the Centre for Economic and Social Rights v Nigeria, African Commission on Human and Peoples' Rights, Comm* No 155/96 (2001) in which the Commission held that Nigeria was in violation of the collective right of the Ogoni people to a satisfactory environment; *Abacha v Fawehinmi,* [2000] 6 NWLR (Pt 668) 228 in which the Nigerian Supreme Court arrived at the same conclusion.

85 *Gbemre v SPDC Nig. Ltd* (n 81) 1; Kaniye SA Ebeku, 'Constitutional Right to a Healthy Environmental and Human Rights Approaches to Environmental Protection in Nigeria: *Gbemre v Shell* Revisited' (2007) 16(3) Rev Euro Compar Int Environ Law 312, 316–19.

86 *Chinda & 5 Others v Shell-BP Petroleum Development Company* [1974], 2 RSLR 1; and *Ogiale v Shell* [1997] (n 15).

87 Kaniye SA Ebeku, 'Constitutional Right to a Healthy Environmental and Human Rights Approaches to Environmental Protection in Nigeria' (n 85) 312–15; KSA Ebeku, 'The Right to a Satisfactory Environment and the African Commission' (2003) 3(1) Afr Hum Rights J 149.

88 A Boyle and MR Anderson (eds), *Human Rights Approaches to Environmental Protection* (Clarendon Press 1998); Kaniye SA Ebeku, 'Constitutional Right to a Healthy Environmental and Human Rights Approaches to Environmental Protection in Nigeria' (n 85) 315.

89 UNGA 48th Session, 5 October 2021, A/HRC/48/L.23/Rev.1.

landmark judgement of the Hague Appeal Court in 2018 in *Urgenda v State of the Netherlands*[90] and the decision in *Ashgar Leghari v Federation of Pakistan*.[91] The use of civil litigation in national courts is very important in defining and enforcing transnational corporate environmental responsibility.

The quest for justice orchestrated by court congestions, inadequate compensation, funding problems, etc., force Nigerian litigants suing for civil damages and compensation for oil spills to seek relief abroad, often in the home jurisdictions of the MNOCs. Some sue under the United States Alien Tort Statute while others go to the UK or the Netherlands in the EU. The next segment of this chapter will discuss these civil claims for damages in the US under the ATS, the UK, and the Netherlands (the EU).

3. Civil Litigations of the Nigerian Oil Spill Matters in the Home Jurisdictions of the Multinational Oil Companies

3.1. Civil Litigation of the Nigerian Oil Spill Matters in the United States Under the Alien Tort Statute (ATS)

The United States' Alien Tort Statute enacted in 1789 states that the 'district courts shall have original jurisdiction of *any* civil action by an *alien* for a tort only, committed in violation of the *law of nations* or a treaty of the United States.'[92] By this provision, the ATS gives foreigners/aliens access to the US federal court and provides them with the basis on which to bring *civil* action in US courts against US and foreign companies for compensation/remedy as a result of violations of customary international law (or *law of nations*) resulting in injury to them, even where the whole incident occurred abroad.[93] As a result of this, the US used to be the preferred jurisdiction for transnational civil litigations even in environmental cases.[94] This changed in 2013 when the US Supreme Court in *Kiobel v Shell*[95] significantly limited the grounds under which foreigners could base their suit on ATS. The *Kiobel case* was brought against the Royal Dutch Shell (RDS) and its Nigerian subsidiary (SPDC) accusing Shell of complicity, aiding and abating in the human rights abuse and violations of customary international law by the Nigerian government against the Ogoni people of the Niger Delta. The US Court of Appeal for the Second Circuit had dismissed the case on the ground that international law does not recognise artificial or legal persons like corporations.[96] According to the court,

90 *Urgenda v State of the Netherlands,* ECLI:NL:GHDHA:2018:2610 (official English translation).

91 *Ashgar Leghari v Federation of Pakistan,* PLD 2018, Lahore 364 [11].

92 Alien Tort Statute (ATS), 28 USC s 1350.

93 Uta Kohl, 'Corporate Human Rights Accountability: The Objections of Western Governments to the Alien Tort Statute' (2014) 63(3) Int Compar Law Q 665–97.

94 Hans van Loon, 'Principles and Building Blocks for a Global Legal Framework for Transnational Civil Litigation in Environmental Matters' (2018) 23 Unif Law Rev 298, 305.

95 *Kiobel et al. v Royal Dutch Petroleum Co et al.,* 569 US 108 (2013); 133 S.Ct. 1659 (2013).

96 *Kiobel et al v Royal Dutch Petroleum Co.,* 621 F.3d 111 (2d Cir. 2010).

corporations cannot be held liable under international law.[97] The US Supreme Court granted certiorari. However, without addressing the issue of corporate personality under international law, the Court unanimously rejected the application of universal jurisdiction to the ATS and dismissed the case for lack of sufficient connection with the United States.

The Court unanimously held that the presumption against extraterritorial application of US law applies to the ATS,[98] and to rebut that presumption and invoke the statute, there must be a link between the defendant and the United States.[99] The link is established where the alleged offence happened within the American territory, or the defendant is an American citizen, or where the defendant's conduct substantially and adversely affects an important American national interest. The mere 'corporate presence' of the RDS in the USA, for example, the fact that its stock is traded in the New York Stock Exchange, was not enough.[100] The case must 'touch and concern the territory of the United States with sufficient force.'[101] So, the claim against Shell based outside the US did not touch the US with sufficient force.

Although all the nine Justices agree with the conclusion that the case should be dismissed for lack of *sufficient* touch with the United States, in his concurring opinion, Justice Breyer (joined by Justices Ginsburg, Sotomayor, and Kegan) disagreed with the reasoning behind the ruling. He stated that for the ATS to apply, the violated international law must be *specific*, obligatory, and universally accepted norms among civilised nations.[102] The requirement of *specificity* means that today's interpretation of the statute must be in line with and comparable to the three actionable conducts established when the statute was enacted in 1789, namely, violation of safe conducts, infringements of the rights of ambassadors, and recovery of damages against pirates.[103] Breyer argued that because the ATS categorically mentioned 'alien,' 'treaties,' and 'the law of nations' in its provisions and applies to pirates, it means that it was definitely intended to apply extraterritorially[104] to compensate victims of 'piracy and its modern-day equivalents' when they operate within US territorial jurisdiction. He further argued that since the crime of robbery and murder committed by pirates on the high seas are committed within ships and against the nations whose flag the ship flies,[105] it is analogous to committing the crime on land within the flag State. And because one of the aims of the ATS is to compensate

97 *Kiobel v Royal Dutch Petroleum Co.* [2010] (n 96).

98 *Morrison v Nat'l Austl. Bank Ltd.*, 130 S. Ct. 2869 (2010) at 2875, 2881. The presumption against the extraterritorial application of the US law to the ATS was established in this case.

99 *Wiwa v Royal Dutch Petroleum Co et al* 226 F3d 88 (2d Cir 2000).

100 *Daimler AG v Bauman, et al.*, 134 S. Ct. 746 (2014); *BNSF Ry. Co. v Tyrrell*, 137 S.Ct. 1549 (U.S. 2017), It should be noted that before now, the US have been criticised for allowing a claim of general jurisdiction based on such minimal contact. *Bristol-Myers Squibb Co. v Superior Court of California*, 137 S.Ct. 1773 (U.S. 2017) on the issue of specific jurisdiction.

101 *Kiobel v Royal Dutch Petroleum Co.* [2013] (n 95).

102 *Sosa v Alvarez-Machain*, 542 US 692 (2004) 723.

103 *Sosa v Alvarez-Machain* (n 102) 723–25.

104 *Sosa v Alvarez-Machain* (n 102) 7.

105 *Sosa v Alvarez-Machain* (n 102).

the victims of piracy, the relevant question is: Who are today's pirates?[106] Breyer stated that they include torturers, perpetrators of genocide – '*common enemies of all mankind.*'[107] Since the ATS provides relief for those harmed by pirates, it will also afford relief for those harmed by torturers, perpetrators of genocide, etc. – *common enemies of all mankind.*

For a State to exercise jurisdiction outside its territory, international law normally requires the State to show some connections to its territory – and nationality – based on principles of sovereign equality and noninterference in the domestic affairs of sovereign States.[108] One exception to this rule under international law is the application of *universal jurisdiction*[109] for heinous crimes like torture, genocide, piracy, serious war crimes, crimes against humanity, and common enemies of all mankind.[110] This is because they violate norms of peremptory character. For this reason, they are universally condemned by civilised nations and any state may claim jurisdiction over them no matter the locus of the crime, the victim's nationality, or that of the offender. This remains true even when the prosecuting nation has no link with the crime, the alleged offender, and the victim.[111] Based on this premise, this work argues that *common enemies of all mankind* should include at some level heavy environmental polluters such as oil spillers. This is because massive oil pollution, especially when it is left uncleaned for years, could be likened to serious war crimes, to the extent that it exposes communities to diseases and ill-health leading definitively to *premature death of a group of people.* Like serious war crimes, which have the hallmark of total indifference to human life and suffering far beyond what is permissible under normal rules of engagement, massive environmental pollution with no serious attempts at proper clean-up and remediation similarly portrays an unjustifiable indifference to the immense suffering, sickness, and ultimate untimely death of some of the world's most vulnerable people due to the activities of the MNOCs. There is no doubt that these companies primarily protect their own economic interest while serving the needs of their industrialised home countries and shareholders without much consideration to the sufferings of the downtrodden masses in the unindustrialised host communities. Since the ultimate end of the actions of these companies results in the untimely death of a group of people and because such heavy environmental polluters ought to be universally condemned by the civilised nations[112] as common enemies of all mankind, it is

106 *Kiobel v Royal Dutch Petroleum Co* [2013] (n 95) 5, per Justice Breyer, repeating the question by the majority in *Sosa v Alvarez-Machain* (n 102) 724–25.

107 *Kiobel v Royal Dutch Petroleum Co* [2013] (n 95) 5.

108 UN Charter Art 2.

109 General Assembly of the United Nations, 'Resolution 70/119' <https://www.un.org/en/ga/sixth/71/universal_jurisdiction.shtml> accessed 3 January 2024.

110 M Cherif Bassiouni, *International Criminal Law Multilateral and Bilateral Enforcement Mechanisms*, Vol 2, 169–80 (3rd edn, Brill | Nijhof, 2008) (discussing the basis for universal jurisdiction over these crimes; and the various mechanisms and modalities of international cooperation in penal matters). Restatement (Third) of the Foreign Relations Law of the United States s 404 (1987).

111 Kenneth C Randall, 'Universal Jurisdiction under International Law' (1987/1988) 66 Tex Law Rev 785.

112 *Sosa v Alvarez-Machain* [2004] (n 102).

submitted that universal jurisdiction should apply to them and claims for damages issuing from their harmful activities should be permitted under the ATS even when the case involves purely extraterritorial conduct.[113]

Additionally, the home States of the MNCs are encouraged to enact laws that would require companies to report the social impacts of their operations and that of their subsidiaries abroad. Although most MNOCs now voluntarily self-report this, there is no existing international mechanism for independent monitoring to ensure compliance neither is there an international obligation to do so.[114] The requirement of these obligations from MNCs would help to improve corporate accountability and responsibility.[115] There are ongoing moves in the EU Parliament to adopt a resolution in support of a binding legislation on Member States to establish rules for corporations to carry out effective due diligence with respect to potential or actual impacts of their operations on human rights and the environment.[116] This is because voluntary due diligence standards have not achieved significant progress in preventing corporate human rights and environmental harm,

Corporate rights and responsibilities must be acknowledged and corporate wrong redressed and punished to avert corporate impunity.[117] Alexandra Carleton suggested the enactment of an international crime of plunder as a crime against humanity and to make it subject to universal jurisdiction and extraterritorial application.[118] This is a good idea and comparing it with the crime of piracy[119] finds support in the concurring judgement of Justice Breyer in the *Kiobel case.*[120] However, to be fully extensive, it must be framed as 'International crime of plunder *and pollution*' (environmental degradation) because plunder and pollution go hand in hand in the exploitation of mineral resources by corporations especially in developing countries. Carleton argued that extraterritorial corporate crimes could be prosecuted just like individuals because in Australia the implementation of the International Criminal Court (ICC) crimes, within Division 268 of the Australian Criminal Code

113 It should be noted that in the *Kiobel case*, all nine justices agreed that the ATS excluded cases involving *purely* extraterritorial conduct, even if the alleged conduct satisfies the international law standards for the application of universal jurisdiction. This is notwithstanding that the Court in *Sosa v Alvarez-Machain,* 542 U.S. 692, 732 (2004) held that only the most serious violations of human rights norms that meet a rigorous '*specific, universal, and obligatory*' standard could be brought under the ATS. Julian G. Ku, 'Kiobel and the Surprising Death of Universal Jurisdiction under the Alien Tort Statute' (2013) 107 Am J Int Law 835, 835.

114 Nadia Bernaz, 'Enhancing Corporate Accountability for Human Rights Violations: Is Extraterritoriality the Magic Portion?' (2013) 117 J Business Ethics 493, 493–511.

115 Bernaz (n 114).

116 Corporate due diligence and corporate accountability – P9 TA (2021) 0073 (10 March 2021, European Parliament) (2020/2129(INL). See also the Corporate Sustainability Due Diligence Directive (CSDDD) adopted by the European Commission on 24 May 2024.

117 Amy J Sepinwall, 'Denying Corporate Rights and Punishing Corporate Wrongs' (2015) 25(4) Business Ethics Q 517, 526–27.

118 Alexandra L Carleton, 'The Gathering Storm around Corporate Liability in Natural Resource Investment: Re-Examining the Recent Past' (2015) 2 Am J Educ Learn 102, 104.

119 Carleton (n 118) 111.

120 *Kiobel et al. v Royal Dutch Petroleum Co et al.*, 569 US 108 (2013).

Act 1995 does not distinguish between natural and legal persons.[121] He further argued that Division 268 of the Australian *Criminal Code* could be considered to have granted Australian Courts universal jurisdiction over extraterritorial corporate criminal conduct amounting to genocide, crimes against humanity, or war crimes as defined under the *Rome Statute.*[122] Several other countries like Canada, the Netherlands, and the United Kingdom, have implemented these crimes in accordance with the Rome (ICC) Statute on the basis of universal jurisdiction applicable to legal and non-legal persons.[123] A move in this direction could present a lasting solution to the problem of extraterritorial corporate environmental liability.

It is important to note that some UK and the domestic courts of the EU Member States are now finding ways to assume jurisdiction and hold parent companies of multinationals liable in their home jurisdiction for damages caused by the harmful practices of their foreign subsidiaries.[124] They allow foreign plaintiffs and victims of environmental pollution from the host jurisdiction to seek justice and compensation from the home jurisdiction of the corporate defendant where the judicial system is better equipped to redress the wrong and grant appropriate remedy.[125] The next segment of this chapter will examine these civil trials in the UK and the Netherlands (an EU Member State).

3.2. Civil Litigation of the Nigerian Oil Spill Matters in the UK Courts

In *Vedanta Resources plc & Or v Lungowe & Ors*[126] the UK courts assumed jurisdiction to determine a case concerning a UK domiciled parent company's accountability for the actions of its Zambian subsidiary. In that case, hundreds of Zambian villagers brought a tort of negligence claim in the English High Court in 2015 against Vedanta Resources plc and its Zambian subsidiary, Konkola Copper Mines plc (KCM) for environmental pollution of their farmland and drinking water caused by toxic discharges from KCM's mining operations at the Nchanga Copper Mine.[127] The claims against KCM were based on its role as the operator of the Nchanga Mine while the claim against Vedanta was because it allegedly controls and directs the mining operations of the KCM. Both Vedanta and KCM challenged the jurisdiction of the English court to try the case. This challenge was dismissed in the High Court in May 2016.[128] Vedanta and KCM appealed and in October 2017, that appeal was dismissed by a unanimous decision of the three

121 Carleton (n 118) 113.

122 Rome Statute of ICC, art 5 – providing for crimes within the jurisdiction of the ICC; Joanna Kyriakakis, 'Australian Prosecution of Corporations for International Crimes: The Potential of the Commonwealth Criminal Code' (2007) 5 (4) J Int Crim Justice 809, 818.

123 Kyriakakis (n 122) 819.

124 *Vedanta v Lungowe* (n 37); *Akpan v Shell* [2021] (52); *Okpabi v Shell* [2021] (n 40).

125 *Vedanta v Lungowe* (n 37) paras 87–102.

126 *Vedanta v Lungowe* (n 37).

127 *Vedanta v Lungowe* (n 37).

128 *Lungowe & Ors v Vedanta Resources plc & Or,* A1/2016/2502 & 2504.

Justices of the Court of Appeal.[129] The appellants appealed to the UK Supreme Court. In a unanimous decision delivered by Lord Briggs on 10 April 2019, the UK Supreme Court dismissed the appeal and ruled in favour of Lungowe.[130] The Court agreed with the Appeal Court that Vedanta could be sued in England under Article 4 of the EU Brussels Regulation;[131] that Vedanta could be used as an anchor defendant for purposes of a potential suit against KCM;[132] that the allegation that Vedanta had taken sufficient part or control in running of the Mine is arguable and requires determination at a trial;[133] and that the proceeding against the two defendants *must* continue in England due to lack of access to justice in Zambia.[134]

This was a wonderful development which opened the possibility of reviewing the appeal court decision in *Okpabi v Shell.*[135] The Okpabi case resembles the *Vedanta case* though it originated from Nigeria and is based on claims from damages caused by oil spills in Nigeria. In the *Okpabi case,* Nigerian farmers and fishermen sued the Royal Dutch Shell (RDS) and its Nigerian subsidiary, the Shell Petroleum Development Company of Nigeria Limited (SPDC) in the UK Courts, for negligence arising from decades of oil spills from SPDC's pipelines and damages to land and the environment issuing from the spills. The plaintiff/appellants claimed that RDS owed them a duty of care either because it controlled SPDC's operation of the oil pipelines and infrastructure or because it had assumed a direct responsibility to protect the appellants from the environmental damage caused by the oil spills.[136]

The Court of First Instance concluded that there was no arguable case that RDS owed the claimants a duty of care; that the claimants have failed to demonstrate that there is a 'real issue' between them and the RDS;[137] and that in the absence of RDS, the anchor defendant, the court does not have jurisdiction over SPDC, a foreign subsidiary company.[138] The claimants appealed and the Court of Appeal by a 2:1 majority dismissed the appeal in February 2018, with Sales LJ dissenting.[139] The majority ruled that RDS could not be held responsible for oil pollution caused by SPDC, because there was insufficient evidence to prove that RDS had enough control over SPDC to establish the necessary degree of proximity with the claimants and that it would not be fair, just, and reasonable to impose a duty of care on RDS.[140] According to Simon LJ who delivered the lead judgement,

129 *Vedanta v Lungowe* [2017] EWCA Civ 1528.
130 *Vedanta v Lungowe* (n 37).
131 *Vedanta v Lungowe* (n 37) para 41.
132 *Vedanta v Lungowe* (n 37) paras 24, 79–83.
133 *Vedanta v Lungowe* (n 37) paras 61–62.
134 *Vedanta v Lungowe* (n 37) paras 87–102.
135 *Okpabi v Shell* [2017] (n 30).
136 *Okpabi v Shell* [2017] (n 30) para 90; *Okpabi v Shell* [2018] (n 32) para 47.
137 *Okpabi v Shell* [2017] (n 30) paras 118–19, 122.
138 *Okpabi v Shell* [2017] (n 30) para 122.
139 *Okpabi v Shell* [2018] (n 32) para 134.
140 *Okpabi v Shell* [2018] (n 32) para 132; *Yaiguaje v Chevron Corporation* (n 35).

> The issuing of mandatory policies plainly cannot mean that a parent has taken control of the operations of a subsidiary . . . such as to give rise to a duty of care in favour of any person or class of persons affected by the policies.[141]

In his dissenting judgement, however, Sales LJ was of the opinion that a good arguable case that deserves to proceed to trial has been made by the appellant against RDS and that the claimants are entitled to treat the parent company as an anchor defendant for the purposes of a potential suit against SPDC.[142] To justify the possibility of increased RDS control over the activities of SPDC, it was noted that during the UNEP environmental assessment of Ogoniland in 2011, the UN agency documented serious issues of oil pollution in the Niger Delta mainly as a result of SPDC's operations, leading to major reputational damage to the company.[143] This led to the inference that the parent company, RDS, may have had a good motive to proactively assume control of the operational decisions and management of oil spill risks from SPDC's pipelines and facilities.[144] Based on this, Sales LJ argued that it is reasonable to infer close control and monitoring of SPDC operations on the ground by the RDS ExCo even if this was not the practice 'in the case of other less troublesome subsidiaries.'[145] This is a plausible reason in support of allowing the appeal and deeper discoveries into the kind of actual control or lack thereof exercised by RDS over the operations of SPDC.

The claimants appealed to the Supreme Court and the Court's decision on 12 February 2021 was consistent with its decision in the *Vedanta* case[146] and in consonance with the reasoning of Sales LJ of the Appeals Court. According to the Supreme Court, it was wrong for the Court of Appeal to hold that the promulgation of group-wide policies or standards by a parent company *can never* in itself give rise to a duty of care.[147] It all depends on the facts of a particular case.

> Even where group-wide policies do not of themselves give rise to such a duty of care to third parties, they may do so if the parent does not merely proclaim them, but takes active steps, by training, supervision and enforcement, to see that they are implemented by relevant subsidiaries. Similarly . . . the parent may incur the relevant responsibility to third parties if, in published materials, it holds itself out as exercising that degree of supervision and control of its subsidiaries, even if it does not in fact do so. In such circumstances its very omission may constitute the abdication of a responsibility which it has publicly undertaken.[148]

141 *Okpabi v Shell* [2018] (n 32) para 89.
142 *Okpabi v Shell* [2018] (n 32) para 134.
143 UNEP (n 20) 43.
144 *Okpabi v Shell* [2018] (n 32) para 162.
145 *Okpabi v Shell* [2018] (n 32) para 161.
146 *Vedanta v Lungowe* [2019] (n 37).
147 *Okpabi v Shell* [2021] (n 40) para 143.
148 *Vedanta v Lungowe* [2019] (n 37) para 53.

The Court further ruled that it was incorrect for the Appeal Court to analyse the duty of care issue in the *Okpabi case* in line with the tripartite test established in *Caparo Industries plc v Dickman*[149] because the liability of parent companies in relation to the activities of their subsidiaries does not present a novel or controversial legal issue[150] but is well established under the general principles of tort of negligence.[151] This thus became the birth of the so-called *Vedanta* test,[152] which simply means, as suggested by the Supreme Court in that case, that the Caparo test and analysis should be applied only to novel and controversial issues of liability in common law negligence.

Additionally, the Supreme Court acknowledged that although the parent company's ownership of the subsidiary may provide it with the opportunity to take control of the management of the operations of the subsidiary and intervene in, supervise, or advise the management of the relevant operations, it does not impose any duty upon the parent to do so.[153] How and to what extent the parent company availed itself of that opportunity is a question of fact[154] to be established through discovery and access to the contents of the documents internal to each of the defendant companies.[155] Considering all the arguments presented, the Supreme Court ruled that there was sufficient material in support of the view that the claimants' case was arguable[156] and should proceed to trial. Following this decision (and in line with the dissenting judgement of Sales, LJ of the Appeal Court in the Okpabi case),[157] the Supreme Court overruled the Court of Appeal and decided the case in favour of the plaintiffs/appellants.[158] According to the Court, the extent of control that RDS has on SPDC is very much in dispute. It warrants proper disclosure[159] and clearly raises triable issues.[160]

149 *Caparo Industries plc v Dickman* (n 33); *Okpabi v Shell* [2021] (n 40) paras 149–51. Test established in the *Caparo case* was based on the HL ruling in *Donoghue v Stevenson* (n 24), that the tort of negligence is committed when the defendant who owes a duty of care breaches that duty and it results in damage to the plaintiff. The criteria for determining duty of care were established in the *Caparo case* as follows: i) the foreseeability of the defendant that the plaintiff would suffer damage; ii) the proximity between the plaintiff and the defendant; iii) whether it is fair, just, and reasonable to assume that a duty of care exists in a specific situation.

150 *Caparo Industries plc v Dickman* (n 33); *Okpabi v Shell* [2021] (n 40) paras 49–54.

151 *Vedanta v Lungowe* [2019] (n 37) para 56; *Robinson v Chief Constable of West Yorkshire Police* [2018] (n 41) para 26.

152 It is not entirely clear that the *Vedanta rule* was recognised by the Hague Appeals Court in the case of *Oguru v Shell* [2021] (n 52) (and parallel cases) in January 2021. Although the Court's analysis somehow reflects the *Vedanta rule* and it was even suggested that it should be made part of the Nigerian law, references were still made to 'foreseeability' and the application of 'fair, just, and reasonable' standards – the hallmarks of the *Caparo* test. *Oguru v Shell* [2021] (n 52) paras 3.30–3.32.

153 *Vedanta v Lungowe* [2019] (n 37) para 49.

154 *Vedanta v Lungowe* [2019] (n 37) paras 44, 49 and 53.

155 *Vedanta v Lungowe* [2019] (n 37) paras 44, 57 & 61.

156 *Vedanta v Lungowe* [2019] (n 37) paras 57–62.

157 *Okpabi v Shell* [2018] (n 32) paras 172–73.

158 *Okpabi v Shell* [2021] (n 40) para 159.

159 *Okpabi v Shell* [2021] (n 40) paras 130–32.

160 *Okpabi v Shell* [2021] (n 40) paras 94–100, 158–60.

This decision is guaranteed to result in deeper discoveries into the kind of control or lack thereof, exercised by RDS over the operations of SPDC to properly decide the issue of liability for pollution and reach a more just conclusion. It would also lead to further discoveries into the opaque and secretive corporate structure of RDS and other mega multinational companies thereby opening the door for more litigations against them in their home jurisdictions for the destructive practices of their subsidiaries in developing countries. It will make it possible to hold the MNOCs accountable for plundering and polluting the Niger Delta environment and thus, make the polluter-pays principle realisable in the region.

Success in this jurisdictional challenge in the *Okpabi case* means the case could go to trial in the UK unless, of course, RDS decides to settle out of court to avoid creating unhelpful precedent and the negative public image that will go with such trial. However, with successes in the UK Supreme Court decisions in *Vedanta v Lungowe*[161] and the Hague Appeals Court ruling in the Nigerian oil spill cases on 29 January 2021, the plaintiffs may be less inclined to agree to such settlement. Progress on this front will level the playing field and significantly help in curbing differential behaviours of these MNOCs in an emerging jurisdiction like Nigeria when compared to their behaviour in advanced jurisdiction such as the UK and the USA.

3.3. Civil Litigation of Nigerian Oil Spill Matters in the Netherlands (EU Member State)

3.3.1. Jurisdictional Issues

In the EU, a company could be sued in tort-based actions in the place of its domicile on grounds of a general jurisdiction provided under the Brussels I Regulation (recast).[162] This would include action for environmental harm even if committed abroad. Under art. 8 of the Brussels 1 Regulations (recast), which deals with connected claims, a subsidiary (or a contractor) based outside the EU can jointly be sued with the parent company, although the subsidiary (or the contractor) is the party that is allegedly responsible for environmental harm. Such joint suit is possible if one of the defendants is domiciled in a Member State 'provided that the claims are so closely connected that it is expedient to hear and determine them together to avoid the risk of irreconcilable judgments resulting from separate proceedings.'[163]

The national law is, however, left to decide whether a subsidiary domiciled outside the EU may be sued in the EU courts where the parent is domiciled. English courts have made this decision by first looking to see if there is 'a real issue' between the claimant and the parent company, the 'anchor defendant,' to avoid using the claim against the parent company as an 'illegitimate hook' to bring the

161 *Vedanta v Lungowe* [2019] (n 37).

162 Regulation (EU) No 1215/2012 of the European Parliament and Council, 12 December 2012 on jurisdiction and the recognition and enforcement of judgement on civil and commercial matters. Brussel 1 Regulation (recast) Art 4(1), read in conjunction with Art 63(1)).

163 Brussels 1 Regulations (recast), art 8(1).

subsidiary before the English courts.[164] In the Netherlands, the court will assume jurisdiction if there is a 'close connection' between the claim against the subsidiary and the parent company.[165] Real dispute must exist at the beginning of the proceedings between the plaintiff and the parent company. It is irrelevant that the parent company is later found not liable.[166] In the light of the UK Supreme Court decision in *Vedanta Resources plc & ors v Longowe & ors*[167] and *Okpabi and Others v RDS plc and SPDC (Nig) Ltd*[168] and the Hague Appeal Court ruling in *Akpan & Milieudefensie v RDS and SPDC Nig. Ltd*,[169] it is safe to conclude that it will be very difficult for a transnational corporation based in the EU and its overseas subsidiary to successfully argue in the court of the parent domicile that they cannot be sued together for serious environmental damage caused overseas by the activities of the subsidiary.

Based on the foregoing, the EU would be a better place to litigate for remedy for environmental damage allegedly caused by the conduct of the overseas subsidiaries in developing countries where the parent company is domiciled in the EU. The USA presents very limited adjudicatory jurisdiction whether the transnational corporation is domiciled within the USA or outside it.

3.3.2. Akpan v Shell

Akpan v Shell[170] is one of a group of cases brought by Nigerian plaintiffs/farmers/fishermen and Milieudefensie[171] against RDS and its Nigerian subsidiary, SPDC, in the Netherlands in 2008. The plaintiffs'[172] suit was based on torts of negligence for alleged damage to their farmlands and fishing ponds because of oil spills from the SPDC pipelines. A set of cases concern oil spills at the Nigerian village of Oruma in 2005,[173] another set concern oil spills at the Nigerian village of Goi in 2004,[174] and a third set concern oil spills at the Nigerian village of Ikot Ada Udo in 2006 and 2007.[175] Although none of the actions happened in the Netherlands, the home State of RDS, the Hague District Court ruled that it has jurisdiction over the

164 *Vedanta v Longowe* [2019] (n 37) paras 20, 22.

165 Dutch Code of Civil Procedure, art 7(1) aligned to the Brussels I Regulations, art 8(1). *Akpan v Shell* [2021] (n 52); *Vedanta v Lungowe* [2019] (n 37).

166 Dutch Code of Civil Procedure, art 7(1) aligned to the Brussels I Regulations, art 8(1). *Akpan v Shell* [2021] (n 52); *Vedanta v Lungowe* [2019] (n 37).

167 Dutch Code of Civil Procedure, art 7(1) aligned to the Brussels I Regulations, art 8(1). *Akpan v Shell* [2021] (n 52); *Vedanta v Lungowe* [2019] (n 37).

168 *Okpabi v Shell* [2021] (n 40).

169 *Okpabi v Shell* [2021] (n 40). See also the parallel cases of *Oguru v Shell* [2021] (n 52); and *Dooh v Shell* [2021] (n 52).

170 *Akpan v Shell* [2013] (n 22).

171 An environmental NGO (Friends of the Earth) headquartered in the Netherlands.

172 Fidelis *Oguru* and Alali Efanga from Oruma village in Bayelsa State; Eric Barizaa *Dooh* from Goi village in Rivers State; and Friday Alfred *Akpan* from Ikot Ada Udo village in Akwa Ibom State of Nigeria.

173 *Oguru v Shell* [2021] (n 52).

174 *Dooh v Shell* [2021] (n 52).

175 Akpan *v Shell* [2021] (n 52).

plaintiffs' case based on its jurisdiction over RDS.[176] The Court decided that the actions against the two defendants (RDS and SPDC) would be joined because they were based on the same tort of negligence under the Nigerian law.[177] In its final ruling in the Akpan case, however, the court dismissed all the claims against RDS[178] because under the Nigerian law the parent company has no *general* duty of care to shield other parties from suffering damages as a result of the actions of their subsidiaries unless there is evidence to show that the parent company controls the actions of the subsidiary and directs or supervises it.[179] Additionally, all the claims initiated by *Milieudefensie* were dismissed because the court held that the oil spill in Nigeria did not affect their rights.[180] But the court ruled in favour of Akpan because SPDC was found negligent for 'insufficiently securing the wellhead at the IBIBIO-1 well prior to the two oil spills in 2006 and 2007 near Ikot Ada Udo in Nigeria.'[181] SPDC was, therefore, ordered to pay compensation for the damages that Akpan suffered as a result of the spill.[182] However, in December 2015, a Dutch Appeals Court ruled that the balance of the claims in *Akpan v Shell* and the two parallel cases should go forward.[183]

On 29 January 2021, the Appeals Court in The Hague delivered judgment in the three cases ruling, *inter alia*, that the party alleging sabotage of the oil pipelines must prove it beyond all reasonable doubt.[184] This is proper because proof of a fact by anyone who alleges its existence is consistent with the Nigerian and Dutch rules of evidence.[185] It is, therefore, not in dispute that Shell has the burden of proof with regards to the third-party sabotage that it claims. Also, under the Nigerian law, the burden of proof in civil proceedings is discharged on the balance of probabilities.[186] However, where commission of crime is in issue or where guilt of crime is asserted in any proceedings, (civil or criminal), it must be proved beyond all reasonable doubt.[187] Pipeline vandalism/sabotage is a criminal offense in Nigeria.[188] Since Shell alleges this criminality, the onus is on the company to prove beyond

176 Article 2(1)23 and Article 60(1)24 of the Brussels Regulation.
177 Dutch Code of Civil Practice (DCCP), Bk 1, Article 7(1); *Akpan v Shell* [2013] (n 22) paras 4.5–4.6.
178 *Akpan v Shell* [2013] (n 22) paras 4.33–4.34.
179 *Akpan v Shell* [2013] (n 22) para 4.24.
180 *Akpan v Shell* [2013] (n 22) para 5.3; Article 3:305a of the Dutch Code of Civil Practice (DCCP).
181 *Akpan v Shell* [2013] (n 22) para 5.1.
182 *Akpan v Shell* [2013] (n 22).
183 *Akpan and Milieudefensie v RDS and SPDC*, ECLI: NL: GHDHA: 2015: 3587. <https://uitspraken.rechtspraak.nl/inziendocument?id=ECLI:NL:GHDHA:2015:3587>; *Dooh and Milieudefensie v RDSandSPDC*, ECLI:NL:GHDHA:2015:3586<https://uitspraken.rechtspraak.nl/inziendocument?id=ECLI:NL:GHDHA:2015:3586>; and *Oguru, Efanga and Milieudefensie v RDS & SPDC*, ECLI: NL: GHDHA: 2015: 3588 <https://uitspraken.rechtspraak.nl/inziendocument?id=ECLI:NL:GHDHA:2015:3588> all accessed 24 February 2021.
184 *Oguru v Shell* [2021] (n 52) paras 5.3–5.10.
185 Nigerian Evidence Act, 2011, s 131(1); Dutch Law, Art 150 DCCP.
186 Nigerian Evidence Act (n 185) s 134.
187 Nigerian Evidence Act (n 185) Art s 135(a).
188 The Special Tribunal (Miscellaneous) Act, 1984 (n 74); Petroleum Production and Distribution (Anti Sabotage) Act, 2004 (n 74) s 1.

reasonable doubt that the particular spillage complained of was the result of pipeline sabotage and without the company's negligence.[189] Because SPDC failed to discharge this burden of proof regarding the oil leakages in Goi[190] and Oruma[191] communities, the company was held liable for damages resulting from the oil spills in those communities.

The plaintiffs also alleged that RDS owed them a duty of care as a parent company of SPDS obligated to ensure that its Nigerian subsidiary carried out oil production in a prudent manner, that it breached that duty of care based on its acts or omissions, which has resulted in harm to the plaintiffs/third parties through the acts or omissions of its subsidiary.[192] The court held that Shell owed and breached that duty of care to the affected villagers in Oruma by not installing leak detection systems (LDS) on the oil pipeline[193] and are, therefore, liable. The Court ordered the RDS and SPDC to instal 'state of the art' LDS that detects a leak quickly, within *minutes to hours*,[194] in their oil pipelines in Oruma community within a year of the ruling or face a daily fine of €100,000 (about GBP 87,004 or US$121,522 at the time) once the year is up, and they have failed to do so.[195] This decision is doubly significant because the installation of LDS will ensure that leaks are automatically stopped without the need for access, and the fine is comparatively higher than the ones imposed under the Nigerian laws.[196] Hopefully, it will have a deterrent effect, forcing Shell to improve on its pipeline maintenance and surveillance. This will in turn reduce acts of oil pipeline sabotage and consequent spills and will be a damper to Shell's differential behaviour with respect to oil pipelines.

The court, however, found that the spills in Ikot Ada Udo village were a result of sabotage.[197] And under the Nigerian law, an oil company is not liable to pay compensation for damages caused by sabotage spills.[198] But, the court ruled that SPDC had committed a tort of negligence against Akpan by not sufficiently securing the IBIBIO-1 well head prior to the spills in 2006 and 2007 and this resulted in the sabotage that was easily perpetrated.[199] SPDC was, therefore, ordered to pay compensation for the damage resulting from the pollution of Akpan's land and fish ponds.[200]

189 *Oguru v Shell* [2021] (n 52) para 5.9.
190 *Dooh v Shell* [2021] (n 52) paras 5.25–5.26.
191 *Oguru v Shell* [2021] (n 52) paras 5.27–5.28.
192 *Oguru v Shell* [2021] (n 52) para 3.26.
193 *Oguru v Shell* [2021] (n 52) paras 6.17–6.26.
194 *Oguru v Shell* [2021] (n 52) para 6.43.
195 *Oguru v Shell* [2021] (n 52).
196 EGASPIN (n 72) Part IX 4.6.2 (a) under which fines of N500,000 (£1055) generally and N100,000 (£211) for every day the offence subsists were imposed; NOSDRA (Est) Act 2006, s 6(2) under which a fine of N500,000 (£1055) is imposed for every day the operator fails to report a spill to the agency.
197 *Akpan v Shell* [2021] (n 52) paras 5.8–5.13.
198 EGASPIN (n 72) Part VIII B, 8.20; Oil Pipelines Act, Cap 338, LFN 1990, s 11(5)(c).
199 *Akpan v Shell* [2021] (n 52) para 6.1.
200 *Akpan v Shell* [2021] (n 52).

This was an affirmation of the lower court's ruling.[201] It stands to reason that the sabotage would not have happened if the well head was well secured. This underpins the argument that a blanket exclusion from payment of compensation under section 11(5)(c) of the Oil Pipeline's Act, 1956 for damages cause by sabotage spill is wrong especially where the operator is negligent, where he ought to have done something to prevent such third-party malicious act or to mitigate the harm resulting therefrom. For instance, in the Oruma spill, the plaintiffs alleged that the oil spills started from SPDC's underground pipeline on 26 June 2005 but could not be remedied until 7 July 2005, leaking an estimated 400 barrels of oil.[202] It is recommended that where negligence or failure to mitigate the damage resulting from sabotage spill is established, the operator's exclusion from payment of compensation for damages caused by such spills should not apply to that, occasioned by his negligence to stop the spill and mitigate damages. Additionally, where negligence is not established but there is, nevertheless, sabotage spills, the operator's exclusion from payment of compensation should not extend to damages occasioned by ongoing spills resulting from his delay in stopping the spill. Where modern LDS and automatic shutdown devices have not been installed in the pipelines, the operator must pay compensations to the victims of the spill for damages resulting from the oil spills (even if occasioned by sabotage) that would not have occurred if such devices had been installed. A legislative reform to change Oil Pipelines Act section 11(5) to reflect this recommendation is apposite. It is hoped that the Dutch Appeals court would take this into consideration in resolving the still outstanding issue surrounding the sabotage spills in the Ikot Ada Udo community. The court has reserved its ruling on this issue to adequately assess the extent of the pollution.[203]

If it is finally concluded that there is still contamination attributable to the 2007 spill, but not to the extent that remediation is required in Nigeria, the court must decide whether to go no further and to simply award compensation.[204] Shell has already stated that 'No remedial action is required at the site [in Ikot Ada Udo] as soil and groundwater values are far below the intervention values set by the EGASPIN.'[205] This line of argument must be discountenanced by the court in determining whether the polluted environment still needs to be remediated. Although UNEP has recommended adherence to national legislation and guidelines on specific issues, it made an *exception* 'in cases where there are sound scientific reasons to adopt a more stringent standard in order to protect public health and welfare.'[206] It is safe to say that the nature and extent of contamination in the Niger Delta[207] warrants the application of a more stringent standard. Additionally, evidence has shown that Shell's clean-up standard in Nigeria is below the risk threshold

201 *Akpan v Shell* [2013] (n 22) para 5.1.
202 *Oguru v Shell* [2015] (n 183) para 1.1.
203 *Akpan v Shell* [2021] (n 52) para 6.2.
204 *Akpan v Shell* [2021] (n 52) para 13.
205 *Akpan v Shell* [2021] (n 52) para 12.3.
206 UNEP (n 3) 86.
207 UNEP (n 3) 8, 37, 55, 192.

recommended by the World Health Organisation (WHO).[208] Since WHO guidelines provide an international standard of sort (albeit non-binding), one can conclude that Shell's clean-up in Nigeria is inadequate and below international best practices. It is recommended that the Hague Court take all these into consideration in resolving the issue of adequacy of remediation in the Ikot Ada Udo community.

The aforementioned decisions of the Dutch Appeals Court in the Nigerian oil spill cases, just like the *Kiobel, Lungowe*, and *Okpabi* cases, indicate that a window is still open for foreigners to bring civil actions for compensation against MNOCs in the US, UK, and the domestic courts of the Member States of the EU for damages from oil spills that occurred abroad in host jurisdictions. Availability of this window of opportunity will help to hold the MNOCs accountable for environmental pollution including oil spills caused by their subsidiaries in an emerging jurisdiction like Nigeria. It will also help to level the playing field on issues of liability for oil spill clean-up and compensation to the victims and ultimately help to curb differential corporate behaviour that is sure to exist without such opportunity.

4. Conclusion

In addition to common law and statutory torts in the Nigerian oil and gas industry, this chapter covers civil litigation of Nigerian oil spill matters in the US, the UK, and the Netherlands (the EU). Court delays and issues with access to justice force Nigerian litigants suing for civil damages and compensation for oil spills to seek for remedy abroad often in the home jurisdictions of the MNOCs. Some sue in the US under the Alien Torts Statute (ATS) while others seek redress in the English and European Courts.

In the US, the jurisdiction for actions based on the ATS against US corporations and their foreign subsidiaries was significantly narrowed down by the US Supreme Court's decision in *Kiobel v RDS & Others*. According to the Court, the presumption against extraterritorial application of the US law applies to the ATS, and to rebut that presumption, the case must touch and concern the US with sufficient force.

On the other hand, the UK courts started to assume jurisdiction to try parent companies of MNCs for the environmental damages caused by the harmful practices, (including oil spills) of their foreign subsidiaries mainly because of lack of access to justice in the unindustrialised host jurisdictions.[209] In the EU (specifically the Netherlands), courts have found ways to assume jurisdiction and hold parent multinational corporations liable for oil spill and environmental damage caused by their Nigerian subsidiaries.[210] This jurisdictional ground is anchored on Article 4(1)

208 UNEP (n 3) 175 – WHO's guidelines are based on a risk threshold of 1 per 100,000, which corresponds to a clean-up standard of 500 mg/kg TPH, but Shell's clean-up was based on a risk threshold of 1 per 10,000, which corresponds to a clean-up standard of 5,000 mg/kg TPH.

209 *Vedanta v Lungowe* [2019] (n 37).

210 *Oguru v Shell* [2021] (n 52); *Akpan v Shell* [2021] (n 52); *Dooh v Shell* [2021] (n 52).

of the Brussels 1 Regulation (recast) when read together with Article 63(1)[211] and on the fact that the parent company is domicile in the EU. Unlike in the US, the issue of *forum non conveniens* does not arise under the Brussels Regulation,[212] and the Dutch Code allows the parent company and the subsidiary to be sued together where the claims are connected.[213] All things considered, the EU presents a broader and better jurisdiction than the US for litigating oil pollution cases originating from Nigeria (or any other country outside the EU) against the parent MNOCs for environmental damage caused by the conduct of the Nigerian (or overseas) subsidiaries where the parent company is domiciled in the EU.

211 *Forum non conveniens* is, however, grounds to deny jurisdiction in the US, if the court is persuaded that a more appropriate forum exists. This has successfully been used by transnational companies in environmental harm linked with human right violations committed abroad – *Yaiguaje v Chevron Corporation* (n 35). This case involves many fora including Canada for the execution of the judgement. *In re Union Carbide Corp. Gas Plant Disaster at Bhopal India in December 1984,* 809 F.2s 195 (US Court of Appeals, 2nd Circuit, 14 January 1987).

212 *Andrew Owusu v N. B. Jackson* CJEU (1 March 2005) C-281/02.

213 Dutch Code of Civil Practice (DCCP), Bk 1, Article 7(1) deals with connected claims, and aligns with article 8(1) of the Brussels I Regulation. *Akpan v Shell* [2013] (n 22) paras 4.5–4.6.

7 Environmental Crime and Corporate Environmental Crime

1. Introduction

Environmental crimes, (often referred to as green crime) are simply acts and omissions that breach environmental laws, harm the environment, or have the potential to do so.[1] It includes an extensive list of illegal activities that contaminate the air, land, and water and threaten public health.[2] Environmental crime is one of the world's most profitable organised criminal activities causing significant damage to the environment, public health, and the economy.[3] According to Interpol environmental crime is the fourth largest criminal activity in the world coming after drug trafficking, counterfeiting, and human trafficking.[4] It grows at the rate of 5–7% annually (two to three times the rate of global economy) with an annual loss of $110–281 billion dollars.[5] Combating environmental crime is very challenging because it is hard to detect, prosecute, and punish.[6] It is multidimensional, involving national, regional, and international fora; chains of events; and many guilty parties over a period. Serious environmental crimes are often connected to crimes that threaten global peace and security such as terrorism, money laundering, smuggling, human rights abuse, fraud and corruption, forgery of documents and misrepresentation, etc. In fact, reports suggest that human trafficking, drugs,

1 S Bell, D McGillivray and O Pedersen, *Environmental Law* (9th edn, OUP 2017) 266. Derica Lambrechts, 'Environmental Crime in Sub-Saharan Africa – A Review and Future Challenges' (2016) 43(2) Politikon 155, 155; Eelis Paukku, 'Environmental Crime in a Welfare State – A Case Study on the Prosecution of Environmental Crimes in Finland 2015–2020' (2022) Int'l J Compar Applied Crim Just 1, 2.

2 'America's Environmental Crime Fighters Brochure' 5 <https://www.epa.gov/sites/default/files/documents/oceftbrochure.pdf> accessed 13 January 24.

3 'The EU's Fight Against Environmental Crime' <https://www.consilium.europa.eu/en/infographics/eu-fight-environmental-crime-2022/> accessed 18 April 24.

4 C Nellemann and others (eds), *The Rise of Environmental Crime – A Growing Threat to Natural Resources Peace, Development and Security. A UNEPINTERPOL Rapid Response Assessment* (UNEP and RHIPTO Rapid Response) (Norwegian Center for Global Analyses 2016) 7 <www.rhipto.org>

5 Nellemann and others (n 4).

6 The EU's Fight against Environmental Crime (n 3).

DOI: 10.4324/9781003435150-7

and arms trafficking use the same route as illegal trade in wildlife and timber across countries and continents.[7]

International environmental crime has been defined to include five broad areas of offences, namely: illegal trade in wildlife and their parts; illegal logging and trading in timber; illegal fishing, which may include fishing without licence, fishing out of season, using banned gear or techniques in fishing, etc.;[8] illegal trade in controlled chemicals (including ozone depleting substances); and illegal disposal of wastes, particularly e- and hazardous wastes.[9]

2. Corporate Environmental Crime and Proof of Environmental Criminal Liability

Braithwaite and Fisse define corporate crime as the 'conduct of a corporation, or employees acting on behalf of a corporation, which is proscribed and punishable by law.'[10] Simpson et al. appear to agree with this when they define corporate crime as 'illegal behaviour by corporations and their agents[11] brought about by greed of corporate managers and/or weak regulation.'[12] Corporate environmental crime is, therefore, committed when a corporation violates environmental legislation negligently, knowingly, or wilfully.[13] Knowing violations are neither accidental nor by mistake but they are 'deliberate, conscious and informed actions.'[14] For instance, an intentional decision to dispose or dump pollutants into a river without a permit or an intentional decision not to install a required air pollution control device or leak detection devices for oil spills. Knowing or intentional violation is considered more egregious and, therefore, generally prosecuted as a crime. In fact, most US federal environmental statutes generally classify knowing violations as felonies.[15]

Conviction for environmental crime normally require proof of *mens rea* or intent. This is usually difficult to prove and makes it difficult to secure conviction

7 'UNEP & INTERPOL Assess Impacts of Environmental Crime on Security and Development' (UNEP-INTERPOL Press Release, 06 November 2013) <https://www.unep.org/news-and-stories/press-release/unep-and-interpol-assess-impacts-environmental-crime-security-and> accessed 10 January 24.

8 Puneet Pathak, 'International Environmental Crime: A Growing Concern of International Environmental Governance' (2016) 13 US-China L Rev 382, 391.

9 Mary Rice (ed), 'Environmental Crime – A Threat to Our Future' Environmental Investigation Agency (EIA) (October 2008) 6–21. https://globalinitiative.net/analysis/environmental-crime-a-threat-to-our-future/ accessed 12 April 2025.

10 John Braithwaite and Fisse Brent, 'Self-regulation and the Control of Corporate Crime' in Clifford Shearing and Philip Stenning (eds), *Private Policing* (Sage Publications 1987) 221.

11 Executive directors and managers.

12 Sally S Simpson and others, 'An Empirical Assessment of Corporate Environmental Crime-Control Strategies' (2013) 103 J Crim L Criminol 231, 232.

13 US EPA Criminal Investigations, 'What Is an Environmental Crime? <https://www.epa.gov/enforcement/criminal-investigations> accessed 13 January 24.

14 US EPA, 'Basic Information on Enforcement' <https://www.epa.gov/enforcement/basic-information-enforcement> accessed 13 January 24

15 US EPA (n 14).

of an environmental offence as a crime and to impose criminal liability. However, successful proof of knowing violation is seen as satisfactory proof of *mens rea* or the intent required for criminal conviction for environmental crime.[16] Nevertheless, knowing discharge may specifically be difficult to prove especially when there was no prior intention to discharge oil as in the case of the 2010 Gulf oil spill. Uhlmann argued that BP's actions may have been reckless in not taking enough precautions to prevent a blowout but did not amount to an intention to cause the blowout and discharge of oil in violation of the US Clean Water Act (CWA).[17] The fact that Transocean[18] and Halliburton[19] objected but eventually acquiesced to BP's deviation from industry norm in drilling makes them negligent. Whether this negligence meets the 'recklessness' standard is arguable, but it meets the requisite standard for criminal prosecution under the US CWA.[20] It should, however, be noted that negligent violations are not usually criminal unless they involve gross negligence or recklessness.[21] So, a high degree of negligence or recklessness could be equated to an intention to have an obvious outcome that such recklessness would normally result in, thus satisfying the requirement for proof of intent.

The drilling company, Transocean, was responsible for the safe operation of the *Deepwater Horizon* and the blowout preventer. The company was, therefore, extensively involved in carrying out BP's problematic decisions, which led to the well blowout and the spill. Unlike Transocean, Halliburton was not involved in the actual drilling of the well and so was minimally involved in carrying out BP's decisions. The company was nevertheless negligent in going ahead with the six centralisers endorsed by BP rather than the 21 it originally recommended. These acts of negligence put human lives and the environment at risk and warrant punishment but may not amount to crime. This was not fully litigated in the end because BP opted to negotiate a comprehensive settlement that resolves both civil and criminal penalties as well as natural resource damage claims and restitution to Gulf coast residents.[22] BP was found to be grossly negligent with 67% culpability for the spill

16 33 U.S.C. § 1319(c)(2)–(3) (e.g., under the CWA). Isabel Wigley and others, 'Environmental Crimes' (2023) 60 Am Crim L Rev 715, 721.

17 David M Uhlmann, 'Environmental Crime Comes of Age: The Evolution of Criminal Enforcement in the Environmental Regulatory Scheme' (2009) Utah L Rev 1223, 1432.

18 Contractors who own and operated the Deepwater Horizon drilling rig leased by BP to drill the Macondo oil well.

19 Halliburton was hired by BP to provide cementing services and the placement of 'centralisers' to stabilise the well during the drilling of the Macondo oil well. BP decided to install only six of the 21 cement centralisers (spacers) recommended by Halliburton, and BP also decided that it was unnecessary to conduct a cement bond test, which might have shown that explosive gas had seeped into pipes during the cementing process. Uhlmann (n 17) 1422.

20 Criminal prosecution under the US CWA requires proof of ordinary negligence as in tort, e.g., failure to use reasonable care. This is the degree of care that someone of ordinary prudence would have exercised in the same circumstances.

21 33 U.S.C. § 1319(c)(2)–(3) (under the Clean Water Act (CWA); s. 1319(c)(1) (CWA); 42 U.S.C. s. 7413(c)(4) (under the Clean Air Act (CAA); Wigley and others (n 16) 721; Uhlmann (n 17) 1431.

22 Uhlmann (n 17) 1433.

while Transocean and Halliburton were held negligent with 30% and 3% culpability respectively. None of BP's engineers or top executives were convicted for the spill and so, there was no jail time.

Where the environmental regulation is violated by a corporation, the violating employee or the officers or managers who authorised the violation or who have the authority to prevent, correct, or stop it, could be prosecuted individually[23] in addition to prosecuting the corporation as corporate 'person.'[24] One advantage of criminal prosecution is that unlike civil penalties, criminal sanctions cannot be passed on to consumers as cost of doing business. However, criminal offences of the employee, committed on behalf of the corporation, within the course and scope of the employee's employment are generally attributable to the corporation through vicarious liability[25] or the doctrine of *respondeat superior*.[26] Parent companies can also be liable for environmental violations of their subsidiaries especially when it could be shown that they are in control of the operations of the subsidiary[27] or when the corporate veil is pierced to reveal the real owner of the subsidiary.[28]

3. Corporate Environmental Compliance and Good Corporate Behaviour

The general presumption is that companies will comply with regulations when the likelihood of getting caught[29] and punished (or the threat of it) for noncompliance is high and will not comply when noncompliance gives them financial gain or competitive advantage. Decisions to comply or not to comply are not always based on the cost-benefit analysis[30] and on the avaricious tendences of corporate executives but may simply derive from a sense of duty and willingness of the corporation to do the right thing.[31] However, studies of corporate environmental crime show that there is a link between managerial environmental moral commitment, a firm's

23 Wigley and others (n 16) 722; The *'Special Executive Liability'* under *Protection of the Environment Operations Act (PEOA) 1998, New South Wale* (NSW) Australia, ss 169, 143(1) & 144(1); *Environmental Protection Act 1970* (Victoria, Australia) s 66B; *EPA v Foxman Environmental Development Services; EPA v Botany Building Recyclers Pty Ltd; EPA v Foxman (No 2)* [2016] NSWLEC 120.

24 Wigley and others (n 16) 723.

25 *Beyene v Hilton Hotels Corp.*, 815 F. Supp. 2d 235, 250 (D.C. Cir 2011).

26 Albert W Alschuler, 'Two Ways to Think about the Punishment of Corporations' (2009) 46 Am Crim L Rev 1359.

27 *Vedanta Resources plc and Other v Lungowe and Others* [2019] UKSC 20, paras 44,49, 53; *Okpabi & Others v RDS & Another* [2021] UKSC 3, para 130–32.

28 *VTB Capital plc v Nutritek International Corp*, [2013] UKSC 5, [2013] 2 WLR 398. In this case, the UK Supreme Court noted that that the relevant actor is the person behind the company and not the company – per Lord Neuberger, 142

29 Paul B Stretesky, 'Corporate Self-Policing and the Environment' (2006) 44 Criminol 671, 674–75; Toni Makkai and John Braithwaite, 'The Dialectics of Corporate Deterrence' (1994) 31 J Res Crime Delinq 347.

30 This posits that a crime would be committed when the benefit outweighs the cost of doing so.

31 Carole Gibbs, 'Corporate Citizenship and Corporate Environment Performance' (2012) 57 Crime Law Soc Change 345, 346.

obligation and willingness to either violate or comply with environmental regulations, and its overall environmental performance.[32] Gibbs noted that corporations that take duty seriously may be less likely to violate the law and more likely to comply.[33] Thus, a firm's sense of obligation has important implications for corporate behaviour and environmental compliance.

The attitude of corporate managers to environmentalism, ethics, and to the overall firm culture is critical to the determination of corporate environmental behaviour. Firms run by managers with strong sense of right and wrong are generally able to resist the temptation of corporate crime. They encourage employee compliance with the law and punish noncompliance appropriately. Improved internal reporting programs, educating employees about whistleblower laws, and incorporating corporate regulatory compliance into employee promotion and salary structure are all known to be good managerial strategies for incentivising environmentally friendly behaviour in employees.[34] However, external pressures (legal,[35] social,[36] and economic)[37] on the corporation and individual manager's (or employee's) personality traits, morality, and attitude to shame[38] as well as severe, certain, and widely published legal sanctions are known to contribute to corporate environmental behaviour and to shaping the outcome of the final decision of the corporate manager to comply with environmental regulations or to engage in corporate illegality and environmental crime.[39] Prosecuting delinquent firms for violations of environmental regulation[40] not only serves as a wakeup call on such a corporation but on other firms in the same industry. It motivates them to take responsive corrective actions in their firm to improve their environmental compliance performance even when such actions are costly.[41]

Corporate crime causes far more damage to the society than all street crimes combined, in terms of loss of life and property, injury to human health, and the environment.[42] Prominent examples include the Love Canal environmental disaster (1978) in Niagara Falls neighbourhood, New York, USA; Three Mile Island

32 Gibbs (n 31) 346.

33 Gibbs (n 31) 346.

34 Melissa Rorie, 'An Integrated Theory of Corporate Environmental Compliance and Overcompliance' (2015) 64 Crime Law Soc Change 65, 92–93.

35 Constraints imposed by regulatory regimes and formal criminal justice sanctions.

36 Influence of the media, politics, public opinion, and organised non-government environmental groups.

37 The ability to profit or the likelihood of suffering financial loss because of certain behaviours.

38 Stretesky (n 29) 675; Nicole Leeper Piquero, Lyn Exum and Sally Simpson, 'Integrating the Desire-for-control and Rational Choice in a Corporate Crime Context' (2005) 22 Justice Q 252.

39 Rorie (n 34) 65, 92; N Gunningham, RA Kagan and D Thornton, 'Social License and Environmental Protection: Why Businesses Go beyond Compliance' (2004) 29 Law Soc Inq 307.

40 Rorie (n 34) 93.

41 D Thornton, N Gunningham and RA Kagan, 'General Deterrence and Corporate Environmental Behaviour' (2005) 27(2) Law Policy 262, 275.

42 Russell Mokhiber, *Corporate Crime & Violence: Big Business Power and the Abuse of the Public Trust* (Random House, Inc. 1989).

nuclear disaster in Pennsylvania, USA (1979), the Bhopal disaster in India (1984); the Chernobyl Nuclear Power Plant disaster in the northern part of Ukraine in the then Soviet Union (1986); Exxon Valdez oil spill in Prince William Sound Alaska, USA (1989); the BP oil spill disaster at the Gulf of Mexico (2010); etc. Noncompliance with health, safety, and environment (HSE) regulations in workplaces is another aspect of corporate crime that is very debilitating especially to employee lives. Examples in this category include asbestos poisoning and air, water, and land pollution. Hazardous consumer products, medical and pharmaceutical products, contaminated food, etc.[43] are products of corporate crimes that could make goods and services dangerous to human health and the environment.

4. Enforcement of Environmental Crime

Noncompliance with environmental regulation may be a civil offence but can also be a crime.[44] Environmental crime is generally handled under public and administrative law proceedings with civil sanctions. Criminal sanctions are only applied in cases of serious environmental offence or where the case involves gross negligence or recklessness.[45] Criminal sanctions are also applied where the law explicitly provides for it, e.g., in the Convention on International Trade in Endangered Species of Wild Fauna and Flora (CITES) (1973);[46] The Basel Convention on the Control of Transboundary Movement of Hazardous Waste, and their Disposal, (1989);[47] etc. But criminalising environmental offences and imposing harsher punishment does not significantly reduce commission of the crime unless it is backed by adequate sanctions and effective enforcement.[48] For instance, in Nigeria, oil bunkering is a criminal offence punishable by death or up to 21 years' imprisonment,[49] but oil bunkering remains rife in Nigeria's Niger Delta partly because no one has ever been convicted for that offence.[50] This evidences deficiency in the enforcement of that law.

Enforcement could be through administrative, civil, and criminal proceedings.[51] In the US, most environmental statutes administered by the US Environmental Protection Agency (EPA) provide these options, and it is the prerogative of the enforcement agency to decide whether to proceed with one form of enforcement or

43 Mokhiber (n 42).

44 JR Fuller, *Introduction to Criminal Justice* (2nd edn, OUP 2021).

45 33 U.S.C. § 1319(c)(2)–(3); s. 1319(c)(1) (under the US Clean Water Act); 42 U.S.C. s. 7413(c)(4) (under the US Clean Air Act; Wigley and others) (n 16) 721.

46 993 U.N.T.S. 243, art 8(1)(1).

47 1673 U.N.T.S. 125, art 4.

48 Paukku (n 1) 3; C Almer and T Goeschl, 'The Sopranos Redux: The Empirical Economics of Waste Crime' (2015) 49(11) Reg Stud 1908.

49 Petroleum Production and Distribution (Anti Sabotage) Act, Cap P12, LFN 2004, s. 1

50 Dickson E Omukoro, 'Environmental Regulations in Nigeria and Liability for Oil-pollution Damage: Musings from Norway and the US (Alaska)' (2017) 8 Int'l Energy L Rev 324, 326.

51 Granta Y Nakayama, 'Office of Enforcement & Compliance Assurance, Memorandum on the US, EPA's Parallel Proceedings Policy' (24 September 2007) 2 <https://www.epa.gov/sites/production/files/documents/parallel-proceedings-policy-09-24-07.pdf> accessed 22 April 24.

a combination of enforcement actions. Parallel proceeding involving both criminal action and civil administrative compliance or clean-up order are frequently used for the protection of the environment and human health.[52] However, both the US EPA and the Department of Justice's (DoJ's) Environmental and National Resources Division (ENRD) are known to generally prefer criminal enforcements over civil penalties because enforcements of environmental law are known to be more effective when there is a likelihood of criminal sanctions.[53] However, there are instances where both criminal and civil proceedings are pursued.[54]

The European Union was the first international body to criminalise serious environmental offences by enacting the EU Environmental Crime Directive (ECD)[55] on the protection of the environment through criminal law. This was adopted on 24 October 2008 and the EU Member States were obligated to transpose the Directive into national law by December 2010. The purpose of the Directive was to supplement existing administrative sanctions with criminal penalties and thereby to strengthen compliance with environmental protection laws. The Directive is known to have improved the enforcement of environmental law in the region[56] and provided adequate sanction to offenders that merit heavier punishment than the administrative and civil penalties could provide. Though the UK left the EU on 31 January 2020, the Directive remains in force in the UK, because the UK still must maintain EU environmental standards to have access to the EU single market.

4.1. Successful Enforcement Models

Despite weak legislation and ineffective enforcement bedevilling environmental crimes, successes have been reported in relation to some enforcement models[57] such as:

1. **Asia's Project Sky-Hole Patching** – This was a regional cooperation of customs enforcement operation against environmental crimes of illegal trade and transportation of ozone depleting substances (ODS) and hazardous waste. This was reportedly organised by the World Customs Organisation's (WCO) Regional Intelligence Liaison Office for Asia and the Pacific (RILO AP) in 2006. Part II of this project was a joint WCO-UNEP project from May–November 2010 resulting in the seizure of thousands of cylinders of smuggled ODS – Chlorofluorocarbons (CFCs), hydrochlorofluorocarbons (HCFCs), and other gases regulated under the international ozone protection agreement.[58]

52 Nakayama (n 51) 3.
53 Almer and Goeschl (n 48) 1908.
54 Wigley and others (n 16) 715, 719.
55 Directive 2008/99/EC
56 Paukku (n 1) 2.
57 Rice (ed), EIA (n 9) 22–23.
58 Rice (ed), EIA (n 9) 22; 'Project Sky-Hole Patching II' <https://www.wcoomd.org/-/media/wco/public/global/pdf/topics/enforcement-and-compliance/activities-and-programmes/environmental-crime/sky-hole-patching/unep_sky_hole_patching_brochure.pdf> accessed 16 April 2024.

2. **The US' Operation Cool Breeze** – This was a national multi-agency coordinated response against the smuggling of CFC through the ports of Miami, Florida in the US in mid-1990s. The smugglers were effectively tracked down and successfully prosecuted.[59]
3. **Indonesia's Operation Hutan Lestari/Sustainable Forest Operations** – This was a massive government effort to combat deforestation by clamping down on illegal logging in Papua, Indonesia in 2005.[60]
4. **India's Wildlife Crime Control Bureau** – This Bureau is a statutory multi-disciplinary body established by the government of India under the Ministry of Environment and Forests to combat organised wildlife crime in the country. It reportedly used a combination of strategic, intelligence-led enforcement and preventive policing to combat illegal trade in Asian big cat parts and derivatives.[61]
5. **Zambia's South Luangwa Conservation Society** – This was an anti-poaching organisation; a local partnership between government park rangers and the South Luangwa Conservation Society (SLCS) to combat poaching in the South Luangwa National Park, Zambia. The SLCS members are people from the local communities who patrol the park and help to gather intelligence on illicit ivory poaching and other illicit wildlife trade.[62]

4.2. Corporate Crime Control Strategies

In their work in 2013, Simpson et al. offered some empirical insight into how effective different corporate environmental crime prevention and control regulatory strategies are, towards the control of company managers' propensity to engage in corporate environmental crime.[63] They considered how command-and-control strategies, self-regulation, and informal sanctions affect the decisions of corporate managers to embark on corporate environmental crime. The aim was to determine the relative effectiveness of these regulatory strategies.

Command-and-control policies usually imposed and monitored by the legal authorities instituted by the government enforce compliance with set rules and impose formal legal sanctions, punishment, or threats of it for non-compliance. This policy impacts corporate crime because corporate managers often make a cost-benefit assessment of an illegal activity and are likely to commit the crime where the benefit of doing so is high, the risk of getting caught is low, and the

59 Rice (ed), EIA (n 9) 22; 'US' Operation Cool Breeze' <https://www.justice.gov/archive/opa/pr/1997/January97/007enr.htm> accessed 16 April 2024.

60 Rice (ed), EIA (n 9) 23.

61 Rice (ed), EIA (n 9) 23; India's Wildlife Crime Control Bureau <http://wccb.gov.in> accessed 16 April 2024.

62 Rice (ed), EIA (n 9) 23; Zambia's Conservation South Luangwa Society <https://cslzambia.org/> accessed 16 April 2024.

63 Simpson and others (n 12) 231.

punishment is not severe.[64] Conversely, they are deterred from committing the crime when detection risk is high and punishment is certain and severe compared to the gains (financial and non-financial). Both sides of this divide tend to be inversely proportional to each other,[65] but it is not as straightforward as it appears because studies show that severity of punishment or frequency of inspection do not always guarantee the same measure of deterrence in corporate crime.[66] However, improved deterrent has been recorded when corporate managers and employees are targeted rather than the company.[67]

Informal sanctions and consequences of crime such as negative environmental news that brings shame, loss of respect, reputational damage, or threat of it for the firm and the manager (dent on corporate image), combined with internal mechanisms like whistle blower protection policies, have been shown to have greater deterrent effect on corporate crime than the risk of formal enforcement and sanctions.[68] However, corporate managers conscious of good corporate citizenship[69] and the impact of their actions on corporate image tend to prefer to self-regulate.[70]

Simpson et al. described **self-regulation** as a combination of effective internal compliance mechanisms (such as accountability, clear communication of expectations, effective monitoring, and appropriate sanctions for violations), pro-social norms, behaviours, and values that benefit other people or the society (such as sharing, helping, cooperating, and volunteering, etc.) and help to achieve regulatory compliance.[71]

Simpson et al. also found that the organisational and individual factors that increase the risk of crime include financial strain, the desire to have an edge over foreign competitors or to save money for the firm. This generally leads managers to engage in price-fixing, bribery, fraud, or EPA violations, etc. Also, declining firm profits may lead managers and employees to resort to criminal practices to improve performance goals and reach set targets.[72] The character and personal traits of the corporate manager (e.g., personal bias, Machiavellian attitude, pride, tendency to control, etc.) could also be an important factor because managers set the direction of the firm.[73]

64 Simpson and others (n 12) 231. Mark A Cohen, 'Environmental Crime and Punishment: Legal/Economic Theory and Empirical Evidence on Enforcement of Federal Environmental Statutes' (1992) 82 J Crim L Criminol 1054, 1063–64.

65 Simpson and others (n 12) 233.

66 Simpson and others (n 12) 236.

67 Sally S Simpson, *Corporate Crime, Law, and Social Control* (CUP 2002) 35–44.

68 Simpson and others (n 12) 237–39.

69 Corporate citizenship is defined as 'the degree to which firm culture promotes or inhibits a moral commitment to society.' Gibbs (n 31) 345, 346.

70 Simpson and others (n 12) 234.

71 Simpson and others (n 12) 237.

72 Simpson and others (n 12) 240–41.

73 Rorie (n 34) 65, 66–67; Paul Babiak and others, 'Corporate Psychopathy: Talking the Walk' (2010) 28 Behav Sci L 174, 190.

Although research shows that **self-regulation** based on informal social controls could be an effective tool in improving corporate environmental compliance, and may in fact, be more effective than deterrence-based interventions,[74] *Sally et al* recommends that less serious violations be left to self-regulation and normative sanctions, while violations that result in serious harm to human health and the environment be more stringently regulated and enforced.[75] Ultimately, the most effective regulatory tools have been found to be credible legal sanctions that are not only severe but target responsible managers, certainty of sanctions, fear of being discovered, as well as the role of social norms and informal sanctions in corporate environmental compliance.[76]

5. Sanctions

Sanctions are punishment for violation of laws. The aim is to prevent the continuing commission of the offence or to deter future violations. Sanction must be appropriate to have the desired deterrent effect. It must neither be too lenient nor too severe compared to the harm caused.[77] Appropriateness of sanctions also connote the form of sanction – criminal prosecution and prison terms, fines, clean-up and restoration orders, compensation, etc. Uhlmann has suggested that criminal prosecution should be reserved for cases involving significant harm[78] or risk of harm to the environment or public health; deceptive or misleading conduct; operating in clear disregard of environmental regulations; and repeat violations of environmental laws.[79]

Imposition of fine as punishment for corporate environmental crime is not always effective because it could be externalised to the public and treated as part of the cost of doing business. Therefore, it does not necessarily produce the required deterrence for corporate offenders. Individuals (including corporate officers) can face imprisonment for their role in the corporate offence. Criminal enforcement's threat of incarceration is important deterrent to violators.[80] Additionally, sanctions against a firm may incentivise other firms in the same industry to take corrective measures so as not to attract the same fate.

Research indicates that a significant number of firms (63%) embark on compliance (or at least check to ensure that compliance mechanisms put in place are working) after hearing of enforcement actions taken against other firms.[81]

74 Simpson and others (n 12) 266.
75 Simpson and others (n 12) 266–67.
76 Simpson and others (n 12) 265; Gunningham, Kagan and Thornton (n 39) 307.
77 MJ Lynch, 'Punishing Environmental Offenders: Criminal Environmental Sentencing in Louisiana, 2004–2014' (2021) 45(2) J Crime Justice 171; Uhlmann (n 17) 1461.
78 'Significant harm' includes serious injuries or deaths, significant environmental damage requiring substantial time and resources for clean-up and restoration.
79 Uhlmann (n 17) 1246.
80 America's Environmental Crime Fighters Brochure (n 2) 5.
81 Thornton, Gunningham and Kagan (n 41) 262, 275.

Corporate managers are known to fear informal social, political, and economic sanctions far more than formal legal sanctions.[82] The informal social sanctions may come in form of negative publicity because of harm resulting from non-compliance with environmental regulation and strong public disapproval of the offence. Such informal sanctions contribute to increase in compliance even if there is low risk of getting caught.[83] They are often spearheaded by local NGOs, politicians, journalists, etc. and often lead to loss of market share, reputation, and goodwill. It also invites hostility from the local community and more scrutiny by government regulators.[84] Most managers, therefore, often opt to comply, self-regulate, and improve their environmental performance and public perceptions as good stewards of the environment.[85] However, it has been observed that low risk of being caught combined with no policy in place to curtail recidivism lowers deterrence and encourages some offenders to continue reoffending if it is economically profitable.[86] Chester Bowles reported that 20% of the population would comply with any regulation, often based on a high sense of duty and commitment; 5% would attempt to evade it because they have very low sense of duty; while the remaining 75% would submit to and follow the rules if the 5% were apprehended and penalised.[87] Thus, this last category, which forms the bulk, would commit to obeying the law conditionally. If there is a widespread perception that the 5% violators are generally not caught and punished, some of the firms in the 75% group may be discouraged and probably attempt not to comply.[88] So, catching and punishing violators reassures the law-abiding companies that they are not short-changing themselves and operating at a competitive disadvantage.

6. Solutions to Environmental Crime

Apart from enforcement efforts through inspections, civil and administrative actions, and criminal prosecution with associated sanctions, many international institutions and instruments have been used over the years to solve or at least control the problem of environmental crime. These include:

- International institutions (e.g., numerous organs of the United Nations, the Interpol, the International Criminal Court (ICC), the World Customs Organisation (WCO))

82 Thornton, Gunningham and Kagan (n 41) 264.

83 C Almer and T Goeschl, 'Environmental Crime and Punishment: Empirical Evidence from the German Penal Code' (2010) 86(4) Land Econ 707.

84 Thornton, Gunningham and Kagan (n 41) 262, 264.

85 Thornton, Gunningham and Kagan (n 41) 262, 264.

86 Paukku (n 1) 4; T Hubanova, O Yara and M Deineha, 'Socio-economic and Legal Aspects of Environmental Crime in Ukraine' (2017) 3(5) Balt J Econ Stud 276–80, MJ Lynch and others, 'The Weak Probability of Punishment for Environmental Offenses and Deterrence of Environmental Offenders: A Discussion Based on USEPA Criminal Cases, 1983–2013' (2016) 37(10) Deviant Behav 1095.

87 Thornton, Gunningham and Kagan (n 41) 262, 266.

88 Dan M Kahan, 'What Do Alternative Sanctions Mean?' (1996) 63 Univ Chi L Rev 591, 604.

- International soft law instruments (e.g., numerous international conventions and protocols)
- Numerous intergovernmental and non-governmental organisations (NGOs)

In addition to the aforementioned list, the following programmes and policies have been created mainly at the national level to fight environmental crime. These are:

- Creation of specialised environmental courts and tribunals
  - Insights from the New South Wales Land and Environment Court (NSW LEC). Australia
- Voluntary Compliance and Self Auditing Programmes
- Targeting directors through the 'Stepping Stone' approach

These will be discussed in the next segment as well as insights from the Australian Protection of Environment Operations (POEO) Act 1997.

6.1. Creation of Specialised Environmental Courts and Tribunals (ECT)

The establishment of specialised environmental courts e.g., the New South Wales Land and Environment Court (NSW LEC) in Australia reportedly led to the enhancement of environmental protection and ecological sustainability in NSW.[89] It has also been observed that such courts reduce delays in the adjudicatory process of environmental matters,[90] promote greater efficiency, and improve the quality of judgements.[91] It could also enable the development of environmental laws and regulations, leading to legal reforms especially in developing countries.[92] Unfortunately, in Nigeria, the PIA 2021 did not provide for the establishment of such specialised court for environmental matters. However, petroleum pollution matters are assigned to the Federal High Courts.[93] A cost-effective improvement to this could be achieved by creating special divisions within the Federal High Courts to handle environmental and oil pollution cases in Nigeria.[94] Whichever option a State chooses – whether to establish ECTs or to designate a special division of an existing High Court to handle environmental matters, the speed in the adjudicatory

89 Rob White, 'Reparative Justice, Environmental Crime and Penalties for the Powerful' (2017) 67 Crime L Soc Change 117.

90 Brian Preston, 'Operating an Environment Court: The Experience of the Land and Environment Court of New South Wales' (2012) 29 Pace Environ L Rev 46.

91 Anders Bengtsson, 'Specialised Courts for Environmental Matters – The Swedish Solution' (2017) 29(3) ELM 115.

92 Akinseye Akinteye, 'Adjudicating the Impact of Oil Spills in Nigeria: The Need for Black Benches in Oil Producing States' (2018) 16(1) Oil Gas Energy L 12.

93 Constitution of the Federal Republic of Nigeria, 1999, s. 251(1)(n); *SPDC Nig. Ltd v Abel Isaiah & others* 608.

94 Akinteye (n 92) 2.

process in environmental cases would improve and this would ultimately help in solving the problem of environmental crime,

ECT – Insights from the New South Wales Land and Environment Court, Australia: In New South Wales (NSW) Australia, the Land and Environment Court (LEC) has a comprehensive and exclusive jurisdiction in planning and environmental matters.[95] The NSW-LEC is at the same level with the highest court at state level. Appeals lie from it to the High Court of Australia.[96] The NSW-LEC has administrative, civil, and criminal functions. It can, therefore, prosecute and punish environmental offences. Most environmental functions of the NSW-LEC could be carried out by the Federal High Court (FHC) in Nigeria when it relates to oil pollution. However, the NSW-LEC has a broader jurisdiction than the Nigerian FHC since it was established to handle all planning and environmental matters.[97]

When a breach of an environmental legislation occurs or when an environmental offence is committed, anybody can potentially appear before the NSW-LEC to institute appropriate environmental proceedings.[98] However, actions are mostly instituted by the Environmental Protection Agency (EPA). Options available to the EPA under the Protection of Environment Operations (POEO) Act include prosecution, on-the-spot fines, warning letters, prevention, and clean-up notices. If the EPA chose to prosecute,[99] the case is generally heard before the LEC.

Before 1 July 1999, under the POEO Act 1997, the sentencing options available to the NSW LECs were imposition of jail sentence, fine, ordering the offender to undertake clean-up actions or to take steps to prevent the offence continuing or recurring, as well as compensation to those who suffered damage to property as a result of the offence or those who incurred costs in taking steps to clean up the harm caused by the offence. However, the maximum fine imposed for most offences does not differentiate between individual and corporate offenders and so does not provide enough deterrent to the latter. To address this problem, several new sentencing options were introduced into the 1997 POEO Act with the aim of restoring the environment, punishing the offender, and preventing a recurrence of the offence.[100] These orders are:

- **Investigation costs order** – aimed at ensuring that the EPA should not pay out of pocket for enforcing the laws it administers. Here, the offender is ordered to

95 The *Protection of the Environment Administration Act 1991* (NSW) Part 3, s. 6(2).

96 The NSW Supreme Court is like the State High Courts in Nigeria while the High Court of Australia is similar to the Nigerian Supreme Court. However, in Nigeria, there is the Court of Appeals before the Nigeran Supreme Court.

97 'New South Wales EPA: Guidelines for Seeking Environmental Court Orders' (2023) <https://www.epa.nsw.gov.au/licensing-and-regulation/legislation-and-compliance/policies-and-guidelines/guidelines-seeking-enviro-court-orders> accessed 16 January 24.

98 M Pearlman, '20 Years of the Land and Environment Court of NSW' (2010) 38(1) Aust Plan 45.

99 This would be in accordance with the NSW EPA Prosecution Guideline (January 2022).

100 New South Wales EPA: Guidelines for Seeking Environmental Court Orders (2023) (n 97).

pay costs and expenses incurred during the investigation of the offence (section 248 (1)).

- **Monetary benefits penalty order** – Ensures that an offender does not profit from committing an offence. Here, the offender is ordered to pay a sum up to the amount of the monetary benefit derived from the offence (section 249 (1)).
- **Publication order** – Mainly reserved for corporate offenders. It orders the offender to publish details of the offence – and the orders made by the court – for example, in a newspaper/TV/Radio and/or in the executive summary of the company's Annual Report (section 250 (1) (a) & (b)). In case of private company, the publication order may include notice of the offence to shareholders; letters to neighbours/the affected community; and letters to customers and/or suppliers of the company. This order is known to produce the most deterrent effect on such offenders because of its effects on the company's reputation and goodwill. It is usually sought if an offence has generated significant interest in the immediate locality.
  A typical publication order should include details of the offence committed, a short description of the relevant facts, the nature of the pollution (where pollution is involved), any aggravating or mitigating features, and a brief description of all orders made/punishment imposed by the Court.
- **Environmental service order (ESO)** – This orders the offender to carry out a specified project for the restoration or enhancement of the environment in a public place or for the public benefit (section 250 (1) (c)). This order could be made in lieu of or in addition to fine. An ESO can deliver concrete environmental benefits such as a project to a community affected by the offence. It is mostly used in conjunction with publication order and on rich defendants on whom the imposition of a fine may not have a deterrent effect. The relevant community would know that the project is undertaken as a punishment for an offence and not just because of the offender's altruistic or philanthropic nature.
- **Environmental audit order** – This orders the offender to carry out a specified environmental audit of the offender's activities to ensure that it is environmentally acceptable and compliant (section 250 (1) (d)).

The aforementioned orders are in addition to or in lieu of fines, custodial sentences, clean up, restoration, and compensation orders that the Court may make. The EPA decides on which order/s to seek, and the court may make one or more orders against the offender.[101] The orders are available even if the offence is proven but no conviction was recorded against the offender under section 10 of the Crimes (Sentencing Procedure) Act 1999.

From the foregoing, the NSW provisions on environmental crime are very comprehensive. It would be good to introduce some or all of them into the Environmental Guidelines and Standards for the Petroleum Industry in Nigeria (EGASPIN), the National Environmental Standards and Regulations Enforcement Agency

101 POEO Act, 1997, s. 244(1)–(3)

(NESREA), and the National Oil Spill Detection and Response Agency (NOSDRA) Acts.

Despite the sanctions enumerated earlier, some argue that social pressures and *threat* of corporate death sentence (stopping a company from doing business) provide more deterrent for corporate environmental crime.[102] Nigeria can borrow a lot from the NSW-LEC and the POEO Act for its environmental guidelines and statutes.

6.2. Voluntary Compliance and Self-auding Programmes

These programmes embody efforts of a regulated entity to voluntarily identify, disclose, correct, and prevent violations of the law. The US EPA has an Audit Policy, a self-policing programme that encourages companies to improve their environmental performance. In exchange for voluntarily reporting to the proper authorities and correcting or preventing environmental violations (whether administrative, civil or criminal), companies get mitigated penalties,[103] a waiver, and/or a promise not to be sued for the violation.[104] This saves time and resources of needless prosecution and improves environmental performance. Otherwise, there is the possibility that some of the environmental damages that would have been voluntarily reported may not be detected by regulators and remedied due to inadequate resources as a result of budget constraint.[105] In line with this programme, the EPA will usually not recommend prosecution to the Department of Justice if the firm genuinely carries out voluntary compliance and self-auditing programmes and identifies, discloses, and corrects violations.[106] Advantages of these policies include increase in regulatory efficiency and improved environmental performance because violations are more quickly detected and corrected.[107] Environmental crime would likewise be reduced or controlled as a result.

Although corporate self-policing policy is an additional tool in the toolbox of the regulatory agencies, studies have revealed that larger companies are more likely to use the audit policy than small companies, and they are generally more likely to report minor violations rather than more serious violations.[108]

102 S Tombs and D Whyte, *The Corporate Criminal: Why Corporations Must Be Abolished* (Routledge 2015).

103 Incentives for Self-Policing: Discovery, Disclosure, Correction and Prevention of Violations, 65 Fed. Reg. 19,618 (11 April 2000).

104 U.S. Department of Justice, 'Factors in Decisions on Criminal Prosecutions for Environmental Violations in the Context of Significant Voluntary Compliance or Disclosure Efforts by the Violator' (1 July 1991, updated 15 April 2015) <https://www.justice.gov/enrd/selected-publications/factors-decisions-criminal-prosecutions> accessed 01 April 2024.

105 Timo Goeschl and Ole Jurgens, 'Criminalizing Environmental Offences: When the Prosecutor's Helping Hand Hurts' (2014) 37 Eur J L Econ 199.

106 Jennifer Maul and others, 'Environmental Crimes' (2017) 54 Am Crim L Rev 1207, 1222.

107 Stretesky (n 29) 671, 672.

108 Stretesky (n 29) 671, 672.

6.3. Targeting Corporate Directors and Officers of the Company for Punishment through the 'Stepping Stone' Approach

In Australia, the 'stepping stone' approach under the *Australian Securities and Investment Commission Act 2001* ('ASIC Act') is used to impose liability on directors who contravene their statutory duties particularly the duty of care by exposing their company to the risk of criminal prosecution, civil liability, or significant reputational damage.[109] The director's civil liability for their company's fault and misconduct is determined on a balance of probabilities. Criminal liability is imposed where the director's conduct in letting the company contravene legislation is reckless or intentionally dishonest.[110] The application of the stepping stone approach to director liability has been variously endorsed by the Australian Courts[111] and may also be used against officers below board level.[112]

This is appropriate because companies can only operate through human beings, whose acts or omissions could be in good or bad faith. For the stepping stone approach to be applied, corporate fault would first be established to form the stepping stone for finding the directors liable for that fault. If the director is found to cause, authorise, or permit corporate conduct that contravenes the *Corporations Act,*[113] that director would be liable for the corporate fault based on the breach of his statutory duty of care, which is, the duty to act in good faith and in the best interests of the company. The director may have a defence under the business judgement rule, which protects the director from liability in relation to decisions made in the best interests of the company.[114]

Environmental crime could be prevented or controlled if the stepping stone approach is extended beyond the breach of the company's *Corporations Act* to environmental legislations. This would align well with the Environmental Protection Act 1994 (Queensland, Australia), which already provides for criminal prosecution for environmental offences[115] and executive officer liability.[116]

109 *ASIC v Fortescue Metals Group Ltd* (2011) 190 FCR 364, 370

110 Abe Herzberg and Helen Anderson, 'Stepping Stones – From Corporate Fault to Directors' Personal Civil Liability' (2012) 40 Fed L Rev 181, 197. Australia's Corporations and Markets Advisory Committee (CAMAC), *Personal Liability for Corporate Fault* (Report 2006).

111 *ASIC v Fortescue Metals Group Ltd* (2011) 190 FCR 364; *ASIC v Citrofresh International Ltd [No 2]* (2010) 77 ACSR 69; *Morley v ASIC* (2010) 274 ALR 205; *ASIC v Macdonald [No 11]* (2009) 256 ALR 199. Although most of these cases relate to corporate securities malpractice, the principle could be applied to corporate environmental crimes.

112 *Morley v ASIC* (2010) 274 ALR 205.

113 Corporations Act (2001) ss 180(1), 181, and 182; Herzberg and Anderson (n 110) 181, 185–86.

114 Corporations Act (2001) s. 180(2); Herzberg and Anderson (n 110) 181, 184.

115 Environmental Protection Act 1994 (Qld) Ch. 8 provides for general environmental offences; and s. 502 provides for orders the Court may make.

116 Environmental Protection Act 1994 (Qld) Pt 2, s. 493 which enjoins executive officers of a corporation to ensure the corporation complies with the Act or be held liable for failing to do so. Such officer could receive the maximum penalty for the corporate offence similar to that received by an individual who commits the same offence.

7. Global and EU Efforts at Combating Environmental Crime

Many international institutions, intergovernmental organisations and Non-Governmental Organisations (NGOs), dedicate their time and efforts to fight environmental crime. These include the United Nations (UN), particularly the UN Office of Drugs and Crime (UNODC); the International Criminal Police Organization – INTERPOL; the International Criminal Court (ICC); The Commission on Crime Prevention and Criminal Justice (CCPCJ) 2007; the UN Environment Programme (UNEP); the World Customs Organization (WCO); the UN Interregional Crime and Justice Research Institute (UNICRI); the World Bank through the International Consortium on Combating Wildlife Crime (ICCWC); the World Bank and the Secretariats of Multilateral Environmental Conventions and Agreements (MEAs) geared towards promoting international cooperation to address global environmental challenges like climate change, loss of biodiversity, pollution, and management of areas beyond national jurisdiction (ABNJ), pollution and waste management; etc. For their work, these international institutions rely on a broad range of international instruments dealing with a wide spectrum of environmental crime. Some of these are:

- The UN Convention against Transnational Organized Crime, (2000)
- Convention for the Prevention of Marine Pollution by dumping of Waste and other Matters, (1972)
- Convention on International Trade in Endangered Species of Wild Fauna and Flora (CITES) (1973)
- The 1989 Montreal Protocol on substances that deplete the ozone layer
- The 1989 Basel Convention on the Control of Transboundary Movement of Hazardous Waste, and their Disposal
- The 2003 United Nations Convention against Corruption (UNCAC)
- The 2021 Kyoto Declaration on Advancing Crime Prevention, Criminal Justice and the Rule of Law etc.

The Fourteenth United Nations Congress on Crime Prevention and Criminal Justice (CCPCJ)[117] adopted the 'Kyoto Declaration on Advancing Crime Prevention, Criminal Justice and the Rule of Law: Towards the achievement of the 2030 agenda for Sustainable Development.'[118] In May 2021, the UN CCPCJ approved the resolution, to prevent and combat crimes that affect the environment and recommended that the UNGA[119] endorse the Kyoto Declaration on the issue.[120] Under paragraph

117 Kyoto, Japan, 7–12 March 2021.

118 Background Note – CCPCJ Expert Discussions on Crimes that Affect the Environment (UNODC 14-16 Feb. 2022) https://www.unodc.org/documents/commissions/CCPCJ/CCPCJ_Sessions/CCPCJ_31/BackgroundNote_ExpertDiscussions_Crimes_that_affect_the_environment_final.pdf accessed 22 May 2025

119 This recommendation to the UN GA was made through the UN Economic and Social Council (ECOSOC)

120 Background Note (n 117)

87 of the declaration, the UN Member States are committed to adopt effective measures to prevent and combat crimes that affect the environment such as illicit trafficking in wildlife, timber and timber products, wastes, and hazardous wastes as well as precious metals and other minerals, etc. They are enjoined to make the best possible use of relevant international instruments and strengthen legislation and international cooperation to address crimes that affect the environment. Based on the recommendation of the CCPCJ, on 19 December 2023, the UNGA adopted a resolution to accelerate environmental crime prevention towards the implementation of the 2030 Agenda for Sustainable Development.[121]

The European Union Action to Fight Environmental Crime (EFFACE) released five policy briefs and 12 case study policy briefs on environmental crime.[122] Policy brief 1, released in October 2014, addressed environmental crime through the criminal justice system and examined the limitations and challenges of the system in addressing environmental crime. It noted the growing challenge of illegal dumping of waste for the EU and suggested how environmental crime could be tackled. Policy brief 2 released in November 2014 addressed organised environmental crime. It calls for greater focus by the EU to combat environmental crime because it has a grave effect on human health, biodiversity, and the economy. Twelve case study policy briefs that followed covered areas such as waste and e-waste, mining, wildlife, fisheries, pollution, etc.[123] Policy brief 15 quantifies the impact of environmental crime and policy brief 16 identifies the strengths and weaknesses of EU's approach to tackling environmental crime. At the time of this writing, policy brief 17 released in March 2016 was the latest policy brief by EFFACE and it explores the pros and cons of harmonising criminal sanctions on environmental crime.[124]

It is still a subject of academic debate whether to make environmental crime a part of broader international law since it traverses national boundaries but with liabilities for the crime different in different countries. As a result of this and to avoid cross-border enforcement issues, the EU has begun the process of harmonising environmental crime in the region.[125] This is a worthwhile venture.

8. The 2010 Deepwater Horizon Oil Spill – A Legal Analysis

Under the US Clean Water Act, any negligent and knowing discharge of oil or hazardous substances into the navigable waters of the United States in violation of

121 UNGA Resolution on 'Enhancing the contributions of the CCPCJ to the accelerated implementation of the 2030 Agenda for Sustainable Development' A/RES/78/225, 19 December 2023.

122 <https://efface.eu/policy-briefs/#:~:text=The%20first%20EFFACE%20Policy%20Brief,systems%20of%20its%20Member%20States> accessed 18 April 2024.

123 EFFACE Case Study Policy Briefs <https://efface.eu/efface-case-study-policy-briefs/index.html> accessed 18 April 2024.

124 EU EFFACE Policy Briefs on Environmental Crime <https://efface.eu/policy-briefs/> accessed 18 April 2024.

125 M Lennan, 'Evaluating the Effectiveness of the EU Environmental Liability and Environmental Crime Directives as Implemented by Scotland and the Rest of the United Kingdom' (2021) 24(1) J Int'l Wildl L Policy 26.

section 1321(b)(3) may be subject to criminal penalties. On 20 April 2010, the BP Deepwater Horizon oil rig (the Macondo well) in the Gulf of Mexico exploded, spilling an estimated 4.9 million barrels of crude oil into the Gulf, killing 11 workers; coating migratory birds with oil; polluting the water, pristine marshes, and clean beaches; and decimating the Gulf environment and economy.[126] The three companies involved were BP, the Macondo well owners; Transocean, the contractors who owned and operated the Deepwater Horizon drilling rig and were hired by BP to drill the Macondo oil well; and Halliburton, hired by BP to provide cementing services and the placement of 'centralisers' to stabilise the well during the drilling of the Macondo oil well. Following this disaster, as was the case in the 1989 Exxon Valdez oil spill in Prince William Sound, Alaska,[127] the US Department of Justice was expected to prosecute BP, Transocean, and Halliburton for criminal violations of the Clean Water Act[128] and the Migratory Bird Treaty Act.[129] Other criminal charges could also be brought under the Marine Mammal Protection Act,[130] the Endangered Species Act,[131] etc. and any violations of drilling regulations.[132]

While the violation of the Migratory Bird Treaty Act is a strict liability offense deemed committed the moment a migratory bird is coated with the spilt oil, the CWA requires proof of negligence and knowing (wilful) violations by the prosecutors. The criminal trials never took place as BP reached a plea agreement to pay $4 billion for criminal penalties for felony manslaughter, environmental crimes, and obstruction of Congress (Contempt of Congress).[133] This was quite substantial considering that before the Deepwater Horizon spill, the largest criminal penalty for environmental crime of oil spill was $150 million fine imposed in the Exxon Valdez case ($125 million for the Exxon Shipping and £25 million for the Exxon Corporation).[134]

In the civil trial that followed the Deepwater Horizon spill, BP was found to be grossly negligent with 67% culpability for the spill while Transocean and Halliburton were held negligent with 30% and 3% culpability respectively. A finalised settlement of $20.8 billion for the environmental and economic damages done to

126 Uhlmann (n 17) 1414–16; National Commission on the BP Deepwater Horizon Oil Spill and Offshore Drilling, *Deep Water – The Gulf Oil Disaster and the Future of Offshore Drilling* (Report to the President, January 2011).

127 Exxon Shipping Co. and Exxon Corp., No 90-CR-00015 (D. Alaska 1991).

128 Clean Water Act s. 309(c)(1), 33 U.S.C. s. 1319(c)(1)(2) (2006) (involving negligent and knowing discharges in violation of 33 U.S.C. s. 1321(b)(3)).

129 Migratory Bird Treaty Act s. 2, 16 U.S.C. ss. 703(a) and 707(a) (2006) (prohibiting the unauthorised taking or killing of migratory birds and providing misdemeanour penalties for any violations of the provisions of the Migratory Bird Treaty Act).

130 Marine Mammal Protection Act s. 102(a), 16 U.S.C. s. 1372(a) and 16 U.S.C. s. 1375(b) (2006).

131 Endangered Species Act s. 9(a), 16 U.S.C. s. 1538(a) and 16 U.S.C. s. 1540(b) (2006).

132 Uhlmann (n 17) 1417–18.

133 US Department of Justice, Office of Public Affairs. Press Release 'BP Agrees to Pay a Record $4 Billion in Criminal Fines and Penalties' (Thursday, 15 November 2012); In the matter of Bp plc and the Office of Administration and Resources Management, US EPA Case No 12–0295, p. 6.

134 *Exxon Shipping*, No 90-CR-00015; Colin Read, *BP and The Macondo Spill – Complete Story* (Palgrave Macmillan UK 2011) 70–71.

the five Gulf states in the 2010 oil spill was announced in October 2015.[135] However, BP's total spill related cost for the Gulf oil spill was about $62 billion.[136] This includes response and clean-up costs, the Clean Water Act administrative and criminal penalties,[137] natural resource damage claims, as well as compensation and economic damage claims by the Gulf Coast residents and businesses.

The aim of criminal prosecution is not only to deliver justice by punishing the offender and protecting the innocent but to prevent reoccurrence of the offence. Examining the relationship between culpable conduct and environmental harm in the context of criminal liability under the US Clean Water Act, David Uhlmann concluded that criminal prosecution alone cannot prevent future oil spills but must be combined with 'rigorous enforcement of drilling laws, and greater emphasis on safety issues.'[138]

Environmental disasters generally occur when corporations place less emphasis on environmental protection and worker safety. For instance, the Love Canal environmental disaster (1978) in the Niagara Falls neighbourhood, New York, USA; the Bhopal disaster in India (1984); etc. Wilful violations of environmental laws or deliberate concealment of such acts amount to environmental crime and would generally warrant criminal prosecution. Evidence indicates, for instance, that BP, Transocean, and Halliburton actions in drilling the Macondo well were below industry standards.[139] A criminal prosecution is, therefore, necessitated not only because it would increase the liability cap beyond that available under civil enforcement[140] but would send a powerful massage about societal condemnation of such a reckless act of environmental damage, avoidable loss of human life, and significant harm to public health and the coastal economy.

The Deepwater Horizon oil spill at the Gulf of Mexico in 2010 was a classic example of corporate environmental crime. It occurred mainly because BP's management prioritised financial gain (profit) over safety and environmental considerations. Uhlmann noted that this is unacceptable and the government enforcement responses to the spill must make this crystal clear.[141]

Transocean and Halliburton management went along with BP's flawed decisions and deviation from industry standards against their own better judgment on risk assessment and warning signs. There were significant regulatory flaws within

135 Coral Davenport and John Schwartz, 'BP Settlement in Gulf Oil Spill is Raised to $20.8 Billion' *New York Times* (05 October 2015) <https://www.nytimes.com/2015/10/06/business/bp-settlement-in-gulf-oil-spill-is-raised-to-20-8-billion.html> accessed 09 March 24.

136 Ron Bousso, 'BP Puts 2010 Gulf of Mexico Penalties at $62 Billion' *Reuters* (London, 14 July 2016) <https://www.reuters.com/article/idUSKCN0ZU2AJ/#:~:text=BP%20said%20in%20October%20it,on%20the%20London%20Stock%20Exchange> accessed 09 March 2024.

137 In the matter of Bp plc and the Office of Administration and Resources Management, US EPA Case No 12–0295, p. 6.

138 Uhlmann (n 17) 1413, 1413–14.

139 Uhlmann (n 17) 1419.

140 Civil penalties are generally limited e.g., in the US, there is a cap on this under the Oil Pollution Act (1990).

141 Uhlmann (n 17) 1461.

the US Mineral Management Services (MMS)[142] and allegations of improper relationship between the regulatory agency and BP officials leading to lax oversight.[143] BP's contingency plan was not based on real data and neither did it anticipate a spill in the magnitude of spill that occurred. The project plan prepared by BP and signed off by the regulators included risk assessment and environmental assessment that were not relevant to the Gulf of Mexico. For instance, the plan referred to walruses and seal rescue[144] even though these animals never lived in the Gulf but are natives to Alaska. This shows that the plan was a 'cut and paste' work from a plan for Alaska. The regulators apparently signed off on the plan without reading it. So, there is enough blame to go round.

More effective deterrence is achieved by holding corporate executives and the officers and directors of the corporation personally liable where the company commits a civil or criminal offence especially if they are in a position to make or influence corporate decisions on the illegal act.[145] This should be in addition to corporate criminal sentence, significant civil penalties, and rigorous corporate compliance programmes that prioritise environmental protection and worker safety. It could also attract loss of government licence to operate in the country although this would not work in Nigeria and other developing countries where oil is the mainstay of the economy. The cumulative effect of the penalties would send a clear message about the seriousness of the negligence and the government's determination to protect the environment and ensure worker safety. It will also be a useful deterrence to other oil companies and their drilling contractors to avoid similar fate by choosing environmental sound practices and compliance with environmental and drilling laws.

9. Conclusion

States generally appear hesitant to treat pollution as crime because most polluting activities generate huge benefits for the State, e.g., mining, oil exploration and

142 Uhlmann (n 17) 1426–28.

143 Tim Dickinson, 'The Spill, the Scandal and the President' *Rolling Stone* (24 June 2010) 56; Ian Urbina, 'Inspector General's Inquiry Faults Regulators' *The New York Times* (24 May 2010, printed edition 25 May 2010, Section A) 16 <https://www.nytimes.com/2010/05/25/us/25mms.html> accessed 15 March 2024; The final report of the National Commission on the BP Deepwater Horizon Oil Spill and Offshore Drilling, issued in January 2011, attributed the spill to 'a lack of regulatory oversight by the government as well as negligence and time-saving measures by BP and its partners.'

144 Read (n 134) 92–93, 160.

145 Michael Nietsch, 'Corporate Illegal Conduct and Directors' Liability: An Approach to Personal Accountability for Violations of Corporate Legal Compliance' (2018) 18(1) J Corp L Stud 151–84; Kara D Schwee, 'Red Sky at Morning: A Look at Responsible Corporate Officer Liability for Cyber Breaches' (2020) 45(3) J Corp L 787–813; Queensland Environmental Protection Act 1994 (Qld) Australia, s. 493; Amy J Sepinwall, 'Denying Corporate Rights and Punishing Corporate Wrongs' (2015) 25(4) Bus Ethics Q 517–34; David M Uhlmann, 'Crimes on the Gulf' (Fall 2010) L Quadrangle 32.

production, etc. The law, therefore, appears to permit pollution to some extent especially when it is a by-product of an important industrial process.[146] Corporations focused on profit are not helping the issue. But the growing awareness of the effect of environmental crime on environmental sustainability has led many States to join the fight against environmental crime.[147]

Environmental offences at domestic level are often dealt with as civil and administrative matter. For instance, in Nigeria, neither the NOSDRA Act (2018) nor the PIA (2021) have a single criminal provision for oil pollution or other environmental offenses. However, the NESREA (Est), Act (2007) incorporated by reference, the Harmful Waste (Special Criminal Provisions, etc) Act 1988 (Decree No. 42) in respect of hazardous substances as defined under section 37 of the NESREA Act.[148] But, section 32(3) the NESREA Act and section 29(1) of the NOSDRA Act gave an officer of the Agency the power to conduct criminal proceedings, with the consent of the Attorney General of the Federation, in respect of offences under the these Acts or any regulations made under them. If well implemented, this could open the door into rigorous prosecution of environmental crime in Nigeria.

Most national pollution laws come into existence following big pollution incidents e.g., the Harmful (Special Criminal Provisions) Act (1988) referenced in the NESREA Act came into existence in 1988 following the toxic waste dump in Koko village, Nigeria, by an Italian company;[149] the US Comprehensive Environmental Response, Compensation and Liability Act (CERCLA or the Superfund),[150] which was enacted in 1980 was in response to the ground water pollution disaster at Love Canal (Niagara Falls, New York) together with other pollution tragedies at that time such as at Time Beach, Missouri and Valley of Drums, Kentucky; the US Oil Pollution Act 1990[151] was enacted following the Exxon Valdez oil spill incident at Prince William Sounds, Alaska, in 1989. These knee-jerk reactions to environmental incidents would hardly solve the problem of environmental crime. There is need to have a comprehensive international framework to curb transnational environmental crime and guide the development of such laws in the domestic fora to make for a global concerted effort in the fight against environmental crime.

146 Evan Hamman, Reece Walters and Rowena Maguire, 'Environmental Crime and Specialist Courts: The Case for a "One-Stop (Judicial) Shop" in Queensland' (2015) 27 Curr Iss Crim Justice 59, 63; R White, 'Environmental Crime and Problem-solving Courts' (2013) 59(3) Crime L Soc Chang 267–68.

147 Puneet Pathal, 'International Environmental Crime: A Growing Concern of International Environmental Governance' (2016) 13 US-China L Rev 382, 384.

148 NESREA Act (2007), s. 27(5). Although NESREA was amended in 2018, that amendment did not affect s. 27(5).

149 The Federal Environmental Protection Agency Act (FEPA)1988 was also enacted at that time. It was renamed NESREA in 2007. This was subsequently amended in 2018.

150 42 U.S.C. s. 96 et seq. (1980).

151 US Oil Pollution Act (1990) 33 U.S.C. ss. 2701 et seq., amended through P.L. 106–580, Dec. 29, 2000.

The European Union took the lead in this direction when it enacted the Environmental Crime Directive[152] criminalising environmental offences in 2008. It adopted minimum standards but gave the member States the option to adopt stricter standards. Although this led to cross-border enforcement problems, it was nevertheless observed that it has equally contributed to cross-border cooperation in fighting environmental crime.[153] It is recommended that other regions – The African Union, the Asia-Pacific region, North America, South America, etc., should borrow a leaf from the EU's ECD. In the end, it would be helpful to negotiate an international treaty on environmental crime to specifically deal with corporate environmental crime and organised groups and cartels that commit and aid the commission of environmental crime. The Rome Statute should also be revised to empower the ICC to prosecute transnational corporations and international environmental crime cartels for crimes against the environment.

152 Directive 2008/99/EC, of the European Parliament and of the Council, 19 November 2008.
153 European Commission, Evaluation of the ECD, 28 October 2020.

8 Insights from Some Legal Frameworks for Strengthening Corporate Due Diligence and Accountability

1. Introduction

To achieve effective protection of the environment, human rights due diligence (HRDD) requires that firms and corporations take responsibility for the social and environmental impact of their operations across global value chains.[1] Most transnational corporations are known to rely on some self-regulating voluntary approach to corporate environmental responsibility along their value chain, but these have challenges due to their non-binding nature.[2] To improve on this, a wave of legal frameworks have been introduced in some advanced jurisdictions for strengthening corporate due diligence and accountability for environmental protection in global value chains. They aim to establish legal liability for companies that fail to undertake due diligence to identify, prevent, mitigate, and address adverse human rights and environmental impacts in their operations, that of their subsidiaries, and along their entire supply or value chains.

These legal frameworks include the EU Corporate Due Diligence and Corporate Accountability Directive (2021); and the EU Corporate Sustainability Due Diligence Directive (CSDDD) (2024) the Queensland Chain of Responsibility Act (CoRA) 2016; the use of surrogate regulators in the form of mandatory financial security requirements, insurance, and other financial institutions; and finally, the EU Environmental Crime Directive (2008). The scope of operations and available sanctions under these legal frameworks and their effects on environmental protection is examined later in this chapter. Insights are sought for oil spills control and clean-up in the Niger Delta.

1 Enrico Partiti, 'The Place of Voluntary Standards in Managing Social and Environmental Risks in Global Value Chains' (2022) 13(1) Eur J Risk Regul 114–37.

2 Chapter One of this book. Evaristus Oshionebo, *Regulating Transnational Corporations in Domestic and International Regimes – An African Case Study* (University of Toronto Press 2009).

DOI: 10.4324/9781003435150-8

2. The Corporate Due Diligence and Corporate Accountability (CDDCA) Directive

The growth in international supply chains has resulted in negative human and environmental impacts.[3] Voluntary compliance by the multinational companies to due diligence standards for their supply chain has not achieved significant progress in preventing human rights and environmental harm, so, the European Parliament decided on the adoption of a binding legislation on due diligence standard. Having regard to Article 225 of the Treaty on the Functioning of the European Union, the EU Regulation 2017/821 on supply chain due diligence obligations, the EU Whistleblower Directive, the European Green Deal, the OECD Guidelines for Multinational Enterprise, etc.,[4] on 10 March 2021, the European Parliament adopted the 'Directive on Corporate Due Diligence and Corporate Accountability.'[5] Under this legislation, the multinational corporations are *mandated* to minimise the negative impacts of their activities on human rights and the environment along their value chain.[6] The Directive enjoins them to identify, prevent, mitigate, account for, address, and remediate human rights violations and negative environmental impacts in their value chains.[7] Companies are enjoined to make public their due diligence strategy and provide a grievance mechanism responding to stakeholders' warnings and concerns.

The value chain due diligence to be taken by a company should be proportionate and commensurate to the risk and severity of adverse impacts of the company's operations.[8] EU Member States are to provide for and enforce proportionate and dissuasive sanctions considering the severity and repetition of infringements.[9] This should be part of the liability regimes put in place to hold corporations liable and ensure that they provide remediation for any harm arising out of adverse impacts (potential or actual) of their activities on human rights, the environment, or good governance.[10]

This legislation affords the EU the opportunity to increase its scrutiny on the impact of companies' businesses on human rights and the environment. Any violation of the requirements by any EU corporation in their value chain would give rise

3 Ionel Zamfir, 'Towards a Mandatory EU System of Due Diligence for Supply Chains' (European Parliamentary Research Service (EPRS), 22 October 2020) <https://www.europarl.europa.eu/thinktank/en/document.html?reference=EPRS_BRI(2020)659299> accessed 30 July 2021.

4 Preamble to the Corporate Due Diligence and Corporate Accountability – P9 TA (2021) 0073 (10 March 2021, European Parliament) (2020/2129(INL). (Hereinafter, 'CDDCA Directive)

5 CDDCA Directive (n 4).

6 CDDCA Directive (n 4) art 1.

7 CDDCA Directive (n 4) art 1(2)

8 CDDCA Directive (n 4) arts. 1(2), 4(4)(iii).

9 CDDCA Directive (n 4) art 18.

10 CDDCA Directive (n 4) art 18. See also European Parliament 'Legislative Train 10.2021' <https://www.europarl.europa.eu/legislative-train/spotlight-JD21/file-corporate-due-diligence?sid=5201> accessed 28 October 24.

to civil liability before European courts.[11] The law applies to large undertakings (public or private) established and operating within the territory of the EU. It also applies to small and medium sized companies if they are publicly listed and any undertaking established outside the EU if they supply goods or provide services within the EU.[12] The law applies to the whole value chain, which is defined to include:

> 'all activities, operations, business relationships and investment chains of an undertaking and includes entities with which the undertaking has a direct or indirect business relationship, upstream and downstream, and which either *supply* or receive products or services from the undertaking.'[13]

Since the MNOCs could be described as 'suppliers'[14] (of a product – oil), any damage they cause along their value chain e.g., damages due to oil spills (upstream or downstream) must be remediated, otherwise sanctions would be applied proportionate to the severity and repetition of infringements.[15] However, it is taken as effective defence if an undertaking can prove that it took all due care to avoid the adverse impact or the harm in question or that the harm would have occurred anyway, even if all due diligence measures had been taken.[16] It is recommended that the Economic Community of West African States (ECOWAS) sub-region and the African Union (AU) adopt similar legislations to curb corporate misconduct relating to human rights and the environment.

It is worth mentioning that before the EU Parliament adopted the Corporate Due Diligence and Corporate Accountability Directive in 2021, France took the lead in enacting and implementing the French Duty of Vigilance Act (*Loi de Vigilance*).[17]

2.1. France Duty of Vigilance Act **(Loi de Vigilance)***, 2017*

Loi de Vigilance[18] enacted in 2017 imposes a general mandatory due diligence requirement for human rights and environmental impacts on large French companies. The enactment followed the public outrage that met the 2013 'Rana Plaza' tragedy in Bangladesh. This was the collapse of the unsafe building of a textile

11 CDDCA Directive (n 4) art 19.
12 CDDCA Directive (n 4) art 2.
13 CDDCA Directive (n 4) art 3(5).
14 CDDCA Directive (n 4) art 3(3) – 'supplier' here means any undertaking that provides a product, part of a product, or service to another undertaking, either directly or indirectly, in the context of a business relationship.
15 CDDCA Directive (n 4) art 18.
16 CDDCA Directive (n 4) art 19(3)
17 Loi de Vigilance, no: 399/2017 du 23 mars 2017 (hereinafter, French Vigilance Law (2017)). Relating to the duty of vigilance of parent companies and donor companies applicable to France's largest companies. (French Vigilance Law). The other due diligence law enacted was the Dutch Due Diligence Act or Child Labour Legislation adopted 2019 but never entered into force.
18 French Vigilance Law (n 17).

factory in Bangladesh that was closely connected to French companies leading to the death of 1,135 workers. The Duty of Vigilance Law requires French companies to monitor and keep a check on the activities of their subsidiaries in all jurisdictions in which they operate.[19] It made France one of the first countries to adopt corporate due diligence requirements to human rights and the environment in their supply chain and it inspired the proposal of the CSDDD by the European Commission.[20] The law applies to French-registered companies and their direct or indirect subsidiaries with over 5,000 employees or more than 10,000 employees worldwide[21] and imposes a civil duty of vigilance on these French companies to identify and analyse the risks to human rights and the environment arising from their business activities and those of their *controlled* subsidiaries, contractors, and suppliers, if there is an established commercial relationship, and the activities are related to this relationship.[22] So, it holds the French companies accountable for breach of due diligence obligations on human rights and the environment by their subsidiaries

The companies are required to develop a vigilance plan, provide regular assessment of their supply chains and subsidiaries to ensure compliance with the plan. In the event of non-compliance, any party with standing may send a formal three months' notice to the company to comply with this obligation and to remedy the damage that the execution of the obligations could have prevented.[23] Penalties for non-compliance include court injunctions and damages as provided for under articles 1240 and 1241 of the Civil Code.[24] Unfortunately, no government agency has been designated to monitor compliance with this law. That responsibility is left with the company or any party with standing. This is a major shortcoming of the law.

In June 2019, Total SA, an oil company (now TotalEnergies) became the first company to receive a formal notice over alleged non-compliance with the Duty of Vigilance law in Uganda.[25] The company allegedly failed to comply with its duty of care regarding climate change, the human and environmental impacts of its

19 Colin Mackie, 'Environmental Due Diligence in Global Value Chains: A Study to Inform Interpretation of Key Terms within a Cross-sectoral EU Directive' Amnesty International, ECCJ, Fern, FPP, Friends of the Earth Europe, & Global Witness (November 2020) 37. https://corporatejustice.org/wp-content/uploads/2021/05/Environmental-Due-Diligence-in-Global-Value-Chains-Prof.-Dr.-Colin-Mackie.pdf accessed 23 April 2025.

20 Dionis Jurić, Antonija Zubović and Edita Čulinović-Herc, 'Large Companies Saving People and the Planet – Reflections on the Personal Scope of the Application of the Corporate Sustainability Due Diligence Directive' (2022) 9(2) Intereulaweast 12.

21 French Vigilance Law (n 17) art 1.

22 French Commercial Code (*Code de commerce*) article L. 225–102–4.-I para 3.

23 French Vigilance Law (n 17) art 1.

24 French Commercial Code (n 22) art 225–102–5.

25 Mariam R Aczel, 'Justice without Borders: Opportunities from France's "Duty of Care" Act Applied to Uganda' (2021) 75 Energy Res Soc Sci 1; Friends of the Earth International (FOEI), 'Oil Company Total Back in Court for Human Rights Violations in Uganda' (27 October 2020) <https://www.foei.org/press_releases/total-uganda-france-court-appeal-human-rights> accessed 23 July 2021.

subsidiary, and suppliers in Uganda.[26] The plaintiffs alleged that Total's identification of risk and potential impact of their activities was inadequate and devoid of proper analysis and ranking as required by the law. However, on 30 January 2020, the court declined jurisdiction. It treated the case as a 'business dispute' and referred it to the commercial courts. This decision was affirmed by the Appeal Court on 10 December 2020 and has been criticised as contrary to the spirit of the Duty of Vigilance Law. This is because the law was designed to make companies liable for the impacts of their activities on human rights and the environment and that cannot be reduced to a purely commercial dispute.[27]

A similar law to the French Vigilance Law was passed by Germany in 2021,[28] the German Supply Chain Act, which went into force on 1 January 2023.[29] These laws are commendable as precursors to the EU's CSDDD because they hold multinational companies accountable for the negative impact of their activities on human rights and the environment and are very important for parent company liability for their activities and those of their subsidiaries, which often operate in developing counties, as well as those of their suppliers, contractors, etc., along their global value chain.

3. Corporate Sustainability Due Diligence Directive (CSDDD)

The European Council adopted the Corporate Sustainability Due Diligence Directive (CSDDD) on 24 May 2024,[30] and it came into force on 25 July 2024.[31] The aim of this Directive, which comes under the EU Green Deal,[32] is to 'foster sustainable and responsible corporate behaviour in companies' operations and across their global value chains';[33] to advance mandatory, uniform legal framework and legal certainty on corporate sustainability due diligence in companies operating in the EU internal market and across their global value chains.[34] Therefore, the new rule requires companies within the scope of the Directive to identify and address

26 FOEI (n 25).

27 Aczel (n 25) 6; FOEI (n 25).

28 *Gesetz über die unternehmerischen Sorgfaltspflichten zur Vermeidung von Menschenrechtsverletzungen in Lieferketten;* hereinafter: *Lieferkettensorgfaltspflichtengesetz*, LkSG).

29 For the scope and application of these laws, see: Jurić, Zubović and Čulinović-Herc (n 20) 12–22.

30 'Concilium Europa: Council Gives Its Final Approval' (24 May 2024) <https://www.consilium.europa.eu/en/press/press-releases/2024/05/24/corporate-sustainability-due-diligence-council-gives-its-final-approval/> accessed 19 December 2024.

31 European Commission, 'Corporate Sustainability Due Diligence Directive (Directive 2024/1760)' (hereinafter CSDDD) <https://commission.europa.eu/business-economy-euro/doing-business-eu/sustainability-due-diligence-responsible-business/corporate-sustainability-due-diligence_en> accessed 19 December 2024.

32 'The Main Aim of the EU Green Deal Is to Become Climate Neutral by 2050' <https://commission.europa.eu/strategy-and-policy/priorities-2019-2024/european-green-deal_en> accessed 05 June 2024.

33 CSDDD (n 31).

34 CSDDD (n 31).

human rights and environmental impacts of their actions, integrate due diligence into their policy, and identify, monitor, prevent, or minimise potential and actual adverse human rights and environmental impacts in their operations and that of their subsidiaries and business partners, ensuring accountability where they have caused actual adverse impacts.[35] The annex of the CSDDD listed human rights and environmental conventions to which companies must demonstrate that they have taken all appropriate measures to align their operations with.[36]

Companies within the scope of the Directive are also required to develop and put into effect a detailed transition plan for climate change mitigation in line with the 2050 climate neutrality objectives of the Paris Agreement and the intermediate targets under the European Climate Law.[37] This is very important because without addressing the impact of corporate activities on climate change the goal of the Paris agreement will never be actualised. In fact, it has been projected that the enactment of more stringent corporate responsibility rules will continue and companies not now within the scope of CSDDD will likely experience pressure from their various regulators, governments, and customers to accept responsibility for the impact of their activities on human rights and the environment.[38] Also, such companies outside the EU would have a market incentive to adjust their practices on human rights and the environment in line with the CSDDD to maintain commercial relationship with the EU. This could make the Directive a new global standard on mandatory environmental and human rights due diligence. It would also afford developing countries better corporate environmental and human rights protection, improved sustainability-related investments, and increased compliance to international standards. So, this legislation is a victory for corporate responsibility because the Directive will steer businesses towards responsible behaviour.

The CSDDD applies to large EU companies and partnerships with 1,000 and above employees and a net global turnover of at least EUR 450 million. It also applies to large non-EU companies with at least EUR 450 million turnover (net) generated in the EU and to ultimate parent companies of a group or a designated subsidiary that falls into one of the previous categories. This last category will capture EU multinational oil companies such as RDS plc, TotalEnergies, and Eni SpA whose subsidiaries operate in Nigeria. However, where the ultimate parent company is just a holding company and does not engage in management, operations, and financial decisions for the group or individual subsidiary companies within the group, then such parent companies are exempt from the obligations under the CSDDD. The largest companies, both EU and non-EU, with turnovers of over EUR 1,500 million and more than 5,000 employees will be required to comply with CSDDD within three years (2027). However, companies with turnover of at least

35 CSDDD (n 31).

36 CSDDD (n 31) Annex, Part 1(2).

37 CSDDD (n 31) art 22.

38 'The Corporate Governance Institute – on CSDDD' <https://www.thecorporategovernanceinstitute.com/insights/news-analysis/corporate-sustainability-due-diligence-directive-guide/> accessed 28 May 2024.

EUR 900 million and over 3000 employees will have to comply within four years, and the rest (within scope) will have to comply within five years.

From the date the CSDDD enters into force, Member States will have two years to transpose the Directive into national law.[39] Although the CSDDD sets minimum requirements, Member States are allowed to set stricter due diligence requirements or to include into scope activities currently excluded from the Directive.[40] Companies that are already subject to national legislation on supply chains and/or human rights e.g., the French Vigilance Law or the German Supply Chain Due Diligence Act will likely augment their existing laws to align with the CSDDD, rather than institute new legislation.

In terms of enforcement, Member States are expected to designate an authority to supervise and enforce the rules.[41] Injunctive orders and/or fines could be imposed by the courts up to a maximum of 5% of the company's net global turnover in the financial year prior to the penalty decision. At the European level, the Commission will set up a European Network of Supervisory Authorities that will bring together representatives of the national bodies to ensure a coordinated approach.[42] Member States will ensure that victims get compensation for damages resulting from an intentional or negligent failure to carry out due diligence obligations.[43] The limitation period is *at least* five years, but Member States can make this longer. Unfortunately, representative actions by third parties (such as trade unions, NGOs, or National Human Rights Institutions) on behalf of victims are not allowed under the CSDDD but Member States are permitted to allow it. A public statement indicating the infringing company and nature of the infringement is also required.[44] However, it is regrettable that the EU Council removed the requirement for companies to link directors' remuneration to their organisations' long-term sustainability and climate transition planning.[45] The Carbon Disclosure Project (CDP) data indicates that doing this motivates top executives and board members to pay attention to climate issues and ensure that specific climate goals are met by their firm/organisation.[46]

Major shortcomings of this Directive, however, include the absence of provision for criminal liability and provisions for holding corporate executives and the directing minds of the organisation personally liable for the wrongful acts of the

39 CSDDD (n 31).

40 ERM, 'Corporate Sustainability Due Diligence Directive – Policy Alert' <https://www.erm.com/insights/corporate-sustainability-due-diligence-directive-csddd/> accessed 28 May 2024

41 CSDDD (n 31).

42 CSDDD (n 31).

43 CSDDD (n 31) art 29.

44 CSDDD (n 31).

45 Pietro Bertazzi, 'Two Sides of the Same Coin: Corporate Climate Action through the Corporate Sustainability Due Diligence Directive (CSDDD) and the EU Disclosure Rules' (24 April 2024) <https://www.cdp.net/en/articles/companies/two-sides-of-the-same-coin-corporate-climate-action-through-the-corporate-sustainability-due-diligence-directive-csddd-and-eu-disclosure-rules> accessed 28 May 2024.

46 Bertazzi (n 45).

organisation. The Chain of Responsibility Act (CoRA) in Queensland, Australia fills this gap.

4. The Queensland Chain of Responsibility Act (CoRA)

There are many abandoned mine sites in Australia. In Queensland alone, the 2007 government review revealed an estimated 15,000 of them.[47] These have serious environmental and human health impact and will cost more than $1 billion dollars to rehabilitate.[48] *The Environmental Protection (Chain of Responsibility) Amendment Act* 2016 (CoRA) was introduced in response to the inability of an increasing number of companies, due to financial difficulties, to rehabilitate or stabilise their sites to prevent environmental harm. CoRA broadened the circumstances in which an environmental protection order (EPO) can be issued by the Department of Environment and Science (DES). Entities responsible for the environmental harm, whether through their ability to profit significantly from the relevant activity or through their ability to influence environmental compliance at the relevant site were captured.[49] CoRA imposes responsibility on these companies and related entities to bear the cost of rehabilitating the sites and not to leave Queensland taxpayers with the clean-up bills.[50] In fact, CoRA was created to go where the money has gone and to target *related persons*. These are persons (not directors) who stand to make large profits from the company's activities and whose decisions have put the environment at risk.[51] The related persons test was designed to catch all artificial corporate structures and profit-shifting schemes both known and anticipated.[52]

In January 2017, the Queensland Government approved the statutory Guideline for the 'Chain of responsibility' Act.[53] This Guideline provides guidance and clarity for the Chief Executive of the Department of Environment in making decisions on whether to issue an EPO to a *related person* to the company[54] for the rehabilitation of the contaminated site.

A 'related person' could be a holding company; persons with a *relevant connection* to the company that is carrying out the relevant activity; associated entities; and persons that have the capacity to influence the extent of the company's environmental compliance or persons capable of acquiring 'significant financial

47 Queensland Auditor General, *Environmental Regulation of the Environmental and Waste Industries* (Queensland Audit Office, Brisbane, Report 15: 2013–14) 1 & 7.

48 Queensland Auditor General, 2014.

49 Chapter 7, Part 5, Division 2 of the EPA.

50 Sally-Ann Joseph, 'An Examination of the Congruence of the Mining Site Rehabilitation Tax Deductions & Queensland's Chain of Responsibility Legislation' (2017) 2017 AJEL 29.

51 Queensland Parliament, Record of Proceedings, 15 March 2016, 693.

52 Queensland Parliament, Record of Proceedings, 21 April 2016, 1459.

53 Environmental Protection (Chain of Responsibility) Amendment Act 2016, *Guidelines* on Environmental Protection Order to 'related persons' under Chapter 7, Part 5, Division 2 of the Environmental Protection Act 1994 (hereinafter The Guideline to the Chain of Responsibility Act).

54 The Guideline to the Chain of Responsibility Act (n 53) para 1.0.

benefit'[55] from the relevant activities of the company.[56] A 'relevant connection' may exist where a person is capable of significantly benefiting financially or has received a significant financial benefit from a company's relevant activities or is (has been) in a 'position to influence'[57] the company's conduct in relation to the way in which – or extent to which – the company complies with its obligations under the EPA.[58]

To be issued with EPO, the related person must be adjudged culpable, for example, where he has participated in helping the company to avoid its environmental obligations. Also, the EPO will only be considered where the primary company at fault has avoided – or attempted to avoid – its environmental obligations or where the enforcement action against the operator will not achieve restoration of the environment.[59] For instance, there were lots of CoRA orders and litigation against Linc Energy and its CEO, Peter Bond.[60]

The culpable related person has an effective defence if he can show that he has taken 'all reasonable steps in the circumstance' to ensure that the company has complied with the EPA. In such a case, the department will not issue him with a CoRA EPO.[61] However, when determining whether a related person took all reasonable steps in the circumstances, the department may consider the foreseeability and probability of the issue or incident occurring, the legal and practical ability to influence the company, etc.[62] Multiple related persons may be held jointly and severally liable for compliance with an EPO.[63] This allows the department to enforce compliance against any of the related persons to ensure that the requirements of the CoRA EPO are carried out. However, any enforcement action taken by the department will be proportionate to the seriousness of the breach.[64]

In conclusion, for the operations of the CoRA and exposure to a related person EPO, the Guideline reinforces the importance of entities to exercise due diligence and environmental responsibility in their management of environmental risks. Entities can take steps to reduce their risk profile by having in place systems that

55 Factors to be considered in determining what amounts to significant financial benefit is provided for under the Guideline to the Chain of Responsibility Act (n 53) para 4.1.1.

56 The Guideline to the Chain of Responsibility Act (n 53) para 1.0.

57 A person in a 'position to influence' may be an officer of the company such as a director or a shadow director acting in an unofficial capacity for the company. The Guideline to the Chain of Responsibility Act (n 53) para 4.1.2.

58 Section 363AB (2)–(4) of the EPA. The Guideline to the Chain of Responsibility Act (n 53) para 4. 1.

59 The Guideline to the Chain of Responsibility Act (n 53) para 5.0.

60 *Bond v Chief Executive, Department of Environment and Science* [2019] QCA 137; *Linc Energy Ltd (in Liq): Longley & Ors v Chief Executive Dept of Environment & Heritage Protection* [2017] QSC 53; *Linc Energy Ltd v Chief Executive Administering the Environmental Protection Act 1994 & Anor* [2014] QSC 172.

61 The Guideline to the Chain of Responsibility Act (n 53) para 5.0.

62 The Guideline to the Chain of Responsibility Act (n 53) para 5.1.

63 The Guideline to the Chain of Responsibility Act (n 53) para 7.0; Section 363AE of the EPA.

64 The Guideline to the Chain of Responsibility Act (n 53) paras 1.1.2; 2(9).

demonstrate that they have taken all reasonable steps in the circumstance in managing environmental risks and in compliance with the applicable CoRA laws.

5. The Use of Surrogate Regulators to Ensure Corporate Environmental Responsibility

Mandatory financial security requirements, insurance, and other financial institutions could be used as forms of surrogate regulators to ensure corporate environmental responsibility. For instance, a government policy may require the provision of financial security as a risk management measure to cover the consequences of industrial accident. In this case, operators must demonstrate that they have the financial capacity to provide this security and to pay for the costs of recovery and remediation from an environmental accident if it should occur. Financial security may also be required in environmentally risky operations such as in oil and gas exploration and production and a variety of industrial processes. Such security may be provided in the form of insurance coverages, bank loans and guarantees, etc.

Insurers have strong incentive to know their clients' environmental record and trajectory. These are taken into consideration in deciding to provide coverage and the amount of insurance premiums to charge. Poor environmental performers pay higher premiums in line with higher risks posed by their activities. So, insurers can set standards of performance and impose sanctions for noncompliance, in the form of higher premiums or refusal to provide coverage. Their ability to do this provides incentive for operators to take due care to minimise pollution and take environmentally responsible decisions in the process of their operation. Insurers can also insist on certain environmental standards of operation as a condition for coverage, for example, the installation of certain risk-reduction technology such as the installation of leak detection systems in oil pipelines to reduce oil pollution. They could also retain the right to visit and inspect the site to ensure that relevant safety measures are in place and well maintained.[65] Failure to comply with the terms of the policy could attract cancellation of the policy, refusal to renew, or renewal with higher premium. With all these checks, the insurance providers assume the role of 'surrogate regulators' and could positively influence corporate environmental conduct.

It has been argued that a mandatory financial security regime such as insurance policy would undermine the 'polluter-pays' principle and disincentivise operators from operating with due care because their liability is covered by insurance, and their risk transferred to the insurance provider.[66] This line of argument ignores the fact that the polluter still pays in a roundabout way, through high premiums. More importantly, the financial security provider, the insurer in this case, will monitor the

65 Colin Mackie, 'The Regulatory Potential of Financial Security to Reduce Environmental Risk' (2014) 26(2) J Environ Law, 189, 197.

66 Valerie Fogleman, 'Setting the Scene; The Financial Security Provisions in the Environmental Liability Directive' 23 <https://ec.europa.eu/environment/archives/liability/eld/workshop08/docs/BIO_ELD_270608_3_background_VF.pdf> accessed 02 August 2021.

operator's activities and provide checks that will ensure he operates with due care, otherwise he would breach the terms of the policy and lose the coverage. Insurers often employ differentiated premiums proportionate to risks, to incentivise positive environmental behaviour among operators. High risks attract high premium and vice versa. However, for this to work well, there must be accurate performance data. For oil spills in Nigeria, dearth of relevant and accurate spill data may impede the accuracy of actuarial calculations and determination of premiums. This could lead to denial of coverage in such high-risk business or coverage with excessively high premium. Government must provide conducive environment for the insurance business to function effectively. Part of this would be for the regulators to make sure, for instance, that accurate spill data is available for people that need to work with them.

Banks and other lending institutions could also be used as surrogate regulators. They generally request that an environmental audit of their corporate clients be carried out to get full information about their environmental practice before advancing a loan.[67] This helps them to assess the risks involved in a particular loan transaction and ascertain the environmental status of the assets they accept as security for the loan.[68] This ultimately helps them to avoid unnecessary litigation for loan recovery and liability resulting from environmentally unsuitable collateral. Also, where the environmental practice associated with a client's operation is dubious and uncertain and too much of a financial risk, banks would generally deny loan to such a client. This would incentivise the client to improve on its environmental footprint, thus making the actions of the banks, in this regard, akin to that of pseudo/substitute or surrogate regulators, influencing their client's environmental behaviour.

6. The EU Environmental Crime Directive (ECD)

In 2008, the EU adopted the Environmental Crime Directive (ECD)[69] on the protection of the environment through criminal law.[70] The Directive created a supranational legal framework for harmonising environmental criminal law across EU Member States.[71] Existing sectoral civil and administrative penalties and compensation systems have not been adequate to protect the environment,[72] so, there was a

67 Neil Gunningham, Martin Phillipson and Peter Grabosky, 'Harnessing Third Parties as Surrogate Regulators: Achieving Environmental Outcomes by Alternative Means' (1999) 8(4) Bus Strategy Environ 211, 217.

68 Gunningham, Phillipson and Grabosky (n 67) 211, 217.

69 Directive 2008/99/EC, of the European Parliament and of the Council (ECD), 19 November 2008.

70 Directive 2008/99/EC, art 1. Though the UK is currently no longer a member of the EU, the Directive remains in force in UK.

71 Ricardo Pereira, 'Towards Effective Implementation of the EU Environmental Crime Directive? The Case of Illegal Waste Management and Trafficking Offences' (2017) 26(2) Rev Eur Comp Int'l Environ L 147–62.

72 ECD (n 69) 3rd Preamble.

need for additional measures to combat growing environmental crime and harmonise it in the national legislation of the EU Member States.[73]

The Directive categorised certain conduct on the environment as criminal offences in the EU when they are committed *intentionally* or with at least *serious negligence*.[74] They include:

> the discharge, emission or introduction of a quantity of materials or ionizing radiation into air, soil or water, which causes or is likely to cause death or serious injury to any person or *substantial damage* to the quality of air, soil or water, plants or animals; the collection, transportation, recovery or disposal of waste . . . which causes or is likely to cause death or serious injury to any person or *substantial damage* to the quality of air, soil or water, plants or animals; the killing, destruction, possession or taking of specimens of protected wild fauna and flora species, except for cases where the conduct concerns a *negligible quantity* of such specimens and has a *negligible impact* on the conservation status of the species; any conduct which causes the *significant deterioration* of a habitat within a protected site; the production, importation, exportation, placing on the market or use of ozone-depleting substances; etc. (emphasis added)[75]

Applying the foregoing to Nigeria (though not in the EU) means that oil spills caused by pipeline sabotage would be classed as environmental crime under the Directive. This is consistent with Nigeria's Petroleum Production and Distribution (Anti Sabotage) Act,[76] currently somewhat moribund, and the Hague Appeal Court's decision in *Oguru v Shell*.[77]

The requirement of due diligence performance of parent companies over the activities of their subsidiaries have also been upheld by the court.[78] The RDS and its Nigerian subsidiary Shell Petroleum Development Company (SPDC) were held jointly liable for the oil spill that occurred near Oruma community in the Niger Delta and ordered to install 'state of the art' leak detection system in their pipelines in the Oruma community within one year of the judgement[79] or face a steep penalty everyday they fail to do so once the year is up.[80] On the footsteps of this, in May 2021, the Hague District Court in *Milieudefensie & Others v RDS*[81] ordered

73 Mitchell Lennan, 'Evaluating the Effectiveness of the EU Environmental Liability and Environmental Crime Directives as Implemented by Scotland and the Rest of the United Kingdom' (2021) 24(1) J Int'l Wildl L Policy 26–37, 31.

74 ECD (n 69) art 3.

75 ECD (n 69) art 3(a)(b)(f)(h-i).

76 The Petroleum Production and Distribution (Anti Sabotage) Act, Cap P12, LFN 2004.

77 *Oguru and Milieudefensie v RDS and SPDC*, ECLI:NL: GHDHA:2021:132, paras 5.3–5.10

78 *Oguru and Milieudefensie v RDS and SPDC* (n 77).

79 *Oguru and Milieudefensie v RDS and SPDC* (n 77) para 6.43.

80 *Oguru and Milieudefensie v RDS and SPDC* (n 77) para 6.43.

81 *Milieudefensie & Others v RDS* – C/09/571932/HA ZA 19–379 (English version); ECLI:NL: RBDHA:2021:5337 (Dutch version) (26 May 2021)

RDS to reduce the carbon dioxide (CO^2)[82] emissions of the Shell group and those of its customers and suppliers by 45% by 2030 compared to 2019 levels, through the Shell group's corporate policy. Although carbon dioxide (a greenhouse gas) is not an ozone depleting substance, increase in its levels lead to decrease in the stratospheric ozone concentration resulting in global warming. Of note is that the EU ECD criminalises *the discharge or emission into air of materials which causes or is likely to cause substantial damage to air quality*[83](emphasis added) when it is done intentionally or at least with serious negligence.[84] So, the Hague district court's order in *Milieudefensie & Others v RDS* not only follows the Hague Appeals Court ruling in *Oguru v Shell* but also the requirement under the EU ECD.

Although the Directive adopts minimum standards, Member States have the option to introduce and maintain stricter standards. This has led to inconsistencies in the transposition of the ECD by EU Member States and significant variation in the determination of the exact meaning of terms like *negligible quantity, negligible impact, substantial damage,* and *significant deterioration*[85] across Member States of the EU. Member States are also left to define the exact meaning of 'serious negligence.'[86] As a result, there were differences and lack of clarity in the levels of criminal responsibilities and penalties provided by different EU Member State in their national legislations.[87] With this, the Directive failed to provide the harmony hoped for in handling environmental crime across the EU. To remedy this and improve uniformity as well as reduce cross-border enforcement issues relating to the Directive, the basis for criminal responsibility for environmental offence must be redefined and clarified.

Under the Directive, offences are punishable by 'effective, proportionate and dissuasive sanctions,'[88] mostly in form of fines. Although prison sentences are also available,[89] they are rarely imposed and rarely executed,[90] even though it has been determined to be the most effective deterrent against intentional and serious environmental crimes.[91] Fines are particularly ineffective as deterrent for corporate environmental crime because they are generally not high enough to deter corporations from such crimes. Besides, they could also be externalised to the consumers or passed on to shareholders. For more effective deterrent, punishment for corporate

82 Although carbon dioxide (a greenhouse gas) is not an ozone depleting substance, increase in its levels lead to decrease in the stratospheric ozone concentration.

83 ECD (n 69) art 3(a).

84 ECD (n 69) art 3(a) & 3(i).

85 ECD (n 69) art 3.

86 ECD (n 69) 29–30.

87 Elzbieta Zebek, 'Important Issues in Select European Union Countries' Criminal Environmental Law in Compliance with Directive 2008/99/EC' (2021) 2 Vestn St Peter Univer L 356–73.

88 ECD (n 69) arts. 5&7.

89 Carole M Billiet and Sandra Rousseau, 'How Real Is the Threat of Imprisonment for Environmental Crime?' (2014) 37 Eur J L Econ 183, 195.

90 Billiet and Rousseau (n 89) 197.

91 Jacob Oberg, 'Criminal Sanctions in the Field of EU Environmental Law' (2011) 2 New J Eur Crim L 402, 423.

environmental crime should target corporate executives who commit the crime for the benefit of the company.[92] The Directive appears to support this by providing that natural and legal persons can be held liable for environmental crime[93] where such offences have been committed for the benefit of the legal person (firm) by any person in a leading position within the firm, acting either individually or as part of an organ of the firm. This is because he has the authority to represent the firm, take decisions on its behalf or exercise control within it.[94] Also, the firm can be held liable where the lack of supervision or control by a person in authority made the commission of the offence possible for the benefit of the firm.[95] Additionally, the liability of firm under articles 6(1) & (2) does not exclude criminal proceedings against natural persons who are 'perpetrators, inciters, or accessories in the criminal offences or such persons who have aided and abated the commission of such offence.'[96] This means that corporate executives and the directing minds of the corporation who have acted on behalf of the corporation in furtherance of the commission of the environmental crime can be held responsible and personally liable for the offences of the corporation and breach of environmental duties under the Directive. This is commendable and would produce a more deterrent effect. In this regard, the Directive mirrors the Queensland CoRA.

7. Conclusion

The CDDCA Directive proposes the introduction of a *mandatory* corporate due diligence obligation to identify, assess, mitigate, and prevent the potential and/or actual adverse impacts of an undertaking's activities and those of its value chains on human rights and the environment.[97] By providing for mandatory corporate due diligence obligations, the Directive follows in the footsteps of the French Vigilance Law[98] enacted in 2017. Both laws impose a general mandatory due diligence requirement for human rights and environmental impact on multinational corporations, enjoining them to minimise the negative impact of their activities on human rights and the environment along their value chain.[99] However, neither of them provides for criminal liability nor for holding corporate executives personally liable for corporate wrongdoing. This is where the Queensland Chain of Responsibility Act (CoRA) and the EU Environmental Crime Directive come in. The Queensland Chain of Responsibility Act imposes a chain of responsibility on companies and 'related entities' to bear the cost of managing and rehabilitating contaminated

92 Oberg (n 91) 424.
93 ECD (n 69) arts. 2(d), 3 & 4.
94 ECD (n 69) art 6(1).
95 ECD (n 69) art 6(2).
96 ECD (n 69) art 6(3).
97 CDDCA Directive (n 4) art 1(2)
98 French Vigilance Law (n 17) art 1.
99 French Vigilance Law (n 17) art 1; CDDCA Directive (n 4) art 1.

sites[100] and prevent saddling the taxpayers with the clean-up bills. The CoRA targets related persons who stand to make large profits from the company's activities; and whose decisions have put the environment at risk.[101] However, under CoRA, a 'related person' considered culpable has an effective defence if he can prove that he has taken 'all reasonable steps in the circumstance' to ensure that the company is compliant or that it took all due care to avoid the harm in question.[102]

In 2008, the EU adopted the Environmental Crime Directive (ECD)[103] to criminalise environmental offences[104] and provide additional deterrence because the existing sectoral civil and administrative penalties and compensation systems have not been adequate to protect the environment.[105] However, the Directive adopted a minimum standard and gave the EU Member States the option to adopt a more stringent standard. This resulted in inconsistencies in the transposition of the Directive into national law by different EU Member States[106] and significant variation in the determination of what amounts to criminal responsibility.[107]

Consequently, there are differences in the levels of criminal penalties provided by different EU Member States in their national legislations and this raises cross-border enforcement issues.

In May 2024, the European Council adopted the CSDDD to advance mandatory and harmonised rule on corporate sustainability due diligence to instil responsible corporate behaviour in human rights and the environment in their operations and along their global value chain. Companies within the scope of the Directive are required to integrate due diligence into their policy and identify, monitor, prevent, or minimise potential and actual adverse human rights and environmental impacts in their operations and that of their global value chain. This is like the mandatory environmental due diligence but more focussed on sustainability.

The CDDCA Directive, the CSDDD, the CoRA, and the ECD have helped in various ways to protect the environment in the different jurisdictions in which they were meant to operate. They have also helped to provide guidance in holding corporation accountable for environmental damage and for pollution control. It is recommended that the ECOWAS sub-region or the AU should adopt similar regulations as the EU and Australia to curb corporate misconduct and negative impact on human rights and the environment. This is essential in view of numerous mining and oil exploration and production going on in Africa and its subregions and associated environmental degradation.

Although none of the legal frameworks discussed in this chapter could provide a complete solution to the problem of oil spills in the Niger Delta, holding the

100 The Guideline to the Chain of Responsibility Act (n 53) para 4.1.2, p. 11.
101 The Guideline to the Chain of Responsibility Act (n 53) para 1.0, p. 3.
102 The Guideline to the Chain of Responsibility Act (n 53) para 5.0, p. 15.
103 ECD (n 69).
104 ECD (n 69) art 1.
105 ECD (n 69) 3rd Preamble.
106 ECD (n 69) art 3.
107 ECD (n 69) art 3.

MNOCs that operate in that region to the standard provided by these frameworks would help in oil spill control and clean-up in the region. So, there is need to provide for mandatory corporate due diligence performance in the continent/region, apply it along the entire value/supply chain of the corporations in a way that would be binding on both the parent company and its subsidiaries.

9 Environmental Review of the Petroleum Industry Act (PIA) 2021 and Suggestions for Improvement

1. Introduction and Historical Perspective

The Nigerian petroleum industry has been poorly managed over the years and most of the laws regulating the industry were outdated and inconsistent with modern standards of managing petroleum exploration and production. As a result, a major overhaul of these laws was needed and the Petroleum Industry Bill (PIB) was, thus, conceived and drafted. It was intended to present a composite, comprehensive, and modern legal and regulatory framework for the Nigerian petroleum industry that will reflect its current needs and changing dynamics of the industry.[1]

The main objective of the PIB was to restructure and reform the regulatory and fiscal frameworks of the Nigerian petroleum industry in order to achieve transparency, efficiency, and growth and to maximise the benefits from the oil and gas industry in Nigeria.[2] It was also envisaged that the law will protect health, safety, and the environment in the course of petroleum operations, deal with funding challenges of the NNPC, and proffer solutions for the thorny issues associated with the host communities.[3] Additionally, it was hoped that the PIB will align the Nigerian oil and gas industry with international best practices and establish a favourable fiscal framework for Nigeria as well as a stable, globally competitive investment climate.[4] These and more are all laudable objectives and goals envisaged by the law, if passed.

The Bill has a long, winding history in Nigeria. Its origin dates back almost 25 years when President Olusegun Obasanjo set up the Oil and Gas Sector Reform Implementation Committee (OGIC) on 24 April 2000[5] headed by Dr Rilwanu

1 Victor Ndoma-Egba, 'An Overview of Parliamentary Debates of the Petroleum Industry Bill' Nigerian Bar Association (NBA) Conference, Abuja, Nigeria, 2015 at the Breakout Session on 'Legal and Regulatory Framework of the Petroleum Industry Bill in Nigeria: Review of Existing Laws and the Petroleum Industry Bill'.

2 PIB 2012, s. 1.

3 PIB 2012, s. 1.

4 Rilwanu Lukman, 'Keynote Address to the Industry by the Hon Minister of Petroleum Resources, Dr Rilwanu Lukman, on the Proposed Petroleum Industry Bill (PIB)' *Abuja* (16 July 2009).

5 Omowumi Iledare, 'An Appraisal of Oil and Gas Industry Reform and Institutional Restructuring in Nigeria' *International Association for Energy Economics*, Fourth Quarter 2008, 23, 23 <https://www.iaee.org/documents/newsletterarticles/408wumi.pdf> accessed 31 October 2024.

DOI: 10.4324/9781003435150-9

Lukman.[6] This committee was charged with the development of a policy framework for the petroleum industry in Nigeria. It later published the National Oil and Gas Policy (NOGP), which attempted to separate the institutions in charge of the commercial aspects of the oil and gas sector of the Nigerian economy from the regulatory and policy-making institutions. President Obasanjo was succeeded by President Umaru Musa Yar'Adua who reconstituted OGIC on 7 September 2007.[7] This led to the first draft of the PIB, which was first introduced to the Nigerian National Assembly in December 2008. However, the bill was stalled in the National Assembly for many years, unable to pass through the legislature, due, in part, to strong opposition from special interest groups, mainly the MNOCs.[8] They were opposed to the imposition of higher taxes, royalties, charges and penalties and failure to address oil theft/bunkering, corruption, oil pipeline vandalism/sabotage, and other security issues in the Niger Delta. There were also concerns about how the bill would impact good faith investments made under the existing petroleum law and the enormous powers the bill bestowed on the government.[9] The bill was reintroduced in the National Assembly in September 2012 during the tenure of President Goodluck Jonathan. It was extensively debated in February 2013, was read, and was referred to the Senate Joint Committee on Petroleum and the Judiciary for further action.[10] Unfortunately, progress was again stalled due to local, sectorial politics, the issue of the Petroleum Host Community Trust Fund and who benefits from it, as well as opposition from the MNOCs.

Apart from the intense debate and opposition from deep-rooted political and economic interests, it was difficult to harmonise all the disparate issues the bill sought to address, and consequently impossible to pass it in its composite form. The non-passage of the bill created uncertainty in the oil industry and stifled investment because investors were not sure what the new law would introduce. The composite bill was unbundled in 2015 into four separate parts to improve the chances of passage into law. by the National Assembly. These were:

1. Petroleum Industry Governance Bill (PIGB) – meant to update, reform, and modernise the Petroleum Act and replace its provisions with a current and more comprehensive petroleum industry law in line with global standards.
2. Petroleum Industry Administration Bill (PIAB) – focused on establishing a transparent and efficient management of petroleum exploration and production as well as the downstream administration of petroleum resources.
3. Petroleum Industry Fiscal Bill (PIFB) – covers financial terms and fiscal reforms relating to taxation, royalties, contractual terms, etc.

6 Dr Lukman was one of the longest-serving heads of both the Nigerian oil industry and OPEC. He served at the head of the two establishments for about 50 years.

7 Iledare (n 5) 23.

8 Olu Ojewale, 'The Gang-up against the PIB' *Realnews* (7 December 2012) <https://realnewsmagazine.net/featured/the-gang-up-against-the-pib/> accessed 31 October 2024.

9 Ojewale (n 8).

10 Ndoma-Egba (n 1).

4. Petroleum Host Community Bill (PHCB) – focussed on the rights of the host and impacted communities. It covers restitution for environmental damages and social costs of resource extraction operations.

The PIGB was the first of these bills to be presented to the Nigerian National Assembly for deliberation. It sought to provide governance and institutional framework for the Nigerian Petroleum Industry and create clear separation between the policy, regulatory, and commercial institutions.[11] It is also meant to promote transparency and accountability in the administration of petroleum resources of Nigeria and foster a conducive business environment for petroleum industry operations.[12] In essence, the PIGB (2017) was meant to update and replace the outdated Petroleum Act 1969 with a more comprehensive and current legal framework in line with global standards.

The Bill trimmed the enormous powers of the Minister,[13] assigning most of the duties performed by the Minister of Petroleum Resources to the Nigeria Petroleum Regulatory Commission (NPRC).[14] For instance, the power to grant, amend, renew, extend, or revoke any petroleum prospecting licence or petroleum mining lease required for petroleum exploration or production now inheres in the NPRC and not the Minister.[15] This is to ensure separation of duties and provide for checks and balances.[16] Also, the NPRC (and no longer the Minister) now oversee the strict implementation of environmental policies, laws, regulations, and standards as they relate to oil and gas operations in Nigeria.[17] The bill mandates that these functions be carried out in a transparent, non-discriminatory manner.[18]

At the time the PIB was being considered, the Department of Petroleum Resources (DPR), headed by the Minister of Petroleum Resources, was responsible for regulating all petroleum operations in Nigeria – issuing oil licenses and leases; overseeing the regulation and monitoring of Health, Safety and Environment (HSE) in the oil and gas industry; and generally monitoring compliance and enforcement of the petroleum laws, regulations, and guidelines in Nigeria. However, the Minister of Petroleum Resources also heads the NNPC.[19] This regulatory arrangement evinces a conflict of interest that the PIGB has tried to deal with by separating the commercial, policy, and regulatory duties of the petroleum institutions in Nigeria.

11 PIGB 2017 (Final Copy) 44, 178 <http://www.petroleumindustrybill.com/wp-content/uploads/2017/05/FINAL-COPY-OF-PETROLEUM-INDUSTRY-GOVERNANCE-BILL-2017-May-15.pdf> accessed 01 November 24.
12 PIGB 2017 (Final Copy) (n 11) Part 1.
13 PIGB 2017 (Final Copy) (n 11) Part 2, s. 2.
14 PIGB 2017 (Final Copy) (n 11) Part 3 – Nigeria Petroleum Regulatory Commission.
15 PIGB 2017 (Final Copy) (n 11) Part 2 – s 2(1)(h); s 6(s).
16 PIGB 2017 (Final Copy) (n 11) Part 2 – s 2(1)(h); s 6(s).
17 PIGB 2017 (Final Copy) (n 11) Part 2 – s 5(h), 6(5)(a)
18 PIGB 2017 (Final Copy) (n 11) Part 2 – s. 6(u)
19 NNPC Act, 1977 No 33, CAP N123, LFN 2004, ss. 10 & 11; G Etikerentse, *Nigerian Petroleum Law* (2nd edn, Dredew Publishers 2004) 21.

Structurally, the PIGB establishes the NPRC,[20] the Petroleum Equalisation Fund,[21] and the incorporation of three commercial entities created by unbundling the NNPC.[22] These are the Nigeria Petroleum Assets Management Company,[23] the National Petroleum Company,[24] and the Nigeria Petroleum Liability Management Company.[25] The NPRC serves as the supervisory body for the Nigerian oil and gas industry and was meant to consolidate the Petroleum Inspectorate, the DPR, and the Petroleum Products Pricing Regulatory Agency (PPPRA).[26]

Until the introduction of the PIA in 2021, the PIB 2012 remained the most comprehensive petroleum bill introduced to the Nigerian National Assembly. It generated an extraordinary amount of interest within and outside Nigeria due to the extent and full span of what it is expected to introduce. The delay in its passage made the oil industry nervous and has somehow stunted planning and investment in that sector because everybody was waiting to know how the new legislation will unfold. The Nigerian National Assembly passed the bill on 2 August 2021, and the president signed it into law on 16 August, thus, making the PIA 2021 the current law governing the Nigerian petroleum industry.

The next segment of this chapter will discuss and analyse the relevant portions of the PIA 2021. In line with the focus of this book, the analysis will be limited to the upstream sector of the Nigerian petroleum industry and to issues that relate to pollution control and environmental protection. To this end, it will focus principally on the objective, functions, and powers of the Nigerian Upstream Regulatory Commission (the Commission), the Nigerian National Petroleum Company Limited (NNPC Limited), Powers of the Minister of Petroleum Resources, Financial Contribution for Remediation of Environmental Damage, Abandonment, Decommissioning and Disposal, as well as Host Communities Development.

The PIA 2021 effectively overrides the PIB 2012 and the PIGB 2017 to become the new law governing the petroleum industry in Nigeria. The objective of the Act is to create efficient and effective governing institutions for the Nigerian petroleum industry with clear and separate roles for the petroleum industry; establish a framework for the creation of a commercially oriented and profit driven national petroleum company; promote transparency, good governance, and accountability in the administration of the petroleum resources in Nigeria; foster a business environment conducive for petroleum operations in Nigeria; and deepen local content practice in the Nigeria oil and gas industry.[27]

20 PIGB 2017 (n 11) Part 3.
21 PIGB 2017 (n 11) Part 4.
22 PIGB 2017 (n 11) Part 5.
23 PIGB 2017 (n 11) Part 6; Part 5, s. 37.
24 PIGB 2017 (n 11) Part 7; Part 5, s. 37.
25 PIGB 2017 (n 11) Part 7; Part 5, s. 86.
26 PIGB 2017 (n 11) Part 3, s. 4(3).
27 PIA 2021, s. 2.

2. Changes Introduced by the PIA 2021

2.1. The Power of the Minister of Petroleum Resources

Among others, the Act gives the Minister of Petroleum Resources power to formulate, monitor, and administer government policy for the petroleum industry; exercise general supervisory functions over the affairs and operations of the industry; and generally promote an enabling environment for investment in the Nigerian petroleum industry.[28] Although the Minister still retained the power to grant and revoke petroleum prospecting licences and petroleum mining leases, he *must* do so upon the advice of the Commission.[29] However, because the Minister exercises general supervisory power over the Commission, it is questionable how much difference from the status quo this change would make to the powers of the minister to grant and revoke petroleum licences. He would still be capable of exerting undue influence on members of the Commission and thereby still retain more powers than legitimately due to him in the granting and revocation of petroleum licences and leases. This may also negatively impact transparency and foster corruption in the administration of the petroleum resources of Nigeria. But in general, the PIA has assigned a considerable number of functions formally performed by the Minister to the Commission. Some of them are reviewed in the following sections:

2.2. Nigerian Upstream Regulatory Commission (The Commission)

The Commission is covered in Chapter One of the PIA 2021.[30] While section 4 deals with its establishment, section 6 enumerates its objectives. These include the responsibility to administer and enforce policies, laws, and regulations relating to all aspects of upstream petroleum operations and to ensure and enforce compliance with all the terms and conditions of all leases, licences, permits, and authorisations issued in respect of upstream petroleum operations.[31] Also, the Commission ensures that the upstream petroleum operations are carried out with minimal waste, and promote healthy, safe, efficient, and effective conduct of upstream petroleum operations in an environmentally acceptable and sustainable manner.[32] It shall implement government policies for upstream petroleum operations as directed by the Minister of Petroleum in accordance with the provisions of the Act;[33] promote an enabling environment for investment in upstream petroleum operations in Nigeria; and ensure strict implementation of environmental policies, laws, and regulations for upstream petroleum operations,[34] etc. Although the Commission appears to perform some of the functions formally performed by the DPR, the

28 PIA 2021, s 3(1)(a)(b) & (e).
29 PIA 2021, s. 3(1)(g)(h).
30 PIA 2021, Chapter 1, Part III, ss 4–28.
31 PIA 2021, s. 6(a)(b)
32 PIA 2021, s. 69(c)(d)
33 PIA 2021, s. 6(g)
34 PIA 2021, s. 6(h)(i).

function of the Commission under the PIA 2021 is to a great extent clearly delineated[35] to avoid the overlap with the functions of the National Oil Spill Detection and Response Agency (NOSDRA), which was a problem before now resulting in conflicts of interest between the DPR (the Upstream Inspectorate) and NOSDRA. For instance, previously, the DPR was responsible for monitoring and surveillance of the oil pipelines[36] from where most of the onshore oil spills come. This function was also that of the Upstream Inspectorate.[37] But it overlapped with the functions of the NOSDRA, which is statutorily charged with oil spill detection and response[38] and by extension also responsible for oil pipeline surveillance. This overlap results in conflict of interests between the DPR/Inspectorate and the NOSDRA. The PIA appears to have avoided this overlap and conflict of interests by clearly delineating the functions of the Commission.[39] However, potential overlap and conflict of roles have also been pointed out between the NOSDRA and the Hydrocarbon Pollution Remediation Project (HYPREP), an agency set up by the government in 2016 for the clean-up and remediation of Ogoniland and other contaminated sites in the Niger Delta following the UN Environment Programme (UNEP) recommendation in 2011.[40] Questions have been raised as to which of these two agencies is responsible for cleaning up freshly occurring spills in Ogoniland especially when the spills occur on already oil polluted land – re-pollution either from oil pipeline vandalism or illegal artisanal refineries.[41] The answer to this is unclear but most likely to be that of NOSDRA.

The PIA also provides that the Commission shall have powers to enforce the provisions of any regulation made for upstream petroleum operations;[42] set standards to promote the adoption of new technologies;[43] and issue guidelines in accordance with the provisions of this Act or any regulations in respect of the upstream petroleum operations;[44] etc. Under the PIGB, the Commission was allowed to retain 10% of the oil revenue to the detriment of the federal, state, and local governments. For this reason, among others, the president declined assent to the bill.[45] The PIA corrected this by providing for appropriation of funds to the Commission

35 PIA 2021, ss. 7, 8 & 9.

36 DPR Functions <https://dpr.gov.ng/functions-of-dpr/> accessed 25 August 2018; *Federal Government of Nigeria v Zebra Energy* (2002) 18 N.W.L.R. Part 798.

37 PIB 2012, ss. 41(2)(c).

38 NOSDRA (Establishment) Act (2006) s. 1<http://nosdra.gov.ng/PDF/nosdraact.pdf> accessed 25 February 2020.

39 PIA 2021, ss. 7–9.

40 UNEP Environmental Assessment of Ogoniland (2011) 9, 25, 167<https://www.unep.org/resources/report/environmental-assessment-ogoniland> accessed 19 December 2024.

41 K Sam, N Zabbey and AP Onyna, 'Implementing Contaminated Land Remediation in Nigeria: Insights from the Ogoni Remediation Project' (2022) 115 Land Use Policy 1, 5.

42 PIA (2021) s. 10(a)(i).

43 PIA (2021) s. 10(d).

44 PIA (2021) s. 10(f).

45 Paul Carsten, 'Nigeria's Presidency Rebuffs Landmark Oil Reform Bill in Current Form' *Reuters*(29August2018)<https://www.reuters.com/article/nigeria-oil/update-1-nigerias-presidency-rebuffs-landmark-oil-reform-bill-in-current-form-idUSL3N1VJ55M> accessed 01 November 24.

by the National Assembly with no specific percentage of the oil revenue attached. In addition to this, other sources of funds for the Commission include fees charged by the Commission for services rendered to licensees, lessees, permit holders, etc; income derived from publications made by the Commission; fees paid to the Commission for using facilities owned and managed by the Commission; etc.[46]

2.3. The Nigerian National Petroleum Company Limited (NNPCL)

The Nigerian National Petroleum Company Limited (NNPCL)[47] is an incorporated national oil company like any private corporation limited by shares and incorporated under the Companies and Allied Matters Act (CAMA).[48] This incorporation practically commercialises the Nigerian National Petroleum Corporation (NNPC)[49] making it a self-financing and self-governing commercial entity independent of the government management and oversight. However, the shares of NNPCL would still be 100% percent government owned.[50] Where the NNPCL has a participating interest or a 100% interest in a petroleum mining lease or petroleum prospecting licence, the company shall pay its share of all fees, rents, royalties, taxes, etc. to the government's Federal Inland Revenue Services (FIRS) as any company incorporated in Nigeria.[51] The NNPCL will be free to reinvest the money it generates and be free to borrow against their assets if they need to do so. They will pay only dividends into the Federation account and pay royalties and taxes to the Federal Inland Revenue Services (FIRS).[52] Although these are wonderful ideas, it remains to be seen how they will work in practice without 'fixing the leakages in the system.'[53] The NNPC is allegedly the most opaque oil company in the world.[54] Since one of the main objectives of the PIA is to 'promote transparency, good governance and accountability in the administration of the petroleum resources in Nigeria,'[55] efforts must be made to produce regulations and guidelines that would ensure a positive improvement on transparency and accountability in NNPCL to give the government and by extension Nigerians a good return on their investment.

The Minister of Petroleum Resources was to ensure that the NNPCL is incorporated within six months from the commencement of the PIA.[56] Within 18 months from the commencement of the Act, the Minister would liaise with the Minister

46 PIA (2021) s. 24(1)(2).
47 PIA 2021, Chapter 1, Part V, ss. 53–65.
48 PIA 2021, Chapter 1, Part V, ss. 52–65
49 Established under the NNPC Act (n 19) s. 1.
50 PIA 2021, s. 53(2)(3).
51 PIA 2021, s. 53(8)
52 PIA 2021, s. 53(8); s. 100(1).
53 Sanusi Lamido Sanusi, 'Why Is NNPC Not Bringing in Dollars?' (Channels TV) <https://www.youtube.com/watch?v=nk8pYIHybqk> accessed 30 June 2024.
54 Sanusi (n 53).
55 PIA 2021, ss. 2(c); 66(1)(f); 67;
56 PIA 2021, s. 53(1).

of Finance to ensure the full commercialisation of the NNPCL.[57] This requirement was complied with a ceremony at the NNPC(L) Towers, Abuja on Friday 17 February 2023.[58] So, the NNPCL was for all intents and purposes fully operational from that date.

Before the PIA 2021, the NNPC had unincorporated Joint Venture Agreements (JVs) and Joint Operating Agreements (JOAs) in the onshore and shallow water areas and Production Sharing Contracts (PSC) for the deep-water blocks. Unlike what is obtainable in many other national oil companies, for instance, in Algeria, Indonesia, Brazil, and Colombia,[59] the cash earned from these agreements and contracts is not available to the NNPC for investment but is deposited into the Federation Account. Then, like any other government department, the NNPC budget for new investments in oil exploration and production must be approved by the government and funded from the Federation Account. This was a very slow process that hindered the ability of NNPC to plan for timely investments as any independent and purely commercial entity would. It is also detrimental to pollution control since the NNPC with the controlling interest in all JVs and JOAs could not always meet cash calls or contribute its quota of funds for clean-up and other purposes relating to the management of the oil business.[60] This contributes to poor oil pipeline maintenance and the consequent oil spills in the Niger Delta. Shell has been known to insist that the government must contribute its own share to meet court-imposed fines for environmental infractions. For instance, in *Chief Pere Ajuwa & Others v Shell Petroleum Development Company Nig. Ltd*,[61] the Federal High Court imposed a judgement of $1.5 billion on Shell, and the company argued that if it must be complied with, the federal government must contribute its prorated portion of the sanction since it owns the controlling interest in the Joint Venture.

The PIA 2021 transforms the NNPC into a private oil company limited by shares, under the same terms and conditions as any other oil company in Nigeria. Thus, the

57 PIA 2021, s. 54.

58 The NNPCL was unveiled by the Nigerian President in July 2022. Its takeover of the NNPC commenced from that date and culminated on 17/02/23 with the full takeover of the assets of NNPC by the NNPCL in a ceremony at the NNPC(L) Towers, Abuja. This marked the birth of a fully commercialised NNPCL and the end of NNPC. Mary Izuaka, 'NNPC Limited Ends Operations as Government Corporation' *Premium Times* (18 February 2023) <https://www.premiumtimesng.com/news/top-news/582778-nnpc-limited-ends-operations-as-govt-corporation.html?tztc=1> accessed 17 December 2024.

59 Inter-Agency Team (IAT), 'Explanatory Memorandum on the Petroleum Industry Bill (PIB)' (2009) 94. https://vanmeursenergy.com/documents/GovernmentMemoOnPetroleumIndustryBill.pdf accessed 24 April 2025.

60 Richard Steiner, 'Double Standard: Shell Practices in Nigeria Compared with International Standards to Prevent and Control Pipeline Oil Spills and the Deepwater Horizon Oil Spill' (*Milieudefensie*, November 2010) 40–42 <https://www.foei.org/wp-content/uploads/2014/01/20101109-rapport-Double-Standard.pdf> accessed 19 December 2024. A specific example could be seen in the crude oil seepage at Shell's Bonny Oil and Gas Terminal Storage Tank 9 on 25 March 2017. The relevant tank has been due for repair for the past five years but this could not be done due to financial constraints. NOSDRA Report of the joint investigation visit of the oil spill incident number 2017–1826306 <https://oilspillmonitor.ng/#/61884.2017_1826306> accessed 19 December 2024.

61 *Ajuwa & Others v SPDC Nig. Ltd* (2011) 18 NWLR (Pt. 1279).

NNPCL and other parties to a joint operating agreement in respect to any upstream petroleum operations may on a voluntary basis restructure their JOA as a joint venture carried out by way of a limited liability company called an incorporated joint venture company (IJVC).[62] These shall not be subject to the provisions of the Fiscal Responsibility Act and the Public Procurement Act.[63] Like the NNPCL, they shall be independent entities – self-financing, self-governing companies with strong commercial orientation and able to generate and manage their cash flow independent of the government. They would have a transparent company operation for the IJVC shareholders with clear rules of accountability.[64] Their revenue will no longer go to the Federation Account, and they would be free to reinvest the money they generate and borrow against their assets if they need to do so. It is envisaged that the newly formed NNPCL will be able to generate enough funds to meet its cash obligations and, thus, satisfy the polluter-pays principle regarding oil pollution in the Niger Delta.

2.4. Powers of the Minister of Petroleum Resources to Grant and Revoke Petroleum Prospecting Licence or Petroleum Mining Lease

The PIA 2021 recognises three type of petroleum licences namely, the petroleum exploration licence, the petroleum prospecting licence, and the petroleum mining lease.[65] A licence or lease may be granted only to a company incorporated under the CAMA and validly existing in Nigeria.[66] The Commission shall be responsible for granting petroleum exploration licences,[67] while the Minister is responsible for granting petroleum prospecting licences and petroleum mining leases on the recommendation of the Commission.[68]

The PIA 2021 provides that upon the written recommendation of the Commission, the Minister of petroleum resources may revoke a petroleum prospecting licence or petroleum mining lease if the licensee or lessee fails to comply with environmental obligations required by applicable law or by the provisions of the applicable licence or lease.[69] This is commendable although there is always a reluctance in the Nigerian petroleum industry to revoke a licence or lease in view of the strategic position of oil in the Nigerian economy and the government's interest in the continuous flow of oil. Other grounds of revocation include where the applicable licensee or lessee fails to conduct petroleum operations in accordance with *good international petroleum industry practices*, the provisions of the PIA, and any other relevant legislation.[70]

62 PIA 2021, s. 65(1).
63 PIA 2021, s. 65(2).
64 PIA 2021, s. 65(3).
65 PIA 2021, s. 70(1).
66 PIA 2021, s. 70(2).
67 PIA 2021, s. 71(1).
68 PIA 2021, s. 3(1)(g).
69 PIA 2021, s. 96(1)(i); s. 120(h)
70 PIA 2021, s. 96(1)(a).

Under the PIA (2021), the clause *good international petroleum industry practices* means:

> Those uses and practices that are, at the time in question, generally accepted in the international petroleum industry as being good, safe, economical, *environmentally sound* and efficient in petroleum operations and should reflect standards of service and technology that are either state-of-the-art or otherwise appropriate to the operations in question and should be applied using standards in all matters that are no less rigorous than those in use by petroleum companies in global operations.[71]

Petroleum Act 1969 referred to the term as 'good oil field practice.'[72] Under this Act, the Minister 'may direct in writing the suspension of any operations which *in his opinion* are not being conducted in accordance with good oil field practice.'[73] He may also revoke any oil prospecting licence or oil mining lease if *in his opinion* the licensee or lessee is not conducting the operations in accordance with good oil field practice. It is noteworthy that the Minister's decision is based solely on his opinion under the 1969 Act. Also, while the 1969 Petroleum Act did not define 'good oil field practice,' the Mineral Oils (Safety) Regulations, 1997, provides that, every petroleum operation, production, and distribution shall be considered adequate if it conforms with the appropriate current Institute of Petroleum safety codes,[74] the American Petroleum Institute (API) codes, and the American Society of Mechanical Engineer (ASME) Codes or any other internationally recognised and accepted systems. Although these institutes publish internationally recognised codes of good oil field practice, these codes are usually tailored towards the provision of specifications for oilfield hardware[75] and are normally interpreted with reference to these specifications.[76] They generally do not relate to environmental standards. In the light of the massive environmental pollution that comes with oil exploration and production, the effects on human health, the ecosystem, and climate change, 'good oil field practice' must be redefined and interpreted to embody the concept of environmental protection and sustainability. This will force the oil companies to adopt pollution-prevention or pollution-reduction methods of oil exploration, production, and distribution and support the achievement of sustainable cities and communities.[77] The PIA (2021) filled this gap by providing a definition of 'good international petroleum industry practice' that includes the concept of environmentally sound petroleum operations.

71 PIA 2021, s. 318.

72 Petroleum Act 1969, s. 8(1)(g) and s. 25(1)(a)(iii); PIB 2012, s. 362.

73 Petroleum Act 1969, s. 8(1)(g).

74 Institute of Petroleum is now renamed Energy Institute, London.

75 Michael AG Bunter, 'World-wide Standards of Good Oilfield Practice . . . the Impact of the Blow-out, Deaths and Spills at the BP Macondo Well, the MC 252/1–01, US Gulf of Mexico' (2013) 11(2) Oil Gas Energy L 3.

76 Bunter (n 75) 3.

77 UN Sustainable Development Goal (SDG) 11.

2.5. Environmental Management Plan

Under the PIA 2021, a licensee or lessee who engages in upstream petroleum operations shall within one year of the effective date of the extant Acts – or six months after the grant of the applicable licence or lease – submit for approval an environmental management plan with respect to projects that require environmental impact assessment to the Commission.[78] This plan shall be in accordance with the existing Acts. The Commission shall approve the environmental management plan if it complies with relevant environmental Acts and the applicant has the capacity or has provided for the capacity to rehabilitate and manage negative impacts on the environment.[79] This is an improvement on the Petroleum Act 1969, which has no requirement for an elaborate environmental management plan. However, section 102(1) of the PIA gives licensees and lessees up to one year from the commencement of the extant Acts to submit a plan or six months from the date of the grant of the license or lease to submit such a plan. While one year may be adequate for the already existing licensees and lessees to come up with a plan, having an environmental management plan should be made a condition precedent to the grant of the licence or lease to the new applicants for such licences or leases. This would be weighed against relevant environmental impact assessment of the project to ensure that the environmental management plan could help to reduce or, in some cases, eliminate the negative impacts of the project.

Section 102(3)(b) of the Act provides that the Commission shall not approve the environmental management programme unless the applicant has the capacity or has provided for the capacity to rehabilitate and manage the negative impacts on the environment. This appears nebulous when read together with subsection (1), which allows the new licensees and lessees six months from the date of grant of the licence or lease to submit a plan. It leaves one to wonder what will happen if the environmental management plan is not approved. Since no sanction is provided, will that be a ground for revocation of a freshly granted licence or lease? Also, since there is always a reluctance in the industry to revoke a licence or lease in view of the huge sums of money often already invested in the business and the fact that oil is the mainstay of the Nigerian economy, it makes sense to demand that the capacity to rehabilitate and manage the negative impacts on the environment be made a condition precedent for granting the licence or lease.

2.6. Financial Contribution for Remediation of Environmental Damage

Section 103 of the PIA 2021 provides for financial contribution for remediation of environmental damage. Prior to the approval of an environmental management plan by the Commission, this section mandates a licensee or lessee to pay a prescribed financial contribution to an *environmental remediation fund* established

78 PIA 2021, s. 102(1)(2).
79 PIA 2021, s. 102(3).

by the Commission for the rehabilitation or management of the negative environmental impacts relating to the licence or lease.[80] The Petroleum Act 1969 has no such provision, so it is a welcome addition to the PIA 2021. It is comparable to the recommendation of the UNEP after its environmental assessment of Ogoniland in 2011. The UN agency recommended that an *Environmental Restoration Fund* for Ogoniland be set up with an initial capital of USD 1 billion to be contributed by the oil industry and the government.[81] Also, the EU Environmental Liability Directive (ELD), based on the polluter-pays principle, requires an operator to provide prior security (funds) for any pollution event from his operations.[82] This could cover oil spills. Where the licensee or lessee fails to rehabilitate or to manage any negative impact on the environment or is unable to undertake such rehabilitation, the Commission may, upon written notice to such licensee or lessee, use all or part of the environmental remediation fund contributed by the licensee or lessee to rehabilitate or manage the negative environmental impact in question.[83] This provision ensures that funds are always available for clean-up of environmental pollution and that such clean-up is done. However, the provision is weak and lacks clarity to the extent that it fails to state what will happen if there are insufficient funds for clean-up in the Environmental Remediation Fund. It is recommended that where the fund is insufficient to meet the remediation costs, the parent company of the immediate polluter[84] and/or all relevant group members to which the immediate polluter belongs, as well as all companies/entities 'associated with' the immediate polluter, be held liable to provide the additional funds needed especially if they have been found to have managed or controlled the immediate polluter.[85] This will broaden the liability group and ensure that funds are made available for oil spill clean-up and environmental remediation.[86]

The Act also provides that the size of the operation and level of environmental risks that may exist shall be taken into consideration in determining the amount of the financial contribution.[87] A licensee or lessee is required to assess its environmental liability annually and to increase its financial contribution. Where the Commission is not satisfied with the assessment and financial contribution, the Commission may appoint an independent assessor to conduct the assessment and

80 PIA 2021, s. 103(1).

81 UNEP Environmental Assessment of Ogoniland (n 40) 15.

82 Directive 2004/35/CE, 2004 (ELD) art 27.

83 PIA 2021, s. 103(4)

84 *Oguru and others v Shell Petroleum NV and others,* ECLI:NL: GHDHA: 2021:133 on 29 January 2021.

85 Millicent Ele, 'Oil Spills in the Niger Delta-Does the Petroleum Industry Act 2021 Offer Guidance for Solving this Problem?' (2022) 13(1) J Sustain Dev L Policy, 130, 151; *Vedanta Recourses Plc & Another v Lungowe & Others* [2019] UKSC 20, para 49.

86 For further analysis, see, Ele (n 85); and Millicent N Ele, 'Cleaning Up the Oil Spill Mess in the Niger Delta with Insights from the Contaminated Land Regimes in the UK and the US' (2021) 7(1) IELR 134.

87 PIA 2021, s. 103(2).

determine the financial contribution.[88] This is an unnecessarily long process that will not augur well for the environment. It is recommended instead that an independent assessor or *standards organisation* be used from the beginning to do the assessment at pre-determined intervals – for example, once every year or every other year – and that specific amounts of contribution be imposed when a predetermined threshold or marker is exceeded. Also, where the licensee has had recurrent oil spills from its pipelines and facilities, the volume of the spill and the length of time before containment should be taken into consideration in determining the amount to be paid into the Fund subsequently. This is because such recurrent spill is an indication that the licensee's or lessee's operation is at a much higher risk of causing environmental damage than any average licensee or lessee in its category. The assessor's fees should be paid from the Environmental Remediation Fund and factored into the relevant licensee's or lessee's contribution. This will render subsection (6) of section 103 of the Act null and void and of no effect. It is hoped that the Environmental Remediation Funds scheme will be managed in such a way to always provide enough funds for cleaning up oil spills and for the remediation of the environment.

2.7. Abandonment, Decommissioning, and Disposal

Decommissioning of oil asset installations in Nigeria was not provided for under the 1969 Petroleum Act but was largely covered under the Environmental Guidelines and Standards for Petroleum Industry in Nigeria (EGASPIN), Part VIIIG.

Under the PIA 2021, decommissioning and abandonment is defined as:

> The approved process of cessation of operations of crude oil and natural gas wells, installations, plants and structures, including shutting down an installation's operations and production, total or partial removal of installations and structures where applicable, chemicals and all such other materials handling, removal and disposal of debris and removed items, *environmental restoration of the area* after removal of installations, plants, and structures[89] (Emphasis added).

The foregoing definition shows that the process of decommissioning and abandonment under the PIA[90] includes environmental restoration of the relevant area. The PIA 2021 elaborately covered decommissioning under sections 232 and 233 comprising 26 subsections. Under Section 232(1), the decommissioning and abandonment of petroleum wells, installations, pipelines, etc. onshore and offshore must be conducted in accordance with good international petroleum industry practice[91] and

88 PIA 2021, s. 103(5)(6)

89 PIA 2021, s. 318.

90 PIA 2021, s. 318.

91 This term, synonymous with 'good oil field practice' under the old Petroleum Act 1969, was defined in s. 318 of the PIA 2021.

guidelines issued by the Commission. The PIA requires that such guidelines meet the standards prescribed by the international maritime organisation on offshore petroleum installations and structures.[92]

It is the duty of the Commission to approve the process of decommissioning or abandonment of oil asset infrastructure.[93] A licensee or lessee may by written notice inform the Commission of its intension to decommission or abandon petroleum operations.[94] Following this notice, the licensee or lessee shall submit to the Commission a programme setting out the cost estimate for the decommissioning, detailed measure to be taken and clear description of the method to be employed for the decommissioning process in line with good international petroleum industry practices and environmental development.[95] This sensitivity to environmental protection and sustainability is commendable. The Act also requires the licensee or lessee to ensure proper maintenance and safeguard of installation and structures in deep and ultra-deepwater environments that have either fallen into disuse or where residues remain after the installations and structures have been partially removed. Any residual liability or damages arising from such structures or their residue remains with the licensee or lessee.[96]

The Act also provides that the potential for reuse of the facility or pipeline in connection with further hydrocarbon developments is considered before decommissioning.[97] This aligns with recycling, reuse, and proper waste management, which are fundamental principles of good environmental practice. The Commission is also enjoined to consider and compare all feasible decommissioning options and that any decision to leave an installation, structure, or pipeline *in situ* (in place) should be made carefully with due consideration to its deterioration and effects on the environment both presently and in future.[98]

The PIA 2021 gives the Commission the power *to recall* any licensee or lessee responsible for the decommissioning or abandonment programme regarding a licence or lease that has expired to carry out its decommissioning and abandonment obligations. This holds true even if the licensee or lessee has sold its interest in the installation or structure *unless* the new company that acquired the property assumed all decommissioning obligations with the approval of the Commission.[99] The UK has a similar but more elaborate call-back provision. The Secretary of State for the Department of Business Energy and Industrial Strategy (BEIS)[100]

92 PIA 2021, s 232(1)
93 PIA 2021, s. 232(2)(3).
94 PIA 2021, s. 232(5).
95 PIA 2021, s. 232(6).
96 PIA 2021, s. 232(6)(d).
97 PIA 2021, s. 232(10)(a)(b)
98 PIA 2021, s. 232(10)(c)(d)(e).
99 PIA 2021, s. 232(13).
100 BEIS replaced the Department of Business, Innovation and Skills (BIS) and the Department of Energy and Climate Change (DECC) in July 2016. However, in February 2023, BEIS was replaced by the Department for Business and Trade (DBT), and the Department for Energy Security and Net Zero (DESNZ) and the Department for Science, Innovation and Technology (DSIT).

issues a notice for decommissioning of an installation under section 29 of the UK Petroleum Act, 1998 to every current or past operator or corporate body that has or has had an equity interest in the infrastructure to be decommissioned and any such section 29 notice holder is obligated to carry out the decommissioning programme. The UK position has a broader pool of responsible parties and thus provides a better assurance that the decommissioning must be done. Section 34 of the UK Petroleum Act, 1998 gives the Secretary of State for BEIS the *call-back power* and enables him to call back and impose decommissioning liability on a section 29 notice holder formerly discharged of its decommissioning obligations due to sale and withdrawal of the notice by the Secretary of State. The withdrawn notice could be re-served under section 34 and decommissioning liability re-imposed on a licensee notwithstanding the fact that such licensee has no existing interest in the asset or installation in question. This is not popular with the industry because it means that in the UK, a section 29 notice holder is potentially liable for decommissioning until it is done. However, the UK position provides better assurance that the decommissioning will be done. It is nevertheless important to note that in the UK, an operator cannot be held responsible for the decommissioning of oil asset infrastructure that was not in existence when he possessed interest in the relevant property.[101] Under the PIA 2021, section 232(13) mirrors the *call-back* provision under section 34 of the UK Petroleum Act 1998 but it is not quite as broad as section 34 because a licensee or lessee that has been formally discharged by the Commission either due to sale or divestment cannot be called back as long as the current owner of the property took up the decommissioning obligation with the approval of the Commission at the point of transfer of the assets. With the current divestment of onshore and shallow water petroleum assets going on in the Niger Delta as Shell and the other MNOCs move offshore, this may present a problem in future when the small indigenous oil companies acquiring such assets from the oil majors may lack the financial resources to carry out the decommissioning.

The Commission is mandated under the Act to ensure that a proper record of all petroleum installations, structures, and pipelines, and their status is kept and made public.[102] This is commendable because it makes records available to enable a proper allocation of decommissioning responsibility, a recall for decommissioning where necessary, and assistance in proper allocation of oil spill clean-up liability. Additionally, it will enhance research and corelation between the relative age of pipelines/oil infrastructure and oil spills in Nigeria and help to clarify how much the age of the pipeline, as opposed to corrosion, maintenance, and even change in ownership, contributes to oil spills.

The Act mandates the Commission to require a licensee and lessee to set up and manage *an abandonment fund* to be used by the licensee/lessee for the purpose of abandonment, decommissioning, and disposal with the approval of the

101 *Apache UK Investment Ltd v Esso Exploration and Production UK Ltd* [2021] EWHC 1283 (Comm); [2021] 4 W.L.R. 85.

102 PIA, 2021 s. 232(14).

Commission.[103] Such funds shall be accessible to the Commission in case the licensee/lessee fails to carry out the obligations under the Act.[104] This is a good backup security that will ensure that the decommissioning is done.

2.8. Host Communities Development

The PIA 2021 provides for the development of host communities.[105] The objective is to promote sustainable prosperity within the host communities; provide direct social and economic benefits from petroleum operations to host communities; enhance peaceful and harmonious co-existence between licensees/lessee and the host communities; and create a framework to support the development of host communities.[106]

Under the PIA,[107] the term 'host communities' means 'communities situated in or appurtenant to the area of operation of a settlor, and any other community *as a settlor may determine* under chapter 3 of this Act' (emphasis added) while a 'settlor' is 'a holder of an interest in a petroleum prospecting licence or petroleum mining lease whose area of operation is located in, or appurtenant to any community or communities.'[108]

The PIA also introduced the incorporation of Host Communities Development Trusts (HCD Trusts)[109] to be funded by contributions from settlors/MNOCs and donations, gifts, grants, or honoraria made to specific trust funds.[110]

The definition of 'host communities' is problematic in its scope because it appears to include as host community only the communities whose land has been annexed by the government and ceded to the settlor for oil exploration and production. This is likely to exclude some oil impacted communities from host communities, making them ineligible to benefit from the HCD Trust. A community may neither be in the operational area of a settlor nor appurtenant to it but nevertheless *impacted* by oil exploration and production. In fact, some communities in the Niger Delta do not have pipelines traversing their land neither are they oil producing, but they are nonetheless impacted by oil spills that may have flowed to their land. Where the spill is in the creeks or has flowed into the creeks, it is normally carried far beyond the place in which it originated.[111] This way they pollute the domestic water supply of distant communities downstream and impact their health even though they are far from the spill point.

103 PIA 2021, s. 233(1).
104 PIA 2021, s. 233(3).
105 PIA 2021, ss 234–57.
106 PIA 2021, s. 234(1).
107 Neither the PIB nor the PIGB proffered a definition for 'host community' and 'settlor.'
108 PIA 2021, s. 318.
109 PIA 2021, s. 235
110 PIA 2021, s. 240.
111 The Bayelsa State Oil and Environmental Commission (BSOEC) Interim Report (1 Nov 2019) 9 <https://www.bayelsacommission.org/news/november-2019-interim-report/> accessed 01 November 24.

Secondly, while the idea of setting up a Trust is fresh and commendable, one issue that may arise relates to which community qualifies as 'host community' for purposes of benefiting from the HCD Trust. The PIA 2021[112] appears to give the settlor (oil company) the authority to make this determination. In section 318, 'host communities' means communities situated in or appurtenant to the area of operation of a settlor, and *any other community as a settlor may determine* under Chapter 3 of this Act. 'For settlors operating in shallow water and deep offshore, the littoral communities and any other community *determined by the settlors* shall be host communities for the purposes of this Act'[113] (emphasis added). This means that the settlors are responsible in part for determining which community qualifies as host community and thus could benefit from the Trust. While international law and oceanography may provide guidance on the interpretation of littoral zones and by extension littoral communities, the PIA did not provide any objective blueprint to guide the settlors' determination of which community could be included as host community. This arguably leaves the determination of the host community to the subjective discretion of the settlor. The danger is that members of any community that feel 'unjustly' disenfranchised from benefiting from the HCD Trust because they have been excluded as host community may still form militant groups to sabotage the smooth running of petroleum operations in the Niger Delta.

The Act provides that the settlor shall incorporate host community development trust (the Trust) for the benefit of the host communities for which the settlor is responsible.[114] Where there are multiple settlors operating under a JOA with respect to upstream operations, the operator appointed under the agreement shall be responsible for compliance with this requirement on behalf of the other settlors.[115] For the purposes of setting up the Trust, the settlor shall, in consultation with the host communities, appoint and authorise a board of trustees ('The Board of Trustees'), which shall apply to be registered by the Corporate Affairs Commission (CAC) as a corporate body under the Companies and Allied Matter Act.[116]

The Act empowers the Commission to make regulations relating to the host community development on areas within its competence and jurisdiction including regulations to establish a grievance mechanism to resolve dispute between settlors and host communities.[117] The Commission shall also make regulations on the administration; guide and safeguard the utilisation of the trust fund; and have the oversight responsibility for ensuring that the projects proposed by the Board of Trustees are implemented.[118] The settlor shall undertake needs assessment that will turn into the community development plan for the purpose of determining the projects to be undertaken by the HCD Trust.[119]

112 PIA 2021, ss 235(3) and 318
113 PIA 2021, s. 235(3).
114 PIA 2021, s. 235(1).
115 PIA 2021, s. 235(2).
116 PIA 2021, s. 235(4).
117 PIA 2021, s. 234(2)(3).
118 PIA 2021, s. 235(6).
119 PIA 2021, s. 235(7).

The HCD Trust is a wonderful idea but the power in setting up the Trust and making decisions on how to utilise the fund is so heavily skewed in favour of the settlor/oil company that it is doubtful if it would do much to arrest the endemic oil pipeline sabotage and the consequent sabotage spills going on in the Niger Delta. It is hoped that subsequent regulations and guidelines covering the issue of host communities and the HCD Trust would provide more clarifications and guidance on them. For instance, there is need to provide clear outline on parameters that must be considered and shown to have been considered by the settlor in making the determination of which communities qualify as host communities.

In an additional attempt to discourage oil pipeline sabotage and prevent sabotage spills, the PIA 2021 provides that where an act of vandalism, sabotage, or other civil unrest occurs that causes damage to petroleum facilities or disrupts oil production within the host communities, the community shall forfeit its entitlement to the Trust fund to the extent of the amount it would cost to repair the damage that resulted from the activity.[120] This provision unjustifiably saddles the host community with the obligation to guard oil pipelines and denies them their entitlement under the HCD Trust if they fail to discharge this wrongfully imposed duty. This is both unfair and unwarranted because it is not the duty of the host community to monitor and protect the oil pipelines. This duty belongs to the owners of the pipelines and infrastructure, *to wit*, the oil companies.[121] However, since the issue of security is a matter for the State in most countries including Nigeria, protecting the oil infrastructure should be the dual responsibility of the MNOCs and the government. It is also particularly unjust to place this responsibility on the host community because the community may not know and may not have colluded with the saboteurs.

3. Areas Not Covered Under the PIA 2021

3.1. Establishment of Environmental Courts and Tribunals

The opportunity to provide for the establishment of environmental courts and tribunals was missed in the PIA 2021. Court congestion and delay especially in environmental and oil pollution matters in the Niger Delta suggest the need for the creation of environmental courts and tribunals (ECTs) to handle environmental and oil pollution matters in Nigeria expeditiously. Scholars have recommended different forms of ECTs. For instance, the establishment of a specialised court for adjudicating the impact of oil spills in Nigeria or the designation of special divisions within the already existing Federal High Courts[122] to handle environmental

120 PIA 2021, s. 257(2)(3).

121 *Bodo v Shell* [2014] EWHC 1973 (TCC).

122 Oil pollution matters are currently adjudicated at the FHC in Nigeria. Constitution of the FRN 1999 (as amended) s. 251(1)(n) and Second Schedule to the 1999 Constitution, Part I, Item 39; *SPDC Ltd* v *Abel Isaiah and others* (2001) 11 NWLR (Pt. 723) 168.

and oil pollution cases in Nigeria.[123] Akinseye Akinteye called this a Black Bench Division within the FHC in oil producing States in Nigeria.[124] This will make use of already existing infrastructure, and judges with relevant expertise will be assigned to that division.[125] Besides, it can be created by the Chief Justice/Judge in an internal management process within their administrative competence and without the need to go through the executive and the legislature. It will also save money. Others have advocated for courts dedicated solely for trying environmental crimes and injustices[126] while others recommend specialised adjudicatory bodies for all environmental matters both civil and criminal.[127] Any of these variants would be a good starting point in Nigeria because it will focus attention on environmental and oil pollution matters in the country,

Research suggests that the establishment of ECTs would help to reduce delays in the adjudicatory process[128] and improve greater efficiency in case management[129] and in the quality of judgment. It will also improve access to justice in environmental and oil pollution matters[130] and enable the development of environmental laws and regulations, thereby accelerating reform and growth in environmental jurisprudence.[131] This is because such courts or division of the FHC would be populated by judges with knowledge and interest in environmental law and related areas of law.[132] In view of the gridlock that may visit the passage of huge legal reforms in the Nigerian National Assembly, it may be more pragmatic to carve out a special division within the already existing Federal High Courts in Nigeria to handle environmental and oil pollution cases. This should be considered whenever the PIA is due for review or through subsequent regulations.

123 Akinseye Akinteye, 'Adjudicating the Impact of Oil Spills in Nigeria: The Need for Black Benches in Oil Producing States' (2018) 16(1) Oil Gas Energy L 2.

124 Akinteye (n 123) 1–22.

125 Akinteye (n 123) 14, 'Black' Bench is used here to depict 'oil' as opposed to 'Green,' which is normally used to represent environmental concerns.

126 Evan Hamman, Reece Walters & Rowena Maguire, 'Environmental Crime and Specialist Courts: The Case for a 'One-Stop (Judicial) Shop' in Queensland' (2015) 27 Current Issues Crim Just 59

127 George Pring and Catherine Pring, 'Environmental Courts & Tribunals: A Guide for Policy Makers' (2016) United Nations Environment Programme <https://wedocs.unep.org/bitstream/handle/20.500.11822/10001/environmental-courtstribunals.pdf?sequence=1&isAllowed=y>accessed 21 January 24. Pring G and Pring C, 'Greening Justice: Creating and Improving Environmental Courts and Tribunals' *The Access Initiative, World Resources Institute* (2009) <https://www.eufje.org/images/DocDivers/Rapport%20Pring.pdf> accessed 21 January 2024.

128 Brian Preston, 'Operating an Environment Court: The Experience of the Land and Environment Court of New South Wales' (2012) 29 Pace Environ L Rev 46.

129 Don C Smith, 'Environmental Courts and Tribunals: Changing Environmental and Natural Resources Law around the Globe' (2018) 36(2) J Energy Nat Resources L 137–40.

130 Anders Bengtsson, 'Specialised Courts for Environmental Matters – The Swedish Solution' (2017) 29(3) ELM 115.

131 Akinteye (n 123) 1, 12.

132 Bengtsson (n 130) 126; Akinteye (n 123) 8.

3.2. Company Law and Parent Company Guarantees

Transnational corporations including MNOCs operate globally, often with negative impact on the environment. Without effective regulation to hem them in, these negative impacts will only increase.[133] The MNOCs that operate in Nigeria do so through their local subsidiaries[134] because the Nigerian law *requires* that all foreign companies desiring to do business in the country be reincorporated in Nigeria.[135] This requirement is maintained under the new PIA 2021.[136] Therefore, in line with the Common Law doctrine articulated in *Salomon v Salomon*,[137] all subsidiaries of the MNOCs in Nigeria are usually wholly incorporated Nigerian corporations with separate legal personalities from their parent MNOCs.

Presently in Nigeria, a parent MNC can only share in the subsidiary's pollution liability if it is found to have participated in the pollution process. This participation is evinced where the parent company *controls* or shares control of the material operations of the subsidiary and not merely because it is a majority shareholder of the company.[138] When this control is established, duty of care is imposed on the parent company in favour of the claimants making the company liable to share in the pollution liability of the subsidiary.[139] The extent to which the parent intervenes in, controls, or supervises the management of the relevant operations of the subsidiary is a question of fact.[140] The parent company could be liable as a co-polluter possessing duty of care to the claimants even if it has only a *de facto* control, for example, where it manages or takes part in the management of part of the subsidiary's activities such as pipeline operations, while the subsidiary maintains full *de jure* control of the company.[141] This means that duty of care could still be imposed on the parent company irrespective of the separate legal personality of the subsidiary company as long as the parent company satisfies the requirement of 'control' albeit *de facto*. To this extent, reincorporation and separate legal personalities of the parent and subsidiary companies are irrelevant when the issue relates to parent company accountability for the pollution liabilities of the subsidiary company.

Non-provision for a parent company guarantee in the PIA 2021 was another missed opportunity. A parent company guarantee is a form of undertaken by the

133 Evaristus Oshionebo, *Regulating Transnational Corporations in Domestic and International Regimes – An African Case Study* (University of Toronto Press 2009) 3.

134 Royal Dutch Shell operates through Shell Petroleum Development Company (SPDC) and Shell Nigeria Exploration and Production Company Limited (SNEPCO); ExxonMobil operates through Mobil Producing Nigeria Unlimited (MPN) and Esso Exploration & Production Nigeria Limited (EEPNL) etc.

135 Companies and Allied Matters Act (CAMA) Cap 59, LFN 1990, s 54; Petroleum Act 1969, Cap P10, LFN 2004, s. 2(2) (now replaced by the new PIA).

136 PIA 2021, s. 70(2).

137 *Salomon v Salomon* [1897] AC 22

138 *Vedanta v Lungowe* (n 85) para 49.

139 *Okpabi and Others v RDS plc and SPDC (Nig) Ltd* [2021] UKSC 3; *Oguru v Shell* (n 84).

140 *Okpabi v Shell* [2021] (n 139) para 44.

141 *Okpabi v Shell* [2021] (n 139) para 147.

parent company to answer for or assume specified liabilities of the subsidiary, under the main contract. The provision of a parent company guarantee would afford the court the chance to examine the nature and content of this guarantee in the light of the liability in issue. For instance, the Nigerian Model Production Sharing Contract 2005 mandates the submission of a parent company guarantee, valid for up to five years beyond the term of the contract, to the NNPC.[142] Some of these guarantees come in the form of assurances to provide technical and financial resources that the subsidiary may need in order to meet their obligations under the contract in a timely manner.[143] Since oil spill is an obvious risk in petroleum exploration and production[144] and its clean-up, the obligation of the oil company, it stands to reason that the liability for oil spill clean-up should have been included as one of the guarantees covered by the parent company under the PIA. The provision of a parent company guarantee covering obligations in connection to the petroleum operations is a mandatory requirement for subsidiary companies on the Norwegian Continental Shelf (NCS).[145] It is recommended that Nigeria adopt this model and include it in the PIA when it is up for review.

From its effective date, the PIA 2021 would repeal about eight existing laws including the NNPC Act.[146] There is, however, the savings provision under section 311 of the PIA, which provides that any Act, subsidiary legislation or regulation, guideline, directive, or order made under any principal legislation repealed or amended by the PIA remain in force to the extent that it is not inconsistent with the Act.[147] This means that the EGASPIN and all regulations made under the old Petroleum Act survived except portions that are inconsistent with the PIA 2021.

4. Conclusion

This chapter was devoted to the analysis and review of the Petroleum Industry Act 2021. In line with the focus of this book, this analysis was limited to the sections that relate to pollution control and environmental protection in the upstream petroleum sector of the Nigerian oil and gas industry. Beginning with a brief historical journey of the PIB/PIGB that culminates in signing the PIA into law, the chapter critically analysed some of the provisions of the Act.

Some of the highlights of the analysis include the creation of the Nigerian Upstream Regulatory Commission (The Commission), commercialising the

142 Nigerian Model Production Sharing Contract 2005, s 6(7).

143 AIPN, Government Petroleum Contract Handbook (for the International Petroleum Industry) Vol 2 on Minimum Exploration Commitments, s 3(8)(5)

144 UNEP Environmental Assessment of Ogoniland (n 40) 150.

145 Preben Willoch and Frode Vareberg, 'Parent Company Guarantee for NCS Licences: Scope and Third-party Claims' (*Energy & Natural Resources, Norway*, 16 May 2016) <https://kontrollpanel.svw.no/wp-content/uploads/2020/06/Parent-company-guarantee-for-NCS-licensees_2019.pdf> accessed 01 November 2024.

146 PIA 2021, s. 310(1).

147 PIA 2021, s. 311(1). See also, PIA 2021, s.317.

NNPC, and turning the corporation into an incorporated national oil company, the NNPC limited, like any company incorporated under the CAMA. It is envisaged that it will promote faster development and expansion of oil and gas business in Nigeria since the company will be independent to make its management and investment decisions without the encumbrance from the government. This is expected to make the NNPCL capable of meeting its cash calls for environmental management including oil pollution clean-up. However, it remains to be seen how this reform will work out since the government still owns 100% of the shares of the NNPCL.

The establishment of the NNPCL also eliminates the overlaps and conflict of interest hitherto existing between the NNPC and the DPR (now the Commission). The functions of the Commission appear clearly delineated to avoid the overlap and conflict of interest between the NOSDRA and the DPR in the old law. The enormous powers of the Minister of Petroleum Resources were trimmed down assigning most of it to the Commission to ensure separation of duties and functions.

Other highlights include the elaborate provisions on environmental management plans, financial contributions for remediation of environmental damage, detailed provisions on abandonment, decommissioning and disposal, as well as on the development of the host communities. In fact, the PIA 2021 made good attempts to improve the management of the petroleum resources and oil pollution control in the Niger Delta, but it did not go far enough in providing for adequate funding for environmental management. It failed to provide for sources of additional funding where the available funds are inadequate to meet the environmental remediation costs. It is recommended that the parent company of the immediate polluter and all persons, companies, and entities 'associated with' the immediate polluter be held liable to provide the additional funds when needed.

The PIA is not perfect, but it is a great improvement on the Petroleum Act 1969. Its objectives are laudable, and it has a lot of progressive provisions in line with modern standards for petroleum operation. Its attempts at making the industry more transparent with improved provisions on environmental protection and sustainability are all commendable but there are also some provisions that are under par and some entirely missed as shown in the preceding analysis. For instance, there was a missed opportunity to provide for the establishment of specialised environmental courts for speedy trials of environmental and oil spill cases, and there was no provision for parent company guarantee to improve the accountability of the parent companies for acts of their subsidiaries in the Niger Delta. It is recommended that these be corrected in subsequent regulations and guidelines or when the Act is up for review.

10 Introducing a *Failure to Prevent* Oil Spill Offence in Nigeria

1. Introduction

A corporation generally commits an offence through its corporate employees, agents, managers, etc. when they act on behalf of the corporation in the course of their employment.[1] This is corporate criminal liability in a nutshell and a company can be prosecuted for the criminal offence in such circumstances. It is a strict liability offence, and the conviction stands even when the corporation is not aware that someone associated with it is committing an offence on its behalf. Croft noted the difficulties in explaining and defining corporate commission of offences particularly when dealing with large, multinational corporations with multi-layered administrative and managerial structure and myriad agents and contractors along the value chain.[2] Campbell sees this as one of the reasons for the shift towards corporate offences by omission.[3]

Liability for corporate offence by omission results when corporations fail to act where there is a legal duty to do so. This is seen mostly in regulated industries where companies are statutorily required to perform stipulated actions and are punished for breach of that duty to act or for that omission especially where it results in harm.[4] From punishing corporate omissions, the law pivoted to another form of omission liability, which is to criminalise and punish corporate *failure to prevent* harm or the commission of an offence. The liability is not dependent on the commission of the substantive offence but on the *failure to prevent* the commission of that offence.

It has been observed that *failure to prevent* offences are rampant in institutions that either tacitly allow it or fail to have systems and policies in place to prevent it.[5] A legal response to corporate *failure to prevent* offence was first expressed

1 Liz Campbell, 'Corporate Liability and the Criminalisation of Failure' (2018) 12(2) Law Financ Mark Rev 57.

2 Penny Crofts, 'Three Recent Royal Commissions: The Failure to Prevent Harms and Attributions of Organisational Liability' (2020) 42 Sydney L Rev 395.

3 Campbell (n 1) 57, 58.

4 Campbell (n 1) 58.

5 Crofts (n 2) 395, 400.

DOI: 10.4324/9781003435150-10

in the 1997 Second Protocol of the Convention on the Protection of the European Communities' Financial Interests.[6] Under this Protocol, each EU Member State is required to ensure that a corporation can be held liable where the lack of supervision or control by the directors and managers of that corporation makes passible the commission of an offence by persons under their authority, for the benefit of that corporation.[7] This formed the basis for Article 18(2) of the Council of Europe Criminal Law Commission on Corruption[8] and eventually led to the creation of the offence of *failure to prevent* bribery by a commercial organisation.[9] This offence was fully codified in the UK Bribery Act, (BA) 2010,[10] which was followed by the Criminal Finances Act (CFA), 2017 criminalising the offence of *failure to prevent* facilitation of UK and foreign tax evasion.[11] This chapter offers an analysis of this omission liability (*failure to prevent* offence) and proposes the enactment of a *failure to prevent* oil spills offence in Nigeria, with extraterritorial application, modelled after the *failure to prevent* bribery under the UK Bribery Act, 2010.[12] If adopted in Nigeria, the new law will apply extraterritorially in oil spill matters to any oil company that has a link with Nigeria, the same way the UK Bribery Act applies extraterritorially to any company with links to the UK.

2. Failure to Prevent Bribery Under the UK Bribery Act, 2010

Previous bribery enactments like the US Foreign Corrupt Practices Act (FCPA 1977)[13] and the OECD Anti-Bribery Convention (1997)[14] have helped in the

6 The Second Protocol of the Convention on the Protection of the European Communities' Financial Interests, 19 June 1997, art 3(2).

7 Council Act of 19 June 1997 drawing up the Second Protocol of the Convention on the protection of the European Communities' financial interests (97C 221/02), OJ C 221 (19 July 1997) p. 11.

8 UK HoL Select Committee on the Bribery Act 2010, Report of Session 2017–2019 'The Bribery Act 2010: Post-Legislative Scrutiny' (HL Paper 303, 14 March 2019) para 169.

9 UK HoL Select Committee on the Bribery Act 2010 (n 8) para 170.

10 UK Bribery Act (BA), 2010 <http://www.legislation.gov.uk/ukpga/2010/23/contents> accessed 05 August 2024.

11 UK Criminal Finances Act (CFA), 2017 <https://www.legislation.gov.uk/ukpga/2017/22/pdfs/ukpga_20170022_en.pdf> accessed 06 August 2024.

12 UK BA, 2010 (n 10).

13 The jurisdictional reach of the 1998 amendment cover non-US persons and foreign-based companies doing business within the United States (Issuers), US persons/companies doing business outside the United States (Domestic Concerns), and all other individuals or companies other than 'issuers' and 'domestic concerns' that do business within the United States. FCPA: 15 U.S.C. s. 78dd 1–3 (2006). The Act applies to parent companies and their subsidiaries if the conduct of their business touches the United States – FCPA: 15 U.S.C. ss. 78dd-l(a), (g), 78dd-2(a), (i)

14 OECD Convention on Combating Bribery of Foreign Public Officials in International Business Transactions and Related Documents (1997) <http://www.oecd.org/daf/anti-bribery/ConvCombatBribery_ENG.pdf> accessed 05 August 2024. This Convention applicable to OECD Member States, establishes legally binding standards to criminalise bribery of foreign public officials in international business transaction. It was signed into law on 17 December 1997 and came into force on 15 February 1999. It has been ratified by all 37 OECD Member States plus

improvement of anti-bribery law enforcement in many jurisdictions[15] and in bringing culpable corporations to book. However, they were focussed on cubbing the commission of the substantive offence of bribery and do not provide for the offence of *failure to prevent* bribery.[16]

The UK Bribery Act (UK BA), 2010 covers this gap by providing for *commercial bribery*[17] and specifically identifying failure of a commercial organisation to prevent bribery as an offence. Section 7(1) and (2) of the UK BA, 2010 provides that:

> A *relevant commercial organisation* ('C') is guilty of an offence under this section if a person ('A') associated with C bribes another person intending (a) to obtain or retain business for C, or (b) to obtain or retain an advantage in the conduct of business for C. But it is a defence for C to prove that C had in place adequate procedures designed to prevent *persons associated with C* from undertaking such conduct.
>
> (emphasis added)

The terms *associated person*[18] and *relevant commercial organisation*[19] are so broadly defined and unique to section 7, giving it very extensive jurisdiction. For instance, the term *associated person* could include agents, contractors, suppliers, very senior, and very junior members of the organisation if the person is serving the organisation and committed the offence of bribery on behalf of the organisation. Also, the term *relevant commercial organisation* need not be a UK company or have a place of business in the UK if it carries on a business – or part of a business – in any part of the United Kingdom.[20]

Failure to prevent bribery under the UK Bribery Act makes a commercial organisation culpable unless it can show that it had in place 'adequate procedures' to prevent the bribery.[21] The Bribery Act, however, did not provide the meaning and scope of 'adequate procedures' but instructs the Secretary of State for Justice to produce a guidance on the issue.[22] The Guidance published in March 2011 sets out six principles that a relevant commercial organisation must follow to prove that

---

seven non-member countries. <https://www.oecd.org/daf/anti-bribery/WGBRatificationStatus.pdf> accessed 05 August 2024.

15 Sarah C Kaczmarek and Abraham L Newman, 'The Long arm of the Law: Extraterritoriality and the National Implementation of Foreign Bribery Legislation' (2011) 65(4) Int Organ 745, 746–49, 754–55; OECD Convention on Combating Bribery (n 14) art 4.

16 Ellen Gutterman, 'Banning Bribes Abroad: U.S. Enforcement of the Foreign Corrupt Practices Act' (2015) 53 Osgoode Hall L J 31, 33.

17 UK BA, 2010 (n 10) s. 7. Kayla Feld, 'Controlling the Prosecution of Bribery: Applying Corporate Law Principles to Define a 'Foreign Official' in the Foreign Corrupt Practices Act' (2013) 88(1) Wash L Rev 245, 273; Engle (n 220) 1182.

18 UK BA, 2010 (ibid) s. 8.

19 UK BA, 2010, s. 7(5)

20 UK BA, 2010, s. 12

21 UK BA, 2010, s. 7.

22 UK BA, 2010, s. 9.

it has adequate procedures in place to combat bribery. These are: proportionate procedures; top-level commitment; risk assessment; due diligence; communication and training; and monitoring and review. The burden is on the defendant commercial organisation to prove on a balance of probabilities that it has adequate procedure in place to combat and deter bribery based on these principles.

It is not clear what the exact parameters and scope of the six principles are because no court has ruled on them. However, the efficacy and validity of the term 'adequate procedures' as a defence has been questioned on the ground that no matter how robust the procedures may be, if they fail to prevent bribery, then they are technically inadequate and would not afford the defendant a protection against liability.[23] This argument appears to imply that once bribery occurs, then the offence of failure to prevent it is deemed committed. Although this may appear true, in practice it is not a given because the court is expected to consider how well the six principles have been implemented as well as the circumstances of each case in making a determination on whether the procedures in place are adequate or not.

It must however be emphasised that the main objective of the failure to prevent the offence of bribery under section7 of the UK Bribery Art is to influence corporate behaviour and good governance towards the rejection of bribery as a way of doing business. Therefore, the justification for the 'adequate procedures' defence is 'to encourage companies to realistically assess the bribery risks they face and put in place proportionate procedures to mitigate them.'[24]

The International Organization for Standardization (ISO) is trying to present ISO 37001 (2016) certification on anti-bribery management systems as a means through which a commercial organisation could show that it has adequate procedures in place.[25] ISO 37001 is a risk management system that provides guidance designed to help an organisation establish, implement, maintain, and improve an anti-bribery compliance programme. It also enables organisations to assure any associated person or company (customers, business associates, potential investors, etc.) that the enterprise is taking appropriate steps to manage bribery risk.[26] The system includes a series of measures and controls that appear similar to but broader than the six principles set out in the guidance published by the UK Secretary of State for Justice as mandated under section 9 of the Bribery Act.[27] In addition to the six principles, ISO 37001 require that the commercial organisation and their business associates take steps to implement formal anti-bribery policies; appoint a compliance officer; establish anonymous reporting systems for whistle-blowers; and establish effective investigation procedures.[28] Therefore, companies could

23 Campbell (n 1) 60.
24 Campbell (n 1) 59.
25 ISO 37001 <https://www.iso.org/standard/65034.html> accessed 29 July 2024.
26 ISO 37001 (n 25).
27 Ministry of Justice, 'The UK BA, 2010 – Guidance' (March 2011) 20–31 <https://www.gov.uk/government/publications/bribery-act-2010-guidance> accessed 20 December 2024.
28 Dulce J Foster, 'What Companies Should Know About the New ISO Anti-Bribery Standard' (Fredriksson & Byron, P.A., Global USA, 9 August 2016) <https://www.lexology.com/library/detail.aspx?g=101d1181-d55b-4060-8036-83fd2c4b5c41> accessed 21 December 2024.

obtain ISO 37001 certification as a way to demonstrate that their management systems meet the required standards or that they are taking reasonable steps to prevent bribery. But this cannot provide an all-time guarantee that the companies' business partners are not participating in corruption. For this reason and regardless of the certification, companies must continue to conduct risk assessment and due diligence as well as regular communication and training to ensure that their agents, consultants, and other associated persons are not participating in bribery.[29] Although ISO 37001 is not going to be legally binding, its implementation is likely to be seen as evidence that the company is taking reasonable steps to implement global best practices for preventing and managing the risks of bribery.

3. Failure to Prevent Facilitation of Tax Evasion Under the UK Criminal Finance Act, 2017

In 2017, the scope of the failure to prevent offence was extended to the corporate offence of failure to prevent the facilitation of tax evasion under the UK Criminal Finances Act (CFA), 2017.[30] Under this Act, a *relevant body*[31] is criminally liable for failure to prevent facilitation of tax evasion offence unless it can prove on a balance of probability that it has put in place compliance procedures *reasonable in all the circumstances* to prevent the crime.[32] This is irrespective of the level and capacity of the *associated person*[33] who committed the crime on behalf of the corporation as long as s/he is acting in that capacity while committing the crime on behalf of the corporation. Procedures need only be reasonable in relation to the risk posed in the circumstances. So, proportionality is important, and the relevant commercial organisation needs to first undertake risk assessment of its organisation to be able to set up procedures that would be considered reasonable in all circumstances to prevent the offence. As in the Bribery Act, the Chancellor of Exchequer was required under section 47 of the CFA to produce a guideline to be followed in putting in place reasonable procedures to prevent the commission of the offence. The Guidance published, mirrored the six principles published by the Secretary of State for Justice to meet the requirement of having in place adequate procedures to prevent bribery. These are: risk assessment; proportionality of risk-based prevention procedures; top level commitment; due diligence; communication and training; and monitoring and review. These could be supplemented by sector-specific guidance from industry bodies with the approval of the Chancellor of Exchequer.[34]

29 Foster (n 28).

30 UK CFA (n 11) ss 45(1) & 46(1).

31 A body corporate or partnership (wherever incorporated or formed). CFA 2017, s. 44(2).

32 UK CFA (n 11) ss 45(2)(a) and 46(3).

33 An 'associated person' of a relevant body could be an employee – or agent of that body – and acts in that capacity or otherwise performs services for or on behalf of that body. CFA, 2017, s. 44(4).

34 UK CFA (n 11) s. 47(7). E.g., ISO Certification; The Guidelines on Money Laundering and Terrorism Financing Risks produced by the European Supervisory Authorities (ESAs).

3.1. The Defence

Like the Bribery Act, it is a complete defence if the relevant corporation can prove that when the offence of facilitation of tax evasion was committed, the organisation had in place *reasonable procedures in all circumstances* to prevent it. As already stated, these procedures mirror the procedures that a relevant commercial organisation must follow to prove that it has in place 'adequate procedure' to prevent the offence of bribery under the UK Bribery Act 2010. The reasonableness of the procedures put in place would depend on the level of risk of committing the offence that the organisation is exposed to. This underscores the need for the company to undertake risk assessment of the organisation on a regular basis, to assess their own specific risks, and identify the areas of high risk in the organisation[35] as this would guide the design and implementation of customised reasonable and proportionate procedure to be put in place to prevent the offence.

The difference between the defence of 'adequate procedure' used in the Bribery Act[36] and 'reasonable procedures' used in the Criminal Finances Act[37] has been a subject of debate.[38] Records show unsuccessful attempts to replace 'adequate procedures' in section 7(2) of the Bribery Act with 'reasonable procedures in all the circumstances.' It was argued that the 'adequate procedures' provide no defence because the occurrence of bribery is proof that the procedures in place are not adequate no matter how robust they might have been.[39] But the same argument could be made if that phrase is replaced with 'reasonable procedures in all the circumstances' because once the offence occurs, it means the procedures in place are not reasonable in all circumstances irrespective of how robust they might have been. The House of Lords declined to make the change concluding that the two phrases have the same import and that neither is more stringent than the other.[40] Although they acknowledged that the phrase 'reasonable in all the circumstances' makes the intended meaning clearer,[41] they, nevertheless, decided that both provide the same measure of defence for a company in which the offence had occurred. It is left for the courts to make the final determination on a case-by-case basis whether the procedure in place was adequate/reasonable in all circumstances to prevent the offence.[42] They are to be guided by the six principles laid down in the statutory Guidance in both the Bribery Act and the Criminal Finances Act.

The first of these principles, ***proportionate procedures***,[43] requires that the procedures put in place by the commercial organisation to prevent the offence must be

35 Jenny Wheater and Elly Proudlock, 'Commentary: UK Corporate Offence of Failure to Prevent the Facilitation of Tax Evasion' (2018) 19(2) Business Law International 178, 183.

36 UK BA, 2010 (n 10) s. 7(2).

37 UK CFA (n 11) s. 45(2); s. 46(3)

38 UK HoL Select Committee Report, HL Paper 303 (n 8) paras 196–211.

39 UK HoL Select Committee Report, HL Paper 303 (n 8) para 199.

40 UK HoL Select Committee Report, HL Paper 303 (n 8) para 211.

41 UK HoL Select Committee Report, HL Paper 303 (n 8) para 232.

42 Wheater and Proudlock (n 35).

43 The UK BA, 2010 – Guidance (n 27) 21.

proportionate to the risks it faces that the offence may be committed. In addition to being proportionate, the procedures must be practical and effectively implemented.[44] The proportionality of risk and adequacy of procedures that the commercial organisation puts in place will also depend on such factors like the nature, size, and complexity of the business,[45] as well as the countries in which the commercial organisation operates. It has been observed that bribery risks vary from country to country[46] and from sector to sector. For instance, the extractive industries particularly in developing countries have been known to present high risks for bribery.[47] As a result, the standard and adequacy of the anti-bribery procedure for a successful defence in the extractive industry should be higher than that in the other business sectors like legal and accounting especially if the extractive industry is in a developing country.[48]

It has been observed that corporate offences tend to be widespread in institutions that have very weak response to organisational misconduct.[49] This makes corporate policies and the attitude of senior management to corporate crime very critical for organisational crime prevention.[50] The second principle, which is ***Top-level commitment***,[51] is, therefore, very important not only in ensuring that the procedures and policies to prevent the offence are properly designed and implemented but in the overall success of the preventive procedures.[52] They should ensure proper governance through active engagement in the firm's approach to addressing financial crime risks.[53] It has also been noted that crime prevention is reduced when senior management promote a culture of integrity within the organisation, put extra measures in place to monitor the crime prevention procedures, and increase the probabilities of getting caught and punished.[54] ***Risk assessment*** was provided as the third principle.[55] This is very important if a firm is to apply proportionate and effective systems and control.[56] A firm should conduct risk assessment to identify and assess the financial crime risks e.g., the bribery/facilitation of tax evasion

44 The UK BA, 2010 – Guidance (n 27) 21.

45 UK Financial Conduct Authority (FCA) – Financial Crime Guide: *A Firm's Guide for Countering Financial Crime Risks* (FCG) 2024, para 1.2.3. <https://www.handbook.fca.org.uk/handbook/FCG.pdf> accessed 30 August 2024.

46 Gillian Dell and Andrew McDevill 'Exporting Corruption – Progress Report 2018: Assessing Enforcement of the OECD Anti-bribery Convention' (2018) <https://www.transparency.org/en/publications/exporting-corruption-2018> accessed 08 August 2024.

47 The UK Bribery Act, 2010 – Guidance (n 27) 26.

48 Dell and McDevill (n 46).

49 Croft (n 2) 400.

50 UK Financial Conduct Authority (FCA) – Financial Crime Guide (n 45) para 1.2.3.

51 The UK Bribery Act, 2010 – Guidance (n 27) 23.

52 Wheater and Proudlock (n 35).

53 UK Financial Conduct Authority (FCA) – Financial Crime Guide (n 45) para 1.2.3.

54 UK Financial Conduct Authority (FCA) – Financial Crime Guide (n 45) para 1.2.3.; Xing Ni and Xubong Su, 'International Anticorruption in China: Effectiveness on Bribery Incidence' (2019) 79(4) Public Adm Rev 538, 538.

55 The UK Bribery Act, 2010 – Guidance (n 27) 25.

56 UK Financial Conduct Authority (FCA) – Financial Crime Guide (n 45) para 2.2.4.

risks to which it is exposed as well as gaps in the control mechanisms. This would inform the proportionality of the procedures to be put in place to prevent the offence.[57] Risk assessment is of additional importance because it would enable the firm to target their financial crime resources on the areas of greatest risk.[58] It must be updated from time to time to align with changes in risks.[59]

Building on risk assessment, the fourth principle provides for the application of ***due diligence procedures***,[60] which require firms to apply the appropriate level of due diligence to manage identified risks, to ensure, for instance, that business relationships are transparent and ethical.[61] These calls for appraisals and continuous monitoring, proportionate and appropriate to the identified risks.[62]

Principle five recommends ***Communication and training***[63] to ensure that employees are regularly trained to improve awareness and understanding of the organisation's procedures and commitment to their proper application. ***Monitoring and review***[64] of the procedures put in place to prevent the offence was provided as principle six.[65] It recommends periodic monitoring, evaluation, review, and update to keep the procedures up to date not only to reflect the changes in risks but also to ensure that the procedures are being adhered to.

Satisfactory performance on these six principles will be acceptable evidence that the procedures put in place by the commercial organisation to prevent the offence is adequate/reasonable in all circumstances to prevent the offence of bribery/facilitation of tax evasion. Records show that following the enactment of the Bribery Act in the UK, there was a general deterrence of transnational bribery,[66] and bribery ceased to be an acceptable way of doing business.[67] Using them as templates for the oil spill prevention in the Niger Delta would likely help to reduce and control that offence in the region. It would also lead to a positive change in attitude to oil spill control and clean-up by the multinational oil companies (MNOCs) operating in the Niger Delta.

57 UK Financial Conduct Authority (FCA) – Financial Crime Guide (n 45) para 3.2.3.
58 UK Financial Conduct Authority (FCA) – Financial Crime Guide (n 45) para 2.2.4.
59 The UK Bribery Act, 2010 – Guidance (n 27) 25.
60 The UK Bribery Act, 2010 – Guidance (n 27) 27.
61 The UK Bribery Act, 2010 – Guidance (n 27) 27; Margaret Ryznar and Samer Korkor, 'Anti-Bribery Legislation in the United States and United Kingdom: A Comparative Analysis of Scope and Sentencing' (2011) 76(2) Mo L Rev 415, 422.
62 The UK Bribery Act, 2010 – Guidance (n 27) 28.
63 The UK Bribery Act, 2010 – Guidance (n 27) 29.
64 The UK Bribery Act, 2010 – Guidance (n 27) 31.
65 The UK Bribery Act, 2010 – Guidance (n 27) 31.
66 UK HoL Select Committee Report, HL Paper 303 (n 8) para 343; Sharfa G Hunter, 'A Comparative Analysis of the Foreign Corrupt Practices Act and the U.K. Bribery Act, and the Practical Implications of Both on International Business' (2011) (18)(1) ILSA J Int'l Comp L 89, 90.
67 Hunter (n 66) 112; Kaczmarek and Newman (n 15) 747.

4. Extension of the Failure to Prevent Approach to Corporate Human Rights Harms and Breach of Duty of Care

Following the extension of failure to prevent offence to facilitation of tax evasion in the UK, there were suggestions to replicate the model not only to all economic crimes[68] but also to human rights abuses[69] and all organisational failure to prevent breach of legal duty of care.[70] Consistent with the requirement of human rights due diligence on companies under the UN Guiding Principles on Business and Human Rights (UNGPs),[71] the UK Joint Select Committee on Human Rights and Business recommended that the government should impose a legal duty to prevent human rights abuses on all companies. According to the Committee, this would strengthen the UK business and human rights framework.[72] As in the failure to prevent bribery/facilitation of tax evasion, a company would have a defence if it could demonstrate that it has in place 'reasonable procedures in all circumstances' to prevent the human rights abuse.

On 11 February 2020, the British Institute of International and Comparative Law (BIICL) published a report in support of this recommendation and addressed the legal feasibility of transposing section 7 of the Bribery Act 2010 into a corporate duty to prevent human rights harms,[73] thus making failure to prevent such harm an offence.

It is envisaged that this proposal would likely pass if introduced in the UK Parliament because of the general movement towards corporate human rights legislation across many jurisdictions. For instance, this is evident in the US Dodd-Frank Wall Street Reform and Consumer Protection Act 2010,[74] which contains due diligence and supply chain reporting requirements for certain industries including those associated with conflict minerals from the Democratic Republic of Congo.[75] There is also the French Corporate Duty of Vigilance Law, 2017[76] which requires

68 Campbell (n 1) 58.

69 Crofts (n 2) 395. P Crofts, 'Criminalising Institutional Failures to Prevent, Identify or React to Child Sexual Abuse' (2017) 6 Int'l J Crime Justice Soc Democr 104–22; Campbell (n 1) 66.

70 Croft (n 2) 422.

71 UN Office of the High Commissioner for Human Rights (OHCHR), *Guiding Principles on Business and Human Rights: Implementing the United Nations 'Protect, Respect and Remedy Framework,'* HR/PUB/11/04, 2011 (UNGPs).

72 UK Joint Select Committee on Human Rights, 'Human Rights and Business 2017: Promoting Responsibility and Ensuring Accountability' paras 191–93 <https://publications.parliament.uk/pa/jt201617/jtselect/jtrights/443/44309.htm> accessed 11 August 2024; Irene Pietropaoli and others, 'A UK Failure to Prevent Mechanism for Corporate Human Rights Harms' p. 6 <https://www.biicl.org/publications/a-uk-failure-to-prevent-mechanism-for-corporate-human-rights-harms> accessed 31 July 2024.

73 Pietropaoli and others (n 72).

74 Dodd-Frank Wall Street Reform and Consumer Protection Act, 2010 <https://www.sec.gov/about/laws/wallstreetreform-cpa.pdf> accessed 11 August 2024.

75 Dodd-Frank Wall Street Reform and Consumer Protection Act (n 74) s. 1502.

76 Law No 2017–399 (27 March 2017 – French Duty of Vigilance Law) on the duty of care of parent companies applicable to France's largest companies.

large French companies to address the adverse impact of their activities on people and the planet by publishing yearly their public vigilance plan on human rights due diligence assessments. An additional reason why this proposal would likely pass if introduced in the UK Parliament is because investors are increasingly integrating environmental, social, and governance (ESG) factors into investment decisions as a way of improving corporate behaviour.[77] The legal feasibility and the implications of extending the corporate omission liability model of *failure to prevent* offence to oil spills in the Niger Delta is examined next.

5. Enacting A New *Failure to Prevent* Oil Spill Offence in Nigeria

Nigeria's oil pollution problem is an outlier in the global energy production with an average frequency of 893 per year in the 12-year period from 2010 to 2021.[78] Some of the spills have accumulated for over 40 years[79] and have decimated the entire Niger Delta environment, causing untold health hazards to the Niger Delta population.[80] The spills came from different pipelines owned and operated by different oil companies, often making clean-up liabilities difficult to apportion. This chapter proposes the enactment of a new *failure to prevent* oil spill offence in Nigeria, with extraterritorial application, modelled after the *failure to prevent* bribery, facilitation of tax evasion offences under the UK Bribery Act, 2010, and the UK Criminal Finances Act, 2017.

Under Nigerian law, the operator/licensee is required to take all practicable precautions (including the provision of up-to-date equipment) to prevent oil spill and where it occurs to immediately control and contain it,[81] irrespective of cause.[82] The operator is also obligated to clean it up as long as the spills are from a pipeline or facility it controls.[83] So, under the current Nigerian law, liability is imposed on the relevant licensee/lessee for harm caused by spills that has occurred or is occurring. Failure to prevent oil spill offence offer a more proactive approach to the prevention and control of oil spill in the Niger Delta. Like the failure to prevent bribery and facilitation of tax evasion, an oil company will be culpable for failure to prevent oil spill offence unless it can prove that it has put in place reasonable procedures in all circumstances to prevent the spill.

77 UK HoL Select Committee Report, HL Paper 303 (n 8) paras 227–30.

78 Chapter 1, Table1 of this book.

79 United Nations Environment Programme (UNEP), 'Environmental Assessment of Ogoniland' (2011) 9 <https://www.unep.org/resources/report/environmental-assessment-ogoniland> accessed 12 August 2024.

80 United Nations Environment Programme (UNEP) (n 79).

81 Petroleum (Drilling and Production) Regulation (1969) s. 25; Environmental Guidelines and Standards for the Petroleum Industry in Nigeria (EGASPIN) (2018), Part VIII B, 1.2.1.

82 Petroleum (Drilling and Production) Regulation (1969) s. 25.

83 *Ryland v Fletcher* (1866) L.R.I. Ex.265 (1868) L.R.[.H.L.] 330. The Nigerian Courts have reaffirmed that the strict liability rule established in this case is applicable to the petroleum industry because the use of land for petroleum operation is a non-natural use – *Umudje v Shell Petroleum Development Co. of Nigeria Ltd* (1975) 11 SC 155.

The new law will impose liability on the licensee/lessee if there is unacceptable risk or likelihood that the offence (oil spill) would be committed. The risk of oil spill is established if there are no reasonable procedures set up to prevent it.[84] The existence of reasonable procedures set up to prevent oil spill is evinced through the satisfaction of the six principles namely: proportionate procedures; top-level commitment; risk assessment; due diligence; communication (including training); and monitoring and review.[85]

Since the frequency and risk of oil spill in the Niger Delta is high, the standard and adequacy of procedures put in place to combat it must be proportionately high to match the risk. Also, with high incidence of oil pipeline vandalism in the Niger Delta, oil company management must commit to putting extra monitoring devices in place for surveillance of oil pipelines and instal leak detection systems and automatic flow reduction devices in the oil pipelines and facilities, otherwise the licensee cannot successfully defend itself against the offence of failure to prevent oil spills.

The MNOCs in the Niger Delta must regularly assess the risk of oil spills in their operational environment and provide adequate/reasonable procedures in all the circumstances to prevent oil spills. In the Niger Delta, the level of risk may be linked to the degree of exposure of the facilities and pipelines to vandalism. Where oil pipeline sabotage is foreseeable and rife, then there is high risk of oil spills, and the operator has a general duty to prevent it or take additional measures to limit it,[86] otherwise, the company would be held liable. They must carry out adequate due diligence procedures to identify and evaluate the environmental and social risks and liabilities associated with the business environment to ensure that the procedures set up to deal with them are adequate and reasonable in all the circumstances.

There should be evidence of constant monitoring, review of facilities, and training of a spill response team as required under the fifth and sixth guidelines[87] to keep them up to date and to ensure effective management of identified or potential risks. Any deficiency in any of these would mean that the company cannot successfully establish that the procedures in place are adequate and reasonable in all the circumstances to meet the prevailing risk situations and prevent spills. The case of Willis Limited regarding its anti-bribery systems and control provide a good example here. The Financial Service Authority (FSA) fined the company £6.9 million pounds in 2011 for failings in its anti-bribery systems and control. The company

84 Financial Service Authority Notice to Willis Ltd <https://www.fca.org.uk/publication/final-notices/willis_ltd.pdf> accessed 16 August 2024.

85 UK BA 2010 (n 10) s. 9 re the UK Bribery Act, 2010 – Guidance or under the UK CFA 2017 (n 11) s. 47 re the UK CFA 2017 – Guidance.

86 *Oguru, Efanga and Milieudefensie v RDS and SPDC, ECLI:NL:GHDHA:2021:132* <https://uitspraken.rechtspraak.nl/inziendocument?id=ECLI:NL:GHDHA:2021:132>; *Akpan and Vereniging Mileudefensie v Royal Dutch Shell plc and Shell Petroleum Development of Nigeria Ltd,* LJN BY9854 (District Court of the Hague, 30 January 2013) para 4.39 and 4.41.

87 UK BA 2010 (n 10) s. 9 re the UK Bribery Act, 2010 – Guidance.

had breached Principle 3 on the adequacy of its risk management systems, Principle 2 on top-level commitment to risk management, and Principle 4 on effective due diligence.[88] Although there was no evidence that the substantive offence of bribery had taken place, the FSA decided that a lack of controls at the company meant there was an 'unacceptable risk' that payments made by Willis to third parties overseas could have been used for paying bribes.[89] There was no need for the prosecution to prove that the substantive offence has been committed. It is that *failure to prevent* the offence that is culpable. The *failure to prevent* approach to corporate liability literally punishes the failure to prevent the offence. This is especially ideal for organisations that operate in high risk, high consequence areas such as petroleum operation and production. These are most likely to cause great harm due to a failure to prevent the substantive offence of oil spills (actual occurrence of the spill). The *failure to prevent* offence attracts the imposition of corporate liability, which could come in form of criminal prosecution, substantial fines, and reputational damages. This omission liability model, therefore, incentivises the corporation to constantly monitor and review their compliance policies and procedure, implement and enforce them, and ensure that their system of response to serious risks (identified and potential) are not only excellent but are constantly updated to meet changes in risks and avoid liability.

5.1. Punishment and Defence

Liability under the prototype offences, failure to prevent offence under the UK Bribery Act 2010, and the Criminal Finances Act, 2017 hold individuals, corporations, and their directors accountable for the failure to prevent the offence of bribery/facilitation of tax evasion. The BA provides that an associated person who bribes or is bribed[90] can be punished by imprisonment for up to ten years or fine or both.[91] The corporate offence of failure to prevent facilitation of tax evasion in and outside the UK is punishable by fine,[92] which could be quite substantial. These sanctions could be imposed on oil companies and their directors for the contravention of failure to prevent the offence of oil spills in the Niger Delta.

Like the failure to prevent bribery/facilitation of tax evasion, an oil company could have a defence for the offence of failure to prevent oil spill if it could show that it has in place 'reasonable procedures in all the circumstances' to prevent oil spills. This should be strictly interpreted by the courts to make it extremely difficult for a corporation to escape liability once spill has occurred or where the procedures put in place have created an unreasonable risk of its occurrence.

88 'FSA Fines Willis Limited 6.9 Million Pounds' <https://www.moneymarketing.co.uk/news/fsa-fines-willis-limited-6-9m/> accessed 30 August 2024.

89 'Financial Service Authority Notice to Willis Ltd' <https://www.fca.org.uk/publication/final-notices/willis_ltd.pdf> accessed 16 August 2024.

90 UK BA (n 10) ss 1, 2 and 6.

91 UK BA (n 10) s. 11(1)(b).

92 UK CFA (n 11) s 45(8) and s. 46(7)

6. Conclusion

The enactment of failure to prevent bribery under the UK Bribery Act, 2010 has generally been acknowledged as a remarkable success in the fight against bribery by commercial organisations.[93] The Transparency International UK describes it as an invaluable tool in incentivising improvements in corporate behaviour.[94] Its extension to the failure to prevent the facilitation of tax evasion under the CFA, 2017 has equally been successful and broader extension to other financial and non-financial crimes including human rights abuses have been advocated.[95]

Although the effectiveness of this *failure to prevent* approach in improving corporate compliance is not yet proven, it must be emphasised that the main objective of the failure to prevent the offence of bribery/facilitation of tax evasion under the BA 2010 and CFA 2017 respectively is to promote changes in corporate behaviour towards the reduction of potential culpable conduct within an organisation.[96] Therefore, the justification for the defence of putting in place 'adequate/reasonable procedures in all the circumstances' is to encourage firms to do proper risk assessment of their organisation and put in place procedures reasonable in all the circumstances to eliminate or at least reduce the offence and its potential harm.[97] So, this corporate liability approach incentivises relevant corporations to take proactive measures to prevent the offence of bribery and facilitation of tax evasion by putting in place reasonable procedures to prevent them.[98] This, in itself, is indicative of its positive impact on corporate behaviour.[99]

To demonstrate that their management systems meet the required standards or that they are taking reasonable steps to prevent the offence, companies could submit to independent third-party evaluation such as Asset Integrity Review, obtain certification from accredited third parties like ISO 37001, or rely on commercial due diligence providers. But these cannot provide an all-time guarantee that a corporation has met and sustained the requisite 'reasonable procedures' standard that would prevent the offence. It may, however, help to keep them on alert regarding the need for continuous risk assessment, due diligence and to update their systems accordingly. In the end, the final decision on whether the system in place meets the reasonable procedures standard rests with the courts. It is recommended that courts strictly interpret the six principles in the Guideline[100] and the requirement to put in place 'reasonable procedures in all the circumstances' to prevent the offence of oil

93 UK HoL Select Committee Report, HL Paper 303 (n 8) para 171.

94 UK HoL Select Committee Report, HL Paper 303 (n 8) para 171.

95 Crofts (n 2) 395. Penny Crofts, 'Criminalising Institutional Failures to Prevent . . .' (n 69); Campbell (n 1) 66.

96 Wheater and Proudlock (n 35).

97 Campbell (n 1) 59.

98 Campbell (n 1) 63.

99 Campbell (n 1) 59.

100 UK BA (n 10) s. 9 re the UK Bribery Act, 2010 – Guidance or the UK CFA 2017 (n 11) s. 47 re the UK CFA 2017 – Guidance.

spills. This will eliminate superficial compliance that appears to but fails to meet the requisite standards.[101]

Using the BA 2010 and the CFA 2017 as template for the failure to prevent oil spills offence means that oil companies operating in the Niger Delta will have to prove on a balance of probabilities that they have adequate/reasonable procedures in place to combat oil spills or they would be held criminally liable for that offence. Sanctions would include imposition of substantial fines on the company and/or jail terms for some top management in addition to cleaning up the spill, remediating the environment, and paying damages and compensations to the victims of the spill. Although some of these are already provided for in Nigeria through the torts of negligence,[102] and the Petroleum Production and Distribution (Anti Sabotage) Act 1975,[103] making *failure to prevent* oil spill an offence in Nigeria would be an additional tool for shaping corporate behaviour towards the fight against oil spills in the Niger Delta.

101 J Braithwaite, V Braithwaite and T Makkai, *Regulating Aged Care: Ritualism and the New Pyramid* (Edward Elgar 2007) 220, 227–30.

102 *Oguru v Shell* (n 86).

103 The Petroleum Production and Distribution (Anti Sabotage) Act, Cap P12, LFN 2004.

Index

Note: Page numbers in *italics* indicate figures, **bold** indicate tables in the text, and references following "n" refer notes.

FSC
www.fsc.org
MIX
Papier | Fördert
gute Waldnutzung
FSC® C083411

Kolibri 360 GmbH
Ferdinand-Jühlke-Straße 7
99095 Erfurt, Deutschland
produktsicherheit@kolibri360.de